Action Learning for Social Action

This book is about action learning in the service of social action and social change. The contributors are all engaged in developing new approaches to the wicked problems found in the world today, including the climate emergency, the circular economy, food poverty and insecurity, homelessness, disadvantage, active citizenship, social entrepreneurialism, and the learning of young women abducted by Boko Haram. They reflect a great diversity of settings in South Africa, Australia, Canada, Nigeria, Mozambique, Hungary, Poland and the UK.

At this time of global crisis rapid technological and social developments sit side by side with apparently impossible challenges needing urgent action. In the Global South, conflicts, terrorism and climatic changes have forced millions of people to abandon their homes and to migrate in search of food and safety. In the Global North, neo-liberal and market-based policies have pursued deregulation, privatisation and the shrinking of the state with consequent increases in homelessness, poverty and ill-health.

Action learning was devised to help people work together in challenging situations to bring about changes from the bottom-up. The people in these stories and cases are not passively awaiting brighter futures but are acting together to create a better world for themselves. They are taking back control in local community regeneration schemes, local energy and housing projects, setting up co-working spaces and inventing new ways of doing business and learning new ways to inhabit the earth. They demonstrate a confidence in an action learning idea that is alive and evolving.

The chapters in this book were first published in the journal *Action Learning: Research and Practice*.

Mike Pedler is Emeritus Professor, Henley Business School, University of Reading, UK and founding editor of the journal *Action Learning: Research and Practice*. He has been working with action learning since 1976, when he first met Reg Revans.

Action Learning for Social Action

Taking Part in Social Change

Edited by
Mike Pedler

Routledge
Taylor & Francis Group

LONDON AND NEW YORK

First published 2021
by Routledge
2 Park Square, Milton Park, Abingdon, Oxon, OX14 4RN

and by Routledge
605 Third Avenue, New York, NY 10017

Routledge is an imprint of the Taylor & Francis Group, an informa business

British Library Cataloguing-in-Publication Data
A catalogue record for this book is available from the British Library

ISBN 13: 978-0-367-50049-8 (hbk)

Typeset in Myriad Pro
by codeMantra

Publisher's Note
The publisher accepts responsibility for any inconsistencies that may have arisen during the conversion of this book from journal articles to book chapters, namely the inclusion of journal terminology.

Disclaimer
Every effort has been made to contact copyright holders for their permission to reprint material in this book. The publishers would be grateful to hear from any copyright holder who is not here acknowledged and will undertake to rectify any errors or omissions in future editions of this book.

Contents

Citation Information

The chapters in this book were originally published in the *Action Learning: Research and Practice*, volume 17, issue 1 (March 2020). Chapter 1 was published in a different issue of the same journal. When citing this material, please use the original page numbering for each article, as follows:

For any permission-related enquiries please visit:
http://www.tandfonline.com/page/help/permissions

Contributors

Mike Pedler Henley Business School, University of Reading, UK.

Cathy Sharp Research for Real, Edinburgh, UK.

Éva Tessza Udvarhelyi School of Public Life, Budapest, Hungary.

Ortrun Zuber-Skerritt COMBER, Faculty of Education, North-West University, Potchef-stroom, South Africa; Faculty of Education, Griffith University, Brisbane, Australia.

Lesley Wood COMBER, Faculty of Education, North-West University, Potchefstroom, South Africa.

George Boak York Business School, York St John University, UK.

Jeff Gold York Business School, York St John University, UK; Leeds Business School, Leeds Beckett University, UK.

David Devins Leeds Business School, Leeds Beckett University, UK.

Annie L. Booth Environmental and Sustainability Studies, University of Northern British Columbia, Prince George, Canada.

Kyle Aben Carbon Professional and Course Instructor, Prince George, BC, Canada.

Todd Corrigall Prince George Chamber of Commerce, Prince George, BC, Canada.

Barbara Otter Prince George Chamber of Commerce, BC, Canada.

Anna Jarkiewicz Faculty of Educational Sciences, Department of Educational Studies, University of Łódź (Poland), Europe.

Adrian Ogun Actionable Knowledge Services (Nigeria) Ltd, Abuja, Nigeria.

Armando Machevo Ussivane Regadio do Baixo Limpopo EP, Xai-Xai, Mozambique.

Paul Ellwood University of Liverpool Management School, UK.

Genevieve Cother Business Action Learning Tasmania Ltd, Launceston, Australia.

Stephen Moss Greener Moss Ltd, Somerset and London, UK. Action Learning Associates Ltd, London, UK.

Chelsea Marshall Nourish Scotland, Edinburgh, Scotland.

Ruth Cook Action Learning Associates, London, UK.

CONTRIBUTORS

Sam Anderson The Junction-Young People, Health & Wellbeing Edinburgh, UK.

Caroline Broadhurst The Junction-Young People, Health & Wellbeing Edinburgh, UK.

Siobhan Edwards The Junction-Young People, Health & Wellbeing Edinburgh, UK.

Michelle Smith The Junction-Young People, Health & Wellbeing Edinburgh, UK.

Paul Levy Brighton Business School, University of Brighton, UK.

David Knowles Brighton Business School, University of Brighton, UK.

On social action*

Mike Pedler

Introduction

The theme for this Special Issue arose from a session at the 2018 Action Learning Conference, where Sonja Antell and Ruth Cook talked about their projects focused on urgent social issues such as poverty, homelessness and food insecurity. It was reminiscent of Revans' characterisation of action learning as *Helping Each Other to Help the Helpless* (1982, 457–492).

Revans' ambition extended well beyond management education to the improvement of the organisations and systems that we depend on and ultimately the societies in which we live. The session came alive for me because of the focus upon social improvement, upon, if you wish, the desire to make the world a better place. Fittingly, the conference was being held in Liverpool, in the world's 5th richest nation, where monuments to industry, empire and slavery mingle with the more recent signs of neglect and decay including homeless people on the streets.

Much of what is called action learning today is for personal and career development rather than for organisational and social improvement. This perhaps reflects an era infused by the individualistic ethos of market fundamentalism and so-called neo-liberalism (Edmonstone 2019), where the social takes a back seat to the quest for personal success.

What is social action?

There are two questions here: what do we mean by action in action learning? And, building on that, what do we mean by social action? Listening to Ruth & Sonja speak In Liverpool, it seemed obvious to me that this was social action – action to help those who suffered the deprivations of poverty or homelessness, but also to benefit the wider society. I put out the call for papers and, to judge by the enthusiastic response, seemed to catch a wave. Since then, I have been thinking more about the notion of social action, with the result that the picture has become richer and more complex, but as ever, not necessarily clearer! The following section is a summary of this thinking, to which some close colleagues made notable contributions.

Action

Action is the first requirement for action learning: it is the origin of significant learning and the outcome point of that learning. The inseparability of action and learning is

---

*Thanks to Chris Blantern, Tom Bourner, John Edmonstone & Jeff Gold for their comments and conversations.

emblematic, as in Revans' epigrams: 'Learning is cradled in the task' and 'Learning involves doing' (2011, 3–5); a view also shared with other 'action modalities' (Raelin 2009) concerned with 'actionable knowledge' (Argyris 1993). Action can be defined as 'someone's doing something intentionally', where someone is an agent or one having agency, that is, the power to act, and the something is an event, brought about by the agent's intent (Honderich 1995: p4/5). But such definitions are slippery and rarely comprehensive. So for example, a person can be said to have done something even when doing nothing, whilst another can say that their most profound act is to change their thinking.

In editing these papers about action learning in the service of social improvement, I have urged contributors to make plain the social impact of their work. but this is not always so straightforward where outcomes might include people not doing things that they might otherwise have done or someone having a radical, but invisible thought. And yet, unlearning something, especially when it is a habit that has become dysfunctional, maybe far more effective than trying more new strategies; a transformative change of heart more powerful in its effects than any number of variations on existing themes.

But what distinguishes such an 'action' from 'inaction' (Vince 2008)? This is hard to do if it remains private to the person and it would also not meet the action learning test. However profound an internal change of heart or mind, it is not an action in these terms unless it is shared with at least one other person. Revans liked to quote the Buddha to stress our moral responsibility in this respect:

> It is better to do a little good than to write difficult books. The perfect man is nothing is he does not diffuse benefits on others, if he does not console the lonely. The way of salvation is open to all, but know that a man deceives himself if he thinks he can escape his conscience by taking refuge in a monastery. (Revans 2011, xiii)

Free will?

Rather like nature/nurture discussion in human development, there is a long-standing debate in the social sciences as to whether *agency* or *structure* is the most significant influence on human behaviour. In this argument, and roughly speaking, agency is the capacity of individuals to make free choices, whilst structure includes all the constraining economic, organisational and social arrangements including cultural factors such as customs, norms, ideologies and languages.[1]

In the social sciences, social constructionism has greatly influenced how we understand the idea of action. From this perspective, how we perceive reality depends on shared assumptions so that many of the things we take for granted and believe to be 'true' are actually constructed in human interaction. To illustrate this point, my colleague Chris Blantern likes to quote Richard Rorty's epigram that even 'Nature has no name for itself'. On the other hand, it is clear that people can sometimes rise above structural constraints to resist and deny what is held to be common sense and true. Alongside many mundane examples, Victor Frankl's (1958) account of how he managed to make sense of, and even transcend, the hellish context of the concentration camp, inspired a generation of humanistic psychologists.

We do not live as atomised individuals, but in communities and societies. As social beings, we are both unfree and free. As persons subject to processes of acculturation and socialisation, and the internalisation of aspects of existing institutional frameworks and current systems of beliefs, ideas and values, we are not entirely free to create the world as we might want it. However, socialisation processes can be resisted and challenged; cultures and institutions are always being questioned and internally contested, with alternative ideas and voices existing alongside the orthodoxies. So we are unfree because we are inevitably constituted by these acculturation processes, creatures of our times; but also free because old institutions and social paradigms can be broken and new ones created. For us, social beings action learning offers a means of doing this work.

Social action

Whilst action learning assumes the possibility of personal agency, and the ability of the learner to encourage themselves and their fellow set members into action, it also holds that both action and learning are social processes. In action learning, participants learn with and from each other and act outside the set with other people in their organisations and communities. Without this involvement of other people, the notion of action hardly makes any sense, and thus all action is social action. In arriving at this view, Revans drew on the Scottish philosopher John Macmurray (1961), who forges a position bridging the poles of the structure/agency debate

Macmurray's achievement was in challenging Kant's idea of the Self as primarily a thinker or knower (an 'egocentric position implying 'extreme logical individualism' 1961, Vol. 1; xvii). Instead, he asserts the prior place of action before thought: 'action is ontologically prior, knowledge arises within action' (1961, Vol. 1, xvi). This is a revolutionary shift which turns Descartes' view of the thinking Self on its head and puts in its place the acting Self: 'I do, therefore I am'. However, Macmurray goes on to argue, the very notion of Self implies an Other and we are always 'persons in relation': 'We exist only as agents, and in our existence, we are parts of the world ... .and ... in action the Self and the Other form a unity' (1961, Vol. 1, 220). Because there is no atomistic individual self unrelated to other people, action can only take place between persons and in the interpersonal world; so, it is not so much 'I do, therefore I am' as 'We do, therefore we are'.

Action in the world

Making plain the social impact of action learning may be difficult where individuals are engaged in invisible shifts or unlearning. but it can also be difficult because action learning happens in the contexts of organisations, communities and other social entities. Revans was very conscious of the need to extend the reach of action learning 'outwards from set to learning community' (2011, 71). He proposes an array of supporting structures to amplify the work of the set ('the cutting edge of every action learning programme' 2011, 7) including sponsors, clients, client groups and supporting assemblies as part of 'the multiplier effect' (2011, 12). These were the means to bring about the organisational and social transformations to which he aspired. Revans' 'general theory of human action ... a science of praxeology.' (1971, 58; 33–67) consists of three systems or spheres: those of personal action and learning, specific project development and the wider whole system of organisations in their environments. Although such elaborate structures are rarely present in action learning programmes these days, the multiplier is visible in a number of these papers, as where Cathy Sharp, for example, talks about the 'unknowable number of different people' taking part in leadership processes (Sharp: 2).

For action learning to be deployed helpfully in social renewal and improvement, a whole systems perspective becomes essential for tackling those knotty issues where there are no simple solutions and where responses require collaboration from several agencies acting together. When I first heard Revans speak in 1976, he told us that action learning was a very simple idea, not new, but enshrined in ancient wisdom. It made sense to me, I got it, then and there. but the experience of trying to use it was any-thing but simple. For a start, nothing was ever incontestably 'successful'. We ran projects and they sometimes worked and they sometimes didn't; or some people were successful to a degree, whilst others showed little progress. Simple cause and effect are hard to trace in the dense networks of big systems and organisations; accidental ironies and unintended consequences could be counted on and successful outcomes, insofar as we could find proof of these, were too removed to be reasonably be tracked back to their origins.

In the face of these sorts of dilemmas, contradictions and intractable problems, action learning scholars have paid a good deal of attention to the idea of Critical Action Learning (CAL) (e.g. Edmonstone 2019; Pedler and Hsu 2014; Rigg and Trehan 2004; Trehan 2011; Vince 2004, 2008, 2012). CAL is a post-Revans response to the convoluted and political nature of action in complex systems of organisation. In dealing with such conundrums, unlearning may be as important as any new learning because things are as they are because of the way we have thought about and dealt with them in the past. Revans was aware of this, warning constantly of the 'idolisation of the past' (2011, 41–50), and even proposing, in a whimsical moment, new professorships 'to tell us not how to acquire knowledge but how to forget it' (1982, 527).

So, we are actors not just in personal relations but in complex systems of organising, where particular actions form part of interactions and ramifications far beyond any individual's reach and awareness. These forms of daily interaction. or micro-organisational acts. also go to make up the character of the organisation: for example, via hierarchical acts or by generative and collaborative actions, by democratic or controlling ones, including or excluding practices and so on. Many or most of these daily acts are habitual and thoughtless, but this is the 'life-world' that both generates actions and conditions them. Taken collectively these daily acts sediment into the structural, informing identities, local cultures, habits of taboo and deference and of how power is created, used and abused. This is also where action learning can sometimes help through the questioning and awareness raising processes that can produce changes of heart and mind where the near-invisible processes of change can begin.

Social justice

What fired me up in Liverpool was not the excitement of trying to make sense of 'social action' (although I have enjoyed this) but because these projects aimed to help improve actual people's lives in the places where they lived. During our email conversa-tions, Tom Bourner asked me whether continuing to explore the possible meanings of social action was producing anything useful? As he observed, more than 2000 years after Plato defined knowledge as justified true belief, philosophers are still debating its meaning. At the same time, few of us would deny that there has been a huge increase in useful human knowledge over these years. Perhaps a 'good enough' meaning of 'social action' would suffice: pondering its nature is all very well, but does it help bring about more social justice?

When the focus of this Special Issue became clear, a first thought was that social action was that taking place in the social sphere, by which I mean taking place in the public services, in local communities, amongst social enterprises and not-for-profit undertakings where the bottom line is social improvement, as distinct from the commercial sphere, where profit is the important consideration. Organisations in the social sphere are concerned with social justice, where the purpose of action is to address a social problem or to realise a social opportunity. Questions of social justice raise Important matter of consequence from any action: who benefits and who loses?

A merit of profit as a goal is that it makes things simpler; in its absence an often competing assortment of social, economic and political values or 'bottom lines' appear. These often reveal themselves as dilemmas or wicked problems that are not ultimately resolvable: should a homelessness charity focus on the immediate crisis or on building accommodation? Should a Local Authority, strapped for cash, close its public libraries or cut support for local bus services? Should a National Park focus on conservation and wilding (and keep people out) or on creating facilities and attract more users?

The papers in this special issue

Most of the papers in this Special Issue demonstrate their awareness of questions of social justice and of the complex and multi-layered context of social action. These accounts also often bring their own definitions of social action to the party. There is a richness to the work illustrated here, both in the issues addressed and in the range of contributors and contexts. Problems tackled include the climate emergency, sustainability and the circular economy, food poverty and insecurity, homelessness, active citizenship, social entrepreneurialism, disadvantaged people and the learning of young women abducted by Boko Harem. This diversity is also reflected in the range of contributors. The researchers, learners and activists reporting their work here are from Hungary, South Africa, Australia, Poland, Canada, Nigeria, Mozambique and the UK. Together these papers are a tribute to some 'little good' that is being done in a world about which we hear so much that is bad. The varieties, adaptations and combinations with other approaches demonstrate a confidence in an action learning idea that is alive and evolving.

It has been difficult to decide the order in which the papers should appear. The normal division into Refereed Papers and Accounts of Practice does not work well because all contributors provide case examples of how action learning is being used in their situations. And, whilst some papers are more academic and theoretical than others, all make contributions to the understanding of the issues in their settings. The order chosen is therefore somewhat arbitrary but begins with the more academic papers and proceeds to those more focused on practice. In reading these papers, readers might like to ponder: *What can we learn about action leaning from applying it to social action?* and also, *What can we learn about social action (and social change) by applying action learning to it?*

- Cathy Sharp's *Practising change together – where nothing is clear, and everything changing* is about leadership in the complex contexts of community wellbeing and health care in Scotland. However, this is less about individual leaders and more about collectivities facing the practical reality of how to practice change together in unstable and ambiguous environments. Illustrated by case examples from Scottish communities, leadership and social action are treated as relational and dialogical practices done by people acting together. Rather than the bounded action learning set, the preferred methodology of action inquiry enables the involvement of 'a larger, more disparate and perhaps unknowable number of 'unusual suspects".

- *Participatory action research as political education* is Éva Tessza Udvarhelyi's approach to working with people experiencing homelessness. housing poverty and difficulties due to physical disabilities in Budapest. A notable insight in Tessza's paper is the view of social action as 'anything that disrupts existing relations of power and exclusion": an example given is a homeless person attending an interview about harassment and discrimination with the head of police. The author and her co-workers' personal engagement and commitment to the work is very obvious throughout this paper, not least in the account of how 'the actor is changed as she learns from the process'.

- Ortrun Zuber-Skerritt and Lesley Wood's account of *The transformative potential of action learning in community-based research for social action* is illustrated with cases from South Africa and Australia. The claim here is that action learning must be developed in a systematic and educational way to enable individuals and communities to learn and develop personally whilst also engaging in social action for their particular needs and contexts. The aim of the work is for people to become both self-directed learners and activists who are able to challenge and disrupt dominant power relationships and traditional ways of conducting research.

- *Action learning & Action research to alleviate Poverty* by George Boak, Jeff Gold and Dave Devins reports on a collaborative project funded by the Joseph Rowntree Foundation to alleviate poverty in the Leeds City Region, UK. Action learning, action research and appreciative inquiry were used in with managers from 12 large local organisations, with the aim of identifying and spreading good practices in employment and procurement policies. The outcomes include the implementation of good practices by the participating 'Anchor' institutions which can have a considerable impact on poverty in their regions by virtue of their size, their spending, and the numbers they employ.

- Annie Booth, Kyle Aben, Todd Corrigall & Barbara Otter's account of *Carbon Management and Community-Based Action Learning: A theory to work experience* tells the story of an undergraduate/graduate action learning initiative co-developed by the University, the Chamber of Commerce and local businesses in Northern British Columbia, Canada. Students work together with local businesses who are aware of climate change and the need for better carbon management to gain practical skills and create carbon footprint analyses. As a student notes, the experience changed the way she approaches her work: 'Since then, I've changed our outreach programming to be nearly zero-waste, prioritized the use of recycled materials, and have encouraged staff participation in community initiatives like Go by Bike Week'.

- In *Using Participatory Action Learning to Empower the Active Citizenship of Young People*, Anna Jarkiewicz, of Lodz University, Poland, deploys Participatory Action Learning (PAL) to develop the active citizenship of young people in schools. Via a European educational project called Future Youth School – Forums (FYS-FORUMS), the aim is to create a model of schooling that promotes the idea of active citizenship. Outcomes include students developing their 'transversal' skills, improving relationships with teachers; and changing their attitudes towards active citizenship, which is reflected in their thinking about social actions and the need to get involved in them.

- *Social Action Learning: Applicability to Comrades In Adversity in Nigeria* by Adrian Ogun, Reginald Braggs & Jeff Gold describes work to help young women students learn from their harrowing experiences of being abducted by Boko Haram in Northern Nigeria. Action learning is found to facilitate student engagement and confidence, enabling them to voice their learning concerns and to develop social and emotional learning. The authors suggest that other victims of war and social violence may benefit from these students' learning experiences, including child soldiers, refugees, internally displaced persons and a wider community that includes the re-orientation of victims of teenage trafficking and sexual grooming.

- Armando Ussivane and Paul Ellwood's title *Action Learning in the Service of Food Security and Poverty Alleviation in Mozambique* speaks for itself. Action learning is brought here to a state enterprise delivering a large food security and poverty alleviation programme in Mozambique. A wide variety of stakeholders including subsistence farmers, community leaders and international private investors were brought together in an unusually large and diverse action-learning set to tackle their apparently intractable differences in the agendas of autonomous stakeholders. In a culture that does not question seniors or confront 'challenges', action learning enabled stakeholder conflicts to be explored and sometimes resolved.

- *Developing the Circular Economy in Tasmania* by Genevieve Cother is an early account of a project to help Tasmanian SMEs to implement circular economy ideas and principles. Participants were offered initial seminars to raise their awareness of key concepts including resource efficiency, sustainability and environmental management before moving on into three action learning sets. Results so far show gains in resource efficiency and waste management and some radical ideas needing further work. An interesting finding of this research suggest that 'an inaugurating theoretical framework is not required to get us moving in the right direction', this affirming Revans' view of the place of P in the quest for radical innovation.

- Stephen Moss's *Transforming the lives of people facing severe and multiple disadvantages* tells the story of an action learning intervention to help organisations working to help people with severe and multiple disadvantages including combinations of homelessness, substance abuse, mental health, domestic violence and abuse and chronic poverty. Apart from supporting the participants with their specific organisations challenges, wider findings included: the considerable tension between implementing 'what works' at scale and facilitating ground-up innovation and participation in communities; better understanding by commissioners of the systems change impacts when they commission new services; and the need for enhanced system level is leadership.

- Chelsea Marshall & Ruth Cook's *Using action learning to tackle food insecurity in Scotland* reports on 'A Menu for Change' run by a collaboration of charitable organisations and three local authorities in Scotland. Action learning sets worked within this complexity of organisations in an action learning system operating at three levels: people with lived experience of food insecurity, representatives from community-level advisory groups and strategic-level groups of senior managers from the councils and third sector. This architecture brought credibility to the sets' work and facilitated resulting actions and recommendations. This experience confirms findings from other papers about the benefits of developing action learning systems when tackling complex social problems.

- *Developing empowered and connected leaders in the social sector: The Rank Foundation's engagement with Action Learning* by Sam Anderson, Caroline Broadhurst, Siobhan Edwards & Michelle Smith describes action learning sets being used to help increase the impact of charities and social enterprises. Two case examples illustrates how the sets can help to connect, sustain and support the social action responses of the local organisations involved: one highlights the importance of diversity and set compositions which reflect the variety by sector, community, age, gender, and sexual orientation; the second explores how set processes help participants to reflect on which actions are most congruent with their values and then support their implementation.

- *Drop-in Action Learning* by Paul Levy & David Knowles outlines the DIAL project where more than 300 people from small and micro-businesses have attended the sessions over the last five years. Based at Brighton (UK), which has a high proportion of entrepreneurs and small businesses, DIAL has focused on helping start-ups to launch successfully, and pre-startups to progress towards the startup. Being community-based means that this business development is also a form of local, social action. This paper examines the effectiveness and potential of DIAL as a new form of action learning including the specific challenges and advantages of the drop-in element and the particular benefits of non-formal meeting spaces such as cafes and pubs.

Note

1. Free will versus determinism is a very old and circular philosophical argument which always reminds me of the Monty Python sketch where the Pythons trek to Paris to see Jean-Paul Sartre. On encountering Mrs. J P Sartre, in a headscarf washing the front steps, they ask if her husband is free. Taking the fag from her lower lip, Mrs. Sartre replies: 'I don't know dearie, he's been trying to decide that for the last 40 years'.

Disclosure statement

No potential conflict of interest was reported by the author.

References

Argyris, C. 1993. *Knowledge for Action: A Guide to Overcoming Barriers to Organizational Change.* San Francisco: Jossey-Bass.

Edmonstone, J. 2019. "Beyond Critical Action Learning? Action Learning's Place in the World." *Action Learning: Research and Practice* 16 (2): 136–148.

Frankl, V. 1958. *Man's Search for Meaning.* Boston: beacon Press.

Honderich, T., ed. 1995. *The Oxford Companion to Philosophy.* Oxford: Oxford University Press.

Macmurray, J. 1961. "The Form of the Personal." London: Faber & Faber.

Pedler, M., and S-w Hsu. 2014. "Unlearning, Critical Action Learning and Wicked Problems." *Action Learning: Research and Practice* 11 (3): 296–310.

Raelin, J. 2009. "Seeking Conceptual Clarity in the Action Modalities." *Action Learning: Research and Practice* 6 (1): 17–24.

Revans R, W. 1982. *The Origins & Growth of Action Learning*. Bromley: Chartwell Bratt.

Revans, R. W. 2011. *ABC of Action Learning*. Farnham: Gower.

Rigg, C., and K. Trehan. 2004. "Reflections on Working with Critical Action Learning." *Action Learning: Research and Practice* 1/2: 151–167.

Trehan, K. 2011. "Critical Action Learning." In *Action Learning in Practice*, edited by M. Pedler, 162–171. 4th ed. Farnham: Gower Publishing.

Vince, R. 2004. "Action Learning and Organisational Learning: Power, Politics and Emotions in Organisations." *Action Learning: Research & Practice* 1 (1): 63–78.

Vince, R. 2008. "'Learning-in-Action' and 'Learning Inaction': Advancing the Theory and Practice of Critical Action Learning." *Action Learning: Research & Practice* 2 (5): 93–104.

Vince, R. 2012. "The Contradictions of Impact: Action Learning and Power in Organisations." *Action Learning: Research & Practice* 9 (3): 209–218.

Practising Change Together - Where nothing is clear, and everything keeps changing

Cathy Sharp ⓘ

ABSTRACT
This paper explores the thinking and practice of 'action inquiry' an embedded learning practice that can help navigate complexity when practising change together. The paper uses examples from social contexts where there are concerns about community wellbeing and health care. These are drawn from collaborative or collective leadership development programmes within public services that seek to bring new attention to the qualities of how people think, converse and interact, as part of their collective professional practice. This treats social action as a relational and dialogical practice, something that we do together as professionals by engaging in reflective inquiry and action. The paper suggests that action inquiry offers a prospect of rekindling the links between 'action learning' and collaborative leadership by developing a co-mission and a mutual commitment to a new type of learning partnership. Action inquiry can be wrapped around and enmeshed within initiatives and programmes that work with complexity, anywhere where effective social action will depend on the quality of relationships that can be developed. This research was funded by two separate Scottish Government commissions, where the author was a learning partner. The paper also draws on the further reflections of some of the practitioners most centrally involved.

Introduction

To explore the thinking and practice of 'action inquiry', this paper draws on the experience of two closely related and distinct leadership development programmes, operating in similar public service contexts.

Firstly, *Collaborative Leadership in Practice* (CLIP) is offered jointly by NHS Education for Scotland, the Scottish Social Services Council and the Royal College of GPs in Scotland. The CLIP programme provides small-scale bespoke facilitation support to locally based partnership groups to develop their collaborative responses to health and social care. The CLIP offer is part of a larger leadership programme that also includes coaching and seeks to support the legislative requirement for the integration of health and social care in Scotland. CLIP groups or sites have addressed a wide range of issues, including improving care for patients living in a very deprived area; addressing community needs for a vulnerable group of frail elderly people living at home; homelessness; and inter-professional and across sector working (Sharp, 2018).

Secondly, *Collective Leadership for Scotland* (CLS) provides facilitative and learning support to people 'working with systemic issues which reach beyond the boundaries of traditional hierarchies and public institutions' (Collective Leadership, 2019). This programme works directly with inter-professional groups as they seek to lead change and offers a bespoke support structure for the groups and for the wider changes they seek to achieve. It has evolved from an earlier 'Enabling Collaborative Leadership Pioneer Programme' which was explicitly experimental in its approach to working and learning in collaboration (Bland and Sharp, 2016). CLS sites have addressed a wide range of issues at local and national levels, including tackling conflict and how to achieve the best outcomes for children and families through better collaborative between schools and social work.

Whilst CLIP and CLS have common and distinct antecedents and practices, both have an emphasis on building capacity for leadership which appreciates and engages with the whole system, including the behavioural and relational aspects, and where openness, learning and willingness to take collective action are at the core. Both programmes have been influential in the development of the thinking and practice of action inquiry, as articulated here and elsewhere (Sharp, 2018a). In particular, this paper focuses on two aspects of learning arising from seeking to work in this way; the new qualities of group conversations that can happen through collaborative action inquiry and the challenges of convening a different approach to embedded leadership development within public services.

Understanding social action in complexity

The kind of context and concerns outlined here should resonate with many readers. Whatever our immediate focus, many of us are working on real, intractable, adaptive or 'wicked' problems (Heifetz and Linsky 2002; Grint n.d.). The term 'wicked' has widespread currency and has come to be associated with an understanding of the web of elements that make many public policy issues so stubborn. Very often collaboration is essential, perhaps even in tackling those 'tame' problems that have been seen before, where the inevitable human aspects make change far from a technical matter.

Perhaps over the last decade, there has been a discernible shift in the Scottish and wider UK policy environment with greater acknowledgement of complexity, including better recognition of the complexity of people's lives, including the often-overlooked richness, strengths or assets of people and communities, alongside the challenges they face (Garven et al, 2016). There is both hunger for change and weariness of 'fixes that fail'; the unintended consequences and further complexities that can be created in seeking to deliver support or solve problems (Seddon, 2008). The practical necessity of collaboration may also arise as a statutory responsibility, for example in Scotland, in Health and Social Care Integration, Community Planning Partnerships and Community Empowerment legislation.

Collaborative or collective leadership programmes support participants to work in collaboration and amidst complexity on real and practical issues, where leadership is understood as a participatory and improvisational practice that recognises the mutuality, reciprocity and interdependencies within any system. Less about individual leaders, collective leadership faces the practical reality of how to practise change together in environments where 'nothing is clear, and everything keeps changing' (Sharp, 2018a). Such dynamic or turbulent conditions have added dimensions of complexity and at times, inertia. There are webs of human intricacies and the convolutions of power, emotions and relationships amongst and between services and organisational systems, amongst staff and managers and people who are intended to benefit.

Such a messy reality offers some 'beacons of light'. These are less about (with noted Brexit irony) 'taking back control' as coming to understand and ceasing to deny or control complexity, perhaps giving up an illusion of control and finding the possibilities for action that each can do, given their role, and alongside others with shared ambitions for wider system change. Leadership becomes a form of collaborative social action that embraces both advocacy and inquiry. CLIP and CLS participants are people who want to change their own worlds from inside 'the system', not necessarily from the bottom-up, but from a starting point of wherever they are. The examples cited here encompass an unknowable number of different people and a wide range of occupations, including Civil Servants, General Practitioners, Social Workers, Teachers, Community Development practitioners and Home Care workers, many of whom would not conventionally be invited to take part in action learning or leadership development.

Action learning or action inquiry

Much leadership development is inadequate for these messy realities (Vince and Pedler, 2018). Raelin suggests that action learning can be a gateway to collaborative leadership as the two approaches are based on common principles (2006). Action learning, particularly critical action learning, does seem ideally suited to help address the many unanswerable and unformulated challenges of leadership amidst complexity (Vince and Pedler, 2018). Current and conventional approaches to action learning, are at times disconcertingly corporate or managerial, and often have a focus on leader development and individual capacities; it does seem as if action learning has not yet adapted to the need for systems or collective leadership in public services. It has been argued that we may need alternative approaches and fresh interpretations of action learning that focus on the nurturing of the 'collective capacity to lead' (Edmonstone et al, 2019).

Whilst not offered as a recipe or blueprint, the underpinning philosophy and practice of action learning has a vital part to play as action-orientated learning that helps to recognise, release and use people's gifts, skills and talents to their fullest potential. Both CLIP and CLS use the idea of *'action inquiry' as* a model of 'practising change together' in environments in situations of complexity where social action has to be bespoke and learning is emergent, a continuous process, not a phase or something imported from elsewhere as 'what works'. The starting point for action inquiry is the level of group, rather than an entry point of the individual from which much action learning starts (Raelin, 2006).

Seeking fresh interpretations of action learning is not to dismiss what's gone before. It's fruitful to draw on different roots and traditions that we find ourselves connected or drawn to, to craft practice of inquiry, the basic act of seeking or searching, to express the idea of curiosity, of asking questions and exploring understandings. It is that which enables us to more fully live our values, to do what we can, wherever we are, and to find allies in that endeavour.

In these shifting sands, there is an increasing understanding of the importance of relationships and language in how we make meaning together. The emphasis on relationships is not about 'who we know', nor about treating relationships as objects or 'things', but about recognising the co-created and dynamic relational processes *in which we are already embedded*, and that learning is a relational achievement (Gergen, 2014, emphasis added). Raelin develops this by talking of leadership as a practice in which people create knowledge as they improvise around a problem that they are confronting (2016). *Leadership as practice* does not focus on the relationship between 'leaders' and 'followers' but looks to the (relational) activity of all those who are engaged, to their social interactions, and to their reflections and adjustments to their ongoing work. This makes leadership development a form of public reflection (Raelin, 2001) that seeks to create a community of inquiry amidst the 'everyday politics', here, of partnership working (Vince and Pedler, 2018).

Collective leaders need help to determine 'wise actions' in real-life situations, enabling them to 'speak differently, rather than argue well' (Rorty, 1989, cited in Raelin, 2016), drawing on participatory, rather than spectator knowledge (Pearce, 2007). This includes knowledge from lived experience and that of practitioners, and valuing ways of knowing that might be expressed in more unconventional, creative ways (Heron and Reason, 2001). Such public reflection makes actions and the assumptions on which they are based more open to inspection, affirmation and challenge.

Complexity demands that we pay attention in new ways as change happens through emergence that begins as small, local actions and variations in practice; the 'adaptive solutions that make sense locally' (Greenhalgh and Papousti, 2018). Small actions can have major effects by shifting the focus of attention and intention, triggering different choices by making visible options that did not previously appear to be available (Burns, 2007).

Several writers on complexity, social theory and research have identified the relevance of action research, as a dialogical, integrative method engaged with practice (Weil, 1997; Burns, 2007; Byrne and Callaghan, 2014; Gergen, 2014). Action and engagement become part of the process of co-production of knowledge and some have argued that it is not possible, even unethical, to engage with complex social systems from the outside (Byrne and Callaghan, 2014). The pedagogy of Paulo Freire (1972) underpins action research as dialogical research that is part of conscientization and empowerment. Freire is often interpreted to mean that only knowledge 'from below' or 'bottom up' is valid. Byrne and Callaghan (2014) make the important point that for Freire, dialogue was 'never a one-way street – everybody taught, and everybody learned' such that all knowledges (note the plural) are incomplete.

Our use of the term 'action inquiry' is an interpretation, and greater alignment, of action learning with action research, as a developmental practice that brings about a new collaborative leadership culture. As part of the extended family of action research and action learning, 'action inquiry' borrows and builds on the idea of 'living life as inquiry' as an action research methodology that emphasises moment-to-moment awareness and qualities of attention (Marshall, 1999). It has been developed through different approaches including those of action science (Argyris et al, 1985; Fisher, Rooke, and Torbert 2003); first, second- and third-person inquiry strategies (Reason and Bradbury 2001); and systemic action research (Burns, 2007). Such 'action inquiry' brings an emphasis on dialogue, collaboration, purpose, values and action (Sharp, 2018). It is a desirable and necessary response to the kind of complex situations and challenges of human services and recognises the essentialness of knowledge co-production.

Collaborative leadership in practice: nurturing the collective capacity to lead

In my role as a learning partner, I have worked with CLIP sites to generate a narrative of their experience and these stories are the basis of this section (Sharp, 2018). In general terms, the CLIP programme has shaped unusual and highly valued protected time, with real and practical consequences from exploring both *what* people are doing in their domain of inquiry and *how* they are working together. The range of CLIP stories illustrates the nature and complexities of the facilitation task to orientate people to real-time learning-in-action. They show how small-scale action inquiry that harnesses learning from the work in which people are involved, can help them to engage and improvise together around uncertain and complex problems in their work environment or community.

Sometimes working in very challenging contexts, CLIP has helped to create more positive group dynamics amongst varied groups professionals working in health and social care. The environment created has allowed multi-disciplinary groups to talk much more openly and productively about their fears, anxieties and hopes for service integration.

Greater attention to safety in groups and growing trust amongst participants has enabled the exploration of common values and purposes and the development of a shared focus on improvement. Safety enables sharing of the positives and the difficulties and disagreements, which gives people greater confidence from which to act. This knowledge of each other from new connections has given them confidence to do more, to create stronger, mutual ambitions. It has brought their shared endeavour of health and social care integration to life as they have become immersed in what the national legislative and policy agenda actually means locally by their engagement as active participants. The approach adopted has conveyed the message that everyone's expertise and ideas are important and has supported new qualities of listening and really hearing other perspectives.

Some of the stories refer directly to the dynamics that can happen amidst meetings at which there is superficial agreement, but no real trust that people are necessarily willing or able to follow through on actions.

> … it's a million times better than it was. I don't like the ducking and diving that goes on. I want people to say what they're thinking and not to kind of go away and plant seeds of doubt in other people's minds that become toxic and grow.

Such behaviour creates additional anxieties and further erosion of trust, there's widespread frustration and time and energy is wasted. This protected and facilitated time reduces anxiety and creates a new sense of 'mutuality', cohesion and openness to others, 'as if the temperature in the room has been turned down'. Individuals have come to a better understanding of themselves and each other by exploring what each other mean by particular terms or ideas. This has often dismantled stereotypes or pre-conceptions and helped them realise how they are often talking at cross-purposes. There is a new quality of compassion for each other, humour is important and there is often relief that issues are no longer being avoided.

Talking about the differences amongst them has shown that they were not always a barrier and may be useful. As a result, they have been able to more skilfully deploy different knowledge, skills, strengths and perspectives to create new ways of working and better services. Some are very clear that this form of learning is something that they must do for themselves:

> We could have put out a 'Dummies Guide to How to Avoid the Problems We Had'– assuming that everyone else would have the same ones. But our approach helped us to see the part that we each played and that accelerated the rate at which we came to understand each other's circumstances.

The ability to talk openly about 'how we want to be with each other' means that more business gets conducted 'in the room', there is an excitement about the mutual purpose of providing better services and previously dormant 'action plans' get enacted.

All professional groups have gained insights into their personal role and the part that they may play as individuals, unwittingly or otherwise, creating negative dynamics or 'stuckness' amongst and with other professionals. As is often the case in more conventional action learning, participants talk about the impact of CLIP on themselves, creating a greater awareness of their own assumptions or pre-conceptions and their own gaps in knowledge, perhaps about another professional group or what resources exist locally. There's a willingness to acknowledge, without defensiveness or embarrassment, that 'whilst we might be enthusiastic, we might also be wrong' and, with a willingness to slow down, there are ways to check this out.

Ending isolation has been of particular importance to some professional groups; for example, GPs who have been part of a CLIP group have become more active influencers and participants in the wider health and social care system and some talk about the further influence on their own practice:

> [I have taken my learning] into my day to day work ... There's more of a focus on the relationship – before I might have said 'this person is ready for residential care', whereas social care would say, 'no, this person is ready for assessment'. Now my view is one aspect of a multi-disciplinary assessment. I'm more willing to explore what options there might be, rather than previously I'd get a 'yes' or 'no' answer and it was a battle of wills!

A common theme is the benefits of CLIP to help both small and larger groups to more fully 'come together' and has enabled fuller participation and inclusion of wider expertise to solve problems collectively. Some CLIP activities have engaged with a larger number of participants, beyond the core inquiry group, which have included clinicians, staff and volunteers from social care, home care staff and people that use services. This extension of action inquiry through a more structured, designed approach to events has enabled fuller participation and greater sharing of experience, expertise and ideas for improvement.

CLIP participants who are not in powerful or privileged professional roles, who are not always invited to take part in 'leadership development' activities have been delighted to be part of this work. Rather than being marginalised, the experience and knowledge of a range of practitioners, including those that work directly with patients or people that use services, has been mobilised in important ways that can ultimately enhance the quality of health and social care, for example, insights about prescribing practices, home care and enhanced patient safety. CLIP has also enabled the fuller use of existing and new evidence, including feedback from people that use services, patient questionnaires and data on housing, health and homelessness; such data can often play an important part in challenging assumptions and generating dialogue:

We were kept on track and moved forward rather than going over the same old issues and no-one dominated the discussion. Looking at the case studies gave us a richness too; one man had had nine different tenancies and over 100 A & E attendances. It just isn't possible, when faced with that data, to say 'our service doesn't do that!' People were quite shocked at some of the case studies and we were much more galvanised.

There is a clear shift in how the CLIP participants speak of themselves as they have developed closer, more purposeful relationships and have found that they are able to learn by paying attention to how they communicate and build networks, with a more collective, group ethos, with valued and practical consequences.

The tone of the CLIP stories is of groups of committed, caring, busy, practical people, who are also anxious, fragile and overloaded. They recognise that their action inquiry is work in progress, that dialogue is not easy but that through it, they are reaching new levels of understanding of themselves and others. Important elements of the new qualities of group conversations include:

- Talking openly about how we want to be with each other
- Enabling fuller participation and sharing of our experience, expertise and ideas for improvement
- Working with language and exploring what each other mean by particular terms or ideas
- Dismantling stereotypes or pre-conceptions of each other
- Recognising when we are talking at cross-purposes and getting it over with more quickly
- Being more compassionate with each other
- Talking about our differences of knowledge, skills, strengths and perspectives and seeing them as an asset, not a barrier
- Being able to create new ways of working and better services and being energised by the possibilities.

Without this support, there is a sense that they would have remained 'stuck'; these issues have often been undiscussable or have only been discussed in private in ways that are not necessarily productive or helpful. Many participants talk about being in a very different place to when they started as a CLIP group.

Co-missioning: convening and facilitating new conversations

There is no suggestion that embarking on a different approach to learning and leadership development is easy. Both the CLIP programme and CLS cast light on the intensive, often difficult and sometimes abortive work of 'convening', well before inquiry participants are ever in a room together and this section draws on the experience of both programmes.

Facilitation is frequently referred to as a process of 'making it easy' or supporting people to learn and there are many different schools of practice. In general terms, the purpose of facilitation can be understood as to help and support people to achieve specific goals, and to enable teams and individuals to analyse, reflect and change their attitudes, behaviours and ways of working (Wadsworth 2001; Dewar and Sharp, 2013).

Whilst both programmes have worked with pre-existing and newly convened groups, there are some distinctions in their models of facilitation. The CLIP use of the term 'facilitation' generally refers to a small-scale intervention by a person external to the immediate context, who helps a group move forward with their collaboration, often when they are puzzled about what to do. This might last for a period of a few months or longer or be most simply short-term help to design and facilitate learning events or workshops.

For CLS, paired facilitation is seen as a critical feature in helping participant sites to work successfully and reflects the complex and systemic nature of the issues being tackled. Two facilitators work in partnership to support groups and enable them to work effectively on their personal and collective leadership and in taking steps to impact on the issue at the centre of their work. There is also a commitment to building wider facilitation capacity by drawing on and developing existing resources from within public services (Collective Leadership, 2019).

In both programmes, there is commonly a focus on relationship building and on developing shared understandings, often through exploration of language and the unconscious and emotional aspects of change. A crucial part of the task is to shift the focus from being solely on the challenges that drive the common endeavour, to also focus on learning, adaptation and adoption of new ways of working together, to develop a commitment to a new type of learning partnership.

We know the first steps are fateful; much depends on what happens at the beginning of the inquiry process (Wicks and Reason, 2009), but it's important to consider when inquiry begins. It can be hard to even get started. Both CLIP and CLS showed that, despite apparent interest, individuals and organisations were at different stages of readiness to explore their own collaborative leadership. Many were challenged by financial austerity, the dominance of 'command and control' styles of leadership, commissioning priorities and management systems and wider issues of professional and political power and accountability. In such a context, the ability to establish relations with an appropriate grouping of people cannot be taken for granted and raises questions of access, legitimacy and the capacity to convene. These questions encounter the tensions, paradoxes and contradictions of seeking to work differently, to create the space, literally and metaphorically, in which participants feel safe enough to begin to share and build trust.

The challenge in both programmes is how to coordinate and align divergent aims and purposes in a way that articulates a 'co-mission' or collective purpose and agenda that people can orient around and begin to define their relational accountabilities with each other (Barge, 2015). Both programmes work to what are often very long lead in times; CLIP runs an application and selection process whereas the CLS offer is highly bespoke and responsive and may take some time, perhaps from an initial taster session, to come to fruition as a 'site'.

The CLIP national delivery team (itself a partnership) found that that willingness for collaboration was not as developed as they expected and that, in general, 'people are not used to having a facilitated conversation'. Amongst applications it was rare to get a genuinely collaborative proposal for resources from across a local partnership and the real sensitivities and challenges of the work were rarely identified directly. These quotes are reflections from the delivery team:

The document that the project team put in was a technical document. Most of our time has been spent talking to people about what's really going on.

What I believe has not yet occurred to most participants is that this is also a development pro-gramme, or at least a place where learning together to support growth and change will be given prominence. This requires a different orientation to 'turning up', more reflection, and a different type of commitment and personal investment than they may be used to bringing to a meeting.

These realities had implications for the progress, pace and nature of the programme, extending the initial 'contracting' process due to the need to establish membership of the inquiry group, common expectations and a shared purpose for the local work. After initial interest, several prospective CLIP sites did not proceed. Many were inevitably focus-ing on the service delivery imperatives, financial pressures and conflict between partners and some were in a state of crisis and unable to engage fully with the offer.

Even where these kinds of challenges did not prevent a CLIP site from going ahead, these contextual issues had a strong influence on what each site wished to focus on; in some cases, it took quite a bit of time to work out where in the local system might the CLIP support be most effective, then to move beyond the most immediate or technical aspects of the work in hand to develop a shared commitment to a deeper level of change. In terms of group relations, for example, this might show up as discontinuity of membership of the group, making it difficult to create and sustain conditions for good communications and creating anxiety about who is not present at any time. To give CLIP a chance of success, a focus on technical fixes and responding to crises had to be turned around, despite the wider context.

The learning in CLS sites also starts with the very first conversations. Writing reflectively about the experience of initiating CLS, one of the CLS team, talks of 'convening (with a small "c")' and 'the wax and wane as a collective dance begins':

Working with a group is fundamentally about the development of a complex set of relationships between: the convenor and the facilitators, the facilitator pairing, between the participants and the facilitators, among the participants themselves and crucially, the participants and their colleagues outside of the group … As each player takes up their roles, a kind of tentative dance begins as they test out what it means to work together in this way, and find out more about each other and everyone's intentions. (Collective Leadership, 2019a)

To assemble a group of people, convenors need to have positional or personal power, be motivated to bring a group together to work on a shared issue and be open to working in a different, often counter-cultural, way:

Our experience suggests there are many motivations: [convenors] have been working with a group for a while and feel they've got a bit stuck, they have tried multiple approaches with little progress, or have a strong gut instinct that there must be another way to work together but they're not sure how to bring it to life. I also have a hunch that they tend to be people who like to bend the rules, even in a small way … (Collective Leadership, 2019a)

One such convenor in Fife was charged by senior managers with taking collective leader-ship work forward for social work and education to achieve best outcomes for children and families. Later he was able to work alongside two CLS facilitators leading to changes in practical ways of working amongst social work and schools. He had to overcome barriers of different perspectives and understanding of the issues and suspicion of a different way of working, rooted in a legacy of several years of senior management leadership programmes and masterclasses. Reflecting on this experience, he provides a compelling account of the very messy realities, stops and starts, breakthroughs and crises;

> I wanted them to work in groups … to identify the real issues and to start working to improve them … this was all accepted and had the support of the Chief Social Work Officer and the Executive Director of Education and Children's Services … But, it just felt fractured, it just felt like it was being viewed as another learning programme and therefore another passive approach to learning. And initially people weren't really engaging with their work groups.

As a pilot, he and his colleagues convened a multi-professional group of 17 individuals who were assumed to be working together.

> We soon found that our assumption that they knew each other and were already working really closely together, was blown away. We said to them it's up to you, however you want to work, there's no blueprint on this, if you want to change the way you work here, you need to think about what that is. So, they were given permission to say what doesn't work … and how could we change it together … which was great.

What eventually arose was not planned, but was an evolving, at times reactive, response to meeting resistance, that shifted the mindset of 'why people were coming together'.

> I'm really, really thankful that a few people got upset and annoyed by the first programme, because actually if they hadn't got annoyed and wanted to quit that programme in the first place, it wouldn't have done as well as it did. If it had just been what I'd designed it to be, it might have been OK … but we'd certainly not be where we are now, three and a half years later. I was told by a key manager [locally] that things have been transformed by the way that the first local pilot worked, so the ripples are being felt in every part of the locality, influenced by the way we started working there.

This approach led to a more productive experience, turning distrust and cynicism into a more authentic and trustworthy approach, able to be adopted across other districts in Fife.

> Support to the group through an action inquiry approach and sticking with that … has created a better dynamic for work, which is a result of the positivity that has emerged from this programme.

Reflections on a second CLS site exploring the question 'How do we tackle conflict in Scotland?' casts light not only on the intractable issues themselves 'when actors from different areas of society have a stake in maintaining rather than resolving the issue' (Collective Leadership, 2019a), but just how many previous efforts have been tried, with the risk of 'wearing down the will of those who seek change':

> We've now tried so many approaches, with varying degrees of success, that we were struggling to find a new one. The number of approaches we've taken to tackling this issue is quite phenomenal. We've tried top-down approaches engaging at an organisational level, on the assumption impact would filter down. We've tried bottom up approaches, working directly with communities, thinking the impact would filter up. We have also had a varied research programme to look at the issue from different perspectives and get a real understanding of how the problem impacts on communities across Scotland. (Collective Leadership, 2019a, p. 21)

Searching for new thinking a Scottish Government policy officer attended a CLS taster session. Over the following ten months, he met regularly with the CLS facilitators to reflect on the possibility of bringing together people who would wish to work collectively and differently. The facilitators supported him to take risks and to set a tone and expectation that this would be a new way of approaching both the issue itself and the ways of working together.

Whilst in the early stages, this CLS example illustrates the importance of this extended period of co-missioning to support a local convener to work differently. His willingness to work openly and in ways that may have been uncomfortable was an important part of the initial success:

> The personal experiences expressed by everyone at the session in the opening discussion were among the most honest, heartfelt and sincere testimonies I have ever heard, and I was quite overwhelmed by them. This was like no other meeting that I have ever had on this issue and it was at this point that I realised that there was something different going on here which was radically out of the ordinary. Through discussion of personal experiences, it was easy to understand why everyone was motivated to be involved in this work. And it was apparent that even the most cynical realised there was an entirely new dynamic emerging from the desire to support change. (Collective Leadership, 2019a, p. 22)

Reflecting afterwards, he refers to the difficulties of 'holding your nerve to do something different' (Collective Leadership, 2019a, p. 25), whilst working in an environment that can be impatient for 'quick wins'. This CLS site found that this dynamic quickly asserted itself in a desire for action through the comfortable and familiar route of formalised working groups, agendas and plans of action. The pull towards the 'known' is very strong and CLS has identified that consistent and long-term facilitation is needed to support and hold the space for change to emerge and become embedded (Collective Leadership, 2019).

Both programmes have explored how an action inquiry approach can bring discipline and accountability to a collective and emergent learning process in ways that improve both the quality of the process of working together and the outcomes. Action inquiry is most effective where a group develop a genuine local commitment to this process, creating or recreating their own action inquiry question, rather than working with an imposed question that might have been valid for corporate sponsors or simply evolved since the initial stages.

Conclusions: practising change together

This is challenging and difficult work and it is often quite an achievement to constitute a viable inquiry group, capable and interested in developing a genuine co-mission. There is a risk of seeing paying attention to learning processes as at odds with working with people or simply getting on with the job. Participants need to understand the essentialness of collaboration, treat change as a normal part of their work and be willing to learn by being prepared to experiment, and reflect on the experience.

The role of convenors and facilitators is vital in modelling and embedding this approach to inquiry and in developing a new type of learning partnership, built on a different orientation to active involvement in personal, professional and leadership development. Despite greater acknowledgement of complexity, of 'wicked' issues and of the importance of relationships, the challenges of access, legitimacy and the capacity to convene are especially difficult in times of financial austerity and retrenchment. This means that the ability to establish relations with an appropriate grouping of people cannot be taken for granted.

This work draws on a range of traditions, theories of leadership and models of change and whilst different approaches and ideas about inquiry, dialogue and facilitation can be accommodated, facilitators may need to adapt their practice to support action inquiry as a *systematic* and *collaborative* endeavour ('leadership as learning') that will assist the sustainability of individual and group learning. There's no doubt that there is scope to deepen and spread the approach. It is unfamiliar perhaps particularly for senior leaders and there has been some resistance or rejection of such an approach, but the CLIP and CLS experience suggests that it can be adopted.

The description of the group experience here has many echoes within Raelin's description of action learning as a gateway to collaborative leadership (Raelin, 2006); perhaps the reframing of action learning as action inquiry might rekindle these links. Mutual moral obligations to cooperation and participation are particularly crucial in a context that needs successful coordination and multiple contributions to achieve positive outcomes, across hierarchies of position, professional rank and organisational sectors. Such complexity means that leadership must become a participatory and improvisational practice, a form of collaborative social action that recognises that relationships are at the heart of practising change and that knowledge co-production is essential. Here the process of learning and change inevitably includes ourselves as individuals and group members, not seen simply as something that other people should do or that is the responsibility of an abstraction referred to as 'the system'. This reframes social action as a relational and dialogical practice that we do together, by engaging in reflective inquiry and action, whoever, and wherever we are.

Distinct from much leadership development, this approach sees learning as emergent and relational, arising from the work that people are already engaged in at the level of the group or team, but from that starting point, spreading both to the individual and pan-organisational levels. This might be characterised as an integration of first, second- and third-person inquiry (Reason and Torbert, 2001), offering the potential to awaken and support inquiry across a wider community, so that participants can continue to learn in collaboration to support social action on problems of public importance.

Unlike action learning, action inquiry starts with second-person inquiry, rather than starting with (and perhaps remaining as) first-person inquiry. The constitution of an action inquiry group drawn deliberately from across professional groups and organisational boundaries, where the members share a common goal, may also set this apart from that of action learning sets, where members may be peers, without necessarily having a common focus for their work that they can only do together.

Conventional access to both action learning and leadership development is often based on hierarchical assumptions regarding who 'leaders' actually are and so risk exacerbating the problems of un-integrated care. Framing this work as action inquiry offers the chance to be less bounded by the notion of membership of an action learning set or narrow notions of who is or might become a leader. It enables the recognition of the contributions and the chance to embrace the involvement of a larger, more disparate and perhaps unknowable number of 'unusual suspects', those often not invited to take part in action learning or leadership development. This illustrates the ethical potential to realise 'social recognition', the acknowledgement of someone's social value to the community, that values their unique abilities, skills and contributions, and expresses respect for the other's particular importance to the community (Haslebo and Haslebo, 2012). Whilst not without challenges, perhaps most hopefully, rather than needing to be part of dedicated action learning or leadership development programmes, such collaborative embedded learning practices can be wrapped around and enmeshed within initiatives and programmes that work with complexity; indeed anywhere where effective social action will depend on the quality of relationships that can be developed.

Acknowledgements

Collective Leadership for Scotland is led by a small collaborative team responsible for the ongoing delivery, growth and development of the programme. Collaborative Leadership in Practice has a small delivery team drawing on staff from NHS Education for Scotland, Scottish Social Services Council and the Royal College of GPs in Scotland. Inevitably over several years, the people centrally involved are numerous and some of the key partners have changed. In seeking to distil and summarise some of the valuable learning, I wish to particularly acknowledge the vital contributions of Julie Higgins, Dot Mclaughlin, Sharon Millar, Kiera Oliver, Roy Lawrence, Karen Lawson, Susan Nevill and Janet Whitley. I would also like to thank the members of my own action learning set. I am extremely grateful for the reviewers' comments that have been of considerable help in concluding this paper. As author, I am responsible for the interpretations made in this paper and any errors or omissions.

Disclosure statement

No potential conflict of interest was reported by the author.

Funding

The work on which this paper is based was funded by the Scottish Government.

ORCID

Cathy Sharp 🆔 http://orcid.org/0000-0002-2753-3099

References

Argyris, C., R. Putnam, and D. McLain Smith. 1985. *Action Science*. Jossey-Bass.
Barge, J. K. 2015. "Consulting as Collaborative Co-inquiry." In *Dialogic Organization Development*, edited by G. Bushe and R. Marshak. Berrett-Koehler
Bland, N., and C. Sharp. 2016. "Practising Collaborative Leadership: Reflection and Learning from the Enabling Collaborative Leadership Pioneer Programme." What Works Scotland. http:// whatworksscotland.ac.uk/wp-content/uploads/2016/05/Pioneer-report-publication.pdf.
Burns, D. 2007. *Systemic Action Research*. Policy Press.
Byrne, D., and G. Callaghan. 2014. *Complexity Theory and the Social Sciences*. Routledge.

Collective Leadership. 2019. "Collective Leadership for Scotland: Year 1 Report." Building the foundations." https://workforcescotland.files.wordpress.com/2019/03/collective-leadership-first-annual-report-march-2019.pdf.

Collective Leadership. 2019a. "Collective Leadership: The Power in Beginnings." Research & Practice Series: Writing Sprint – February 2019. Accessed October 14 2019. https://workforcescotland.files.wordpress.com/2019/03/collective-leadership-the-power-in-beginnings-february-2019.pdf.

Dewar, B., and C. Sharp. 2013. "Appreciative Dialogue for Co-facilitation in Action Research and Practice Development." *FoNS 2013 International Practice Development Journal* 3 (2): 7. http://www.fons.org/library/journal.aspx.

Edmonstone, J., A. Lawless, and M. Pedler. 2019. "Leadership Development, Wicked Problems and Action Learning: Provocations to a Debate." *Action Learning: Research and Practice* 16 (1): 37–51. doi:10.1080/14767333.2019.1568967.

Fisher, D., D. Rooke, and B. Torbert. 2003. *Personal and Organisational Transformations*. Boston: Edge Work Press.

Freire, P. 1972. *Pedagogy of the Oppressed*. Penguin.

Garven, F., J. McLean, and L. Pattoni. 2016. *Asset-Based Approaches: Their Rise, Role and Reality*. Dunedin.

Gergen, K. 2014. "From Mirroring to World-Making: Research as Future Forming." *Journal for the Theory of Social Behaviour*. doi:10.1111/jtsb.12075.

Greenhalgh, T., and C. Papousti. 2018. "Studying Complexity in Health Services Research: Desperately Seeking an Overdue Paradigm Shift." *BMC Medicine* 16: 95. doi:10.1186/s12916-018-1089-4.

Grint, K. n.d. *Wicked Problems and Clumsy Solutions: The Role of Leadership*. Cranfield University.

Haslebo, G., and M. L. Haslebo. 2012. *Practicing Relational Ethics in Organisations*. Taos.

Heifetz, R. A., and M. Linsky. 2002. *Leadership on the Line*. Harvard Business School Press.

Heron, J., and P. Reason. 2001. "The Practice of Co-operative Inquiry. Research 'With' Rather Than 'on' People." In *Handbook of Action Research*, edited by P. Reason and H. Bradbury. Sage

Pearce, W. B. 2007. *Making Social Worlds. A Communication Perspective*. Oxford: Blackwell.

Raelin, J. 2001. "Public Reflection as the Basis of Learning." *Management Learning* 32 (1): 11–30. doi: 10.1177%2F1350507601321002.

Raelin, J. 2006. "Does Action Learning Promote Collaborative Leadership?" *Academy of Management Learning & Education* 5 (2): 152–168.

Raelin, J. 2016. "Imagine There Are no Leaders: Reframing Leadership as Collaborative Agency." *Leadership* 12 (2): 131–158. Sage.

Reason, P., and H. Bradbury. 2001. "Introduction: Inquiry and Participation in Search of a World Worthy of Human Aspiration." In *Handbook of Action Research*, edited by P. Reason and H. Bradbury, 1–14. London: Sage.

Reason, P., and W. R. Torbert. 2001. "The Action Turn: Towards a Transformational Social Science." *Concepts and Transformations* 6 (1).

Seddon, J. 2008. *Systems Thinking in the Public Sector: The Failure of the Reform Regime ... and a Manifesto for a Better way*. Triarchy Press Ltd.

Sharp, C. 2018. "Learning and Outcomes from Leadership for Integration." Final Report, April, NHS Education for Scotland. Accessed November 10 2019. http://bit.ly/2qlslli.

Sharp, C. 2018a. "Collective Leadership: Where Nothing Is Clear, and Everything Keeps Changing." New Territories for Evaluation, Workforce Scotland. Accessed November 10 2019. http://bit.ly/2H3ycJN.

Vince, R., and M. Pedler. 2018. "Putting the Contradictions Back Into Leadership Development." *Leadership & Organization Development Journal* 39 (7).

Wadsworth, Y. 2001. "The Mirror, the Magnifying Glass, the Compass and the Map: Facilitating Participatory Action Research." In *Handbook of Action Research*, edited by P. Reason and H. Bradbury, 420–432. London: Sage.

Weil, S. 1997. "Social and Organisational Learning in a Different key: An Introduction to the Principles of Critical Learning Theatre and Dialectical Inquiry." In *Systems for Sustainability: People, Organisations and Environments*, edited by F. Stowell, R. Ison, and R. Armsonet. New York, NY: Plenum.

Wicks, P. G., and P. Reason. 2009. "Initiating Action Research, Challenges and Paradoxes of Opening Communicative Space." *Action Research* 7 (3): 243–262.

Participatory action research as political education

Éva Tessza Udvarhelyi

ABSTRACT

In this paper, I discuss participatory action research (PAR) as a way to support social and political engagement and develop civil society. After a short overview of my personal journey to participatory action research, I describe a general structure that I have developed for organizing PAR projects and a short introduction to the state of civil society in Hungary. I then summarize three PAR projects in Budapest between 2011 and 2018. All three revolved around the issue of affordable and adequate housing and were designed as part of the movement for the right to housing in Hungary. The paper concludes with some of the most important implications I drew from this work regarding the development of civil society and critical consciousness.

Introduction

In this paper, I discuss participatory action research (PAR) as a way to support social and political engagement and develop civil society. After a short overview of my personal journey to participatory action research, a general structure for carrying out PAR projects and a short introduction to the state of civil society in Hungary, I summarize three PAR projects that I have been involved in between 2011 and 2018 in Budapest. All three projects revolved around the issue of affordable and adequate housing and were designed as part of the movement for the right to housing in Hungary. I conclude the paper with some of the most important implications I drew from this work regarding the development of civil society and critical consciousness.

PAR as political education – a personal journey

I started out my life as a social scientist with an interest in the notions of cleanliness and purity. In 2002 I found a newspaper article reporting on a new program by the municipality of Budapest to clean the city's underground pedestrian passages from graffiti, illegal vendors and homeless people. As my co-researcher and I spent the next three years examining the connections between the ideas of cleanliness and social exclusion (see Udvarhelyi and Török 2006), I got more and more disturbed by what we had discovered. Both elected politicians and public officials wanted to convince us that these measures were in the interest of the 'decent' residents of the city such as ourselves (with housing and a middle-class status). In other words, as it turned out, homeless people were chased away from public spaces in my name and to serve my imagined needs.

In fact, I come from a safe middle-class background with many privileges. Among these are a secure home and access to quality education. While I was vaguely aware of these as I grew up, the above research project forced me to take a harder look at my own social position. This research was more than just a school project for me – it made me think about my role in reproducing social injustices and about my responsibility in shaping society. It was a process of awakening that led me to discover my political self and become an activist for housing rights in 2005.

Later, I realized that if the research was something that could politicize and liberate me, it can have the same effect on other people, too, especially those who suffer from the most serious forms of exclusion. However, in the traditional university setup, these people are rarely or never present – or if they are, they are almost always the objects of research. Their ideas and needs are being studied by other people, but their own voice is rarely heard. As I was struggling with these issues, I discovered the world of participatory action research. In PAR, people who are affected by a social issue are not studied as in a laboratory but actively engage in research to understand the roots of their problems and take action to change the situation. In this case, research goes way beyond the walls of the university and becomes a path towards full citizenship. In other words, with the help of PAR, people who are traditionally excluded from formal academic spaces are able to have the same experience as me: first ask, then understand and finally transform the world they live in.

Civil society in Hungary

Civil society organizations such as NGOs, informal groups and grassroots social movements are central to the functioning of a healthy democracy. In Hungary, the freedom of citizens to assemble and organize themselves was seriously limited for the four decades of state socialism between 1948 and 1988. After the regime change in 1989, civil society blossomed as citizens found their new power to establish organizations around issues of interest or concern.

In the 1990s, as former opposition groups became formalized, new civil society groups emerged around issues including environmental protection, ethnic minorities and human rights. Cultural and civic organizations were founded to pursue autonomous activities that had not been allowed in the previous regime. In the first 20 years after the regime change, civic engagement was considered a positive influence in Hungarian politics and civil society organizations had an important role in both making demands on the state and filling in the gaps in areas where the state did not function properly. At the same time, as many civil society organizations became professionalized and started to depend more heavily on state and EU funding, they also started to withdraw from critical public engagement and today, most organizations tend to stay in the realm of social, cultural or community services.

While the legalization and institutionalization of civil society was essential to the democratic transition of Hungary, socialization into democratic governance and everyday democratic practices has lagged behind. Public school methods are still based on rote memorization and most children are not exposed to critical thinking or any form of critical engagement with social, economic or political issues. In the nonformal education sector, there are a few organizations that develop the democratic skills of children and young people, but hardly any organizations that address the democratic education of adults. NGOs working with marginalized adults such as unemployed people, women or the Roma tend to provide social and supportive services and rarely promote political and social participation. By turning into service-providing organizations, civil society produces clients rather than citizens, which weakens the community's potential to exercise control over the state. At the same time, in the past 9 years, the Hungarian state has become more authoritarian and the safeguards of a strong and independent civil society have become dangerously weak. According to the 2018 Freedom House report, Hungary's rating as a democracy has declined on all scales of measurement and the country's media is categorized as only partly free.

In all, citizen activism and political engagement in Hungary have been limited by historical circumstances and this is made even worse by the current semi-authoritarian regime. In the School of Public Life, we address both issues by providing political education to adults for free. While most of our pedagogical work takes the form of trainings and workshops, we use participatory action research as a long-term and embedded approach to promote political consciousness and citizen action.

Participatory action research

Appadurai (2006) defines research as the capacity to make disciplined inquiries into the things we need to know, but do not know yet. In this sense, as he puts it, all human beings are researchers, as we all make decisions that require us to make explorations beyond what we currently know. Today, however, especially in Hungary, research is often considered a privilege of a small academic elite and there is only sporadic productive interaction between the academic sphere and citizens involved in grassroots organizations. By connecting knowledge production, critical thinking, and democratic social action, participatory action research has the potential to bridge the gap between academia and citizen engagement and serve as a tool for democratic education and the development of civil society (Han 2014).

PAR is a form of inquiry where 'ordinary, underprivileged people … collectively investigate their own reality, by themselves or in partnership with friendly outsiders, take action of their own to advance their lives, and reflect on their ongoing experience' (Rahman 2008, 49). On the one hand, PAR emphasizes learning through cycles of reflection, action and evaluation that lead to both relevant, embedded and grounded knowledge and sustained social involvement. On the other, PAR brings together the commitment of social movements, their members' experience and expertise, and scholars skilled in the craft of research with access to the resources of academia. In this way, by establishing a democratic and critical process of knowledge production, PAR is able to produce results that are both theoretically significant and socially transformative.

Among the many variations of action research, critical participatory action research puts emphasis on two main elements. First, as Torre et al. (2012) point out,

> critical participatory researchers are bound by a set of critical and participatory commitments … with a principled purpose of working against unjust, oppressive structures … [C]ritical

participatory projects are crafted toward Impact Validity, anticipating from the start how to produce evidence that can be mobilized for change. (175–181)

The second important element of critical PAR is deep participation (Billies 2010), which means that all researchers – regardless of their academic background – participate in all the aspects of the study as active and fully fledged members. In this way, everyone is involved in a co-learning process on an equal footing.

I have been organizing workshops and trainings in the School of Public Life to promote PAR as an inclusive and emancipatory approach in both science and activism. In these trainings, we have developed a general model to carry out participatory action research that (1) leads to the raising of critical consciousness, (2) is built on deep participation and (3) leads to transformative social action. Below is a short summary of the steps we usually take to implement these projects.

Original idea for research

The original idea for a PAR project can come from many different sources including those directly affected, organizers, activists or even experts. In our practice, what matters is that this idea or need is always embedded in or serve the purposes of a grassroots movement for social justice. In this sense, our PAR projects are not just one isolated project among many, but a structured process of learning and discovery to support long-term personal and organizational development.

Initiating team

While PAR is based on a process of co-learning and co-creation, a smaller group of people can take responsibility to plan and launch the process. In our practice, it is good for this team to include at least three kinds of people: someone familiar with PAR as a critical approach, someone who has personal experiences with the concrete topic and someone experienced in community organizing.

Timeline and budget

Before we actually engage in research, the initiating team has to plan the PAR process in general terms, e.g. when to start, when to finish, how many people can be involved etc. Taking available resources into account is also very important. If we decide to offer co-researchers a stipend or any kind of financial compensation, the fundraising has to start on time so that there is financial security throughout the whole process.

Open call for participants

In my experience, PAR is a wonderful way to engage in social action and reflection people who are traditionally outside of activism and politics. This is why we always recruit researchers through an open in addition to engaging the existing members of a community. In our practice, the initiating team is responsible for involving the most diverse and most motivated co-researchers based on their written applications and a personal interview.

Three-day training

Our PAR projects always start with a three-day training where all the researchers get together to learn about each other and the whole project as well as about PAR as an approach. This is also the opportunity to start co-designing the details of the research process, to collectively create a code of ethics and finalize the budget for the research, which will all serve as the basis for our further collaboration.

Weekly meetings

After the initial training, our research groups usually meet once a week for three hours, which is compulsory for everyone involved. At these meetings, we discuss, manage and evaluate our research project and also plan our individual work. It is important that these meetings are facilitated (ideally in rotation) and accessible to everyone. We always offer snacks and drinks and we take and distribute notes for both our own institutional memory and those who did not attend.

Finding the big question and the subquestions

We tend to take at least a month to formulate the main question of our research and to list all the sub-questions we want to find answers to. This is usually done in a deductive way by asking as many relevant questions as possible and then finding the ones that we feel most crucial. Importantly, this is where the research group starts to take control over from the initiating team and we often significantly deviate from the original research question.

Research design

After we have formulated our question(s), together we learn about the methods available to us for finding answers to them. This is an intensive learning period where even those who have never studied research methods or have any kind of education need to be able to follow. Having looked at all the possibilities, we collectively make a decision about the methods we want to use.

Developing research tools

Once we have decided about the general approach and the methods of the research (which can be anything from body-mapping to statistical surveys), we have to develop our own data collection tools (e.g. interview questions, personal diary schedule etc.) and learn to use them. This can take a relatively long time as we develop each tool, test and re-design them and we also learn to master them (e.g. with practice interview sessions). However, it is of key importance to the participatory aspect of PAR that all researchers understand our methods and master the different tools as much as possible.

Data collection

This is when we put to practical use all the tools we have collectively developed. Of course, not everyone has to be involved in all aspects of data collection (e.g. someone may be great at interviewing but hate to go to the library and vice versa), but it is still crucial that everyone in the group participate in data collection in some way and that more traditionally trained researchers don't take over the process.

Summary and analysis of data

This can take place in an iterative way and we do not need to wait for all the data to arrive. It is possible that we need to ask for external help with certain techniques of interpretation (e.g. statistical analysis). At the same time, it is important that we make the analysis of data as accessible as possible for those with little experience or education and this is why it is a good idea to use as many discussions, visualizations and manual sorting as possible.

Dissemination of results

In PAR, making an impact is as crucial as producing knowledge. To this end, it is necessary to produce a comprehensive research report written in language that everyone understands and that we make it available to everyone for free. In addition to the research report, there are many platforms and approaches we can take to get our findings to as many people as possible including exhibitions, conferences, press releases, performances, workshops, op-eds etc.

Taking action

In PAR action does not have to occur as an isolated act at the end of the project. Quite the opposite: action can be something that is a natural part of the research process itself. Action can be anything that disrupts existing relations of power and exclusion. For example, this is what happens when a homeless person makes an interview with the head of police about harassment and discrimination. It is also very important to initiate more tangible and critical interventions that have long-lasting impact in the field where we work (as shown in the concrete examples below).

Assessment and follow-up

Throughout the PAR process, it is very important to engage in critical reflection about what is happening with the group, the research process and the individuals involved. This can take the form of individual or group work and it is important not only to document it but also to hold ourselves accountable to our own feedback. Finally, it is crucial to devote time towards the end of the project to discuss the future of both the group and its individual members as a basis for further social and political question.

Participatory action research and action learning

Action learning is an approach that has been most widely adopted in organizational development as a way to solve a problem collectively while also creating the foundations for further personal learning and development. While it has most often been used in a (business) management context, it is not completely free of broader political implications and critical action learning is based on more conventional forms of action learning infused with elements from critical social theory, which leads to a more critical stance towards power relations, organizational dynamics and the strengthening of political awareness (Trehan and Pedler 2016).

Action learning and participatory action research share many commitments, methods and elements, which include a focus on group work, reflexivity, learning from peers, process-based and facilitated work and orientation to action. Of course, there are also many differences, one of which is the more limited scope of action learning as an approach to solve particular problems and facilitate the learning and working of a particular team, while PAR tends to have a much broader mandate to challenge existing power relations while understanding and exploring oppressive social structures.

It can be very useful to put action learning and participatory action research into conversation with each other to share practices and approaches and to offer critical input to shape practices related to both. PAR can offer a social justice orientation to action learning that reinforces the voices of more marginalized people and the need for structural social transformations and not only the solution of specific or intragroup problems. Action learning, on the other hand, can offer a rich source of methods and techniques to approach problems and tensions that almost inevitably arise in PAR groups (as in any other group). Using action learning techniques to develop the relationship and power differences among researchers in a PAR project seems very productive and very much in line with the philosophy and practice of participatory action research.

PAR in Hungary

In Hungary, participatory approaches to science and knowledge production are not widely accepted or applied. As a result, participatory action research is neither frequently used, nor institutionalized in any way. There is a relatively small circle of academics who engage in this practice in a systematic way (see the authors in the 2011/5 volume of *AnBlokk* or the 2017/1–4 volume of *Kovász* journals), a few grassroots organizations have used this approach to support their advocacy work and so far only two books have been published about PAR in Hungarian (see Pataki and Vári 2011; Udvarhelyi and Dósa 2019). In the following, I will give an overview of the PAR projects that I have been involved in the past 10 years, which all share a commitment to deep participation, critical consciousness and social change.

From 2010 to 2012, I was involved in a participatory action research project with homeless people about their experiences of discrimination (for a more detailed description, see Udvarhelyi 2014). While this project became an important part of my PhD dissertation, its real significance lies in the fact that it was integrated into the work of the Budapest-based grassroots housing advocacy group, The City is for All. My idea for the research emerged from many years of experience working on homelessness and with homeless people as fellow activists. While in our everyday conversations, discrimination, harassment and even brutality from the state appeared very frequently, there was basically no scientific research about this topic and it was largely overlooked in public and professional discourses. With homeless activists of The City is for All and newly recruited researchers who had all experienced street homelessness, we set out to document this phenomenon through the discussion of personal stories, a survey with 400 homeless people, interviews with representatives of public agencies and statistical data. Our findings showed that homeless people see themselves as second-class citizens because of encounters with the state where they are treated as different from and less than 'regular citizens' in areas such as public transportation, interaction with the police and the health care system. The dissemination of the findings took years and many homeless researchers joined The City is for All to continue working on this topic. The most significant outcome of the research was a legal procedure against the Budapest Police Department for its discriminatory identity checks of homeless people. In this procedure, the findings of our PAR project played a key role and in 2015 the Budapest Police Department was forced to acknowledge the existence of discriminatory identity checks and enter into an agreement with us to ensure that police officers follow fundamental rules of equal treatment.

From 2015 to 2017 the School of Public Life launched a participatory action research project with a group of people living in housing poverty to explore the formerly invisible history of grassroots citizen action around housing in Hungary throughout the twentieth century (for more details, see Csécsei et al. 2017). The need to be aware of our own history became clear to me in 2009 when housing rights activists from New York helped us found The City is for All and we could not come up with any positive Hungarian examples of poor people achieving justice for themselves through struggle. The main aim of this project was to explore and raise awareness about the often-forgotten traditions of citizen activism in the contemporary housing movement and more generally in Hungary. Co-creating the design of this research was more difficult because it required methods of historical inquiry that few of us in the group had knowledge about or experience in. However, with the help of a volunteer historian, we became familiar with various ways of working with digital databases, archives, libraries and photo collections. In the end, we managed to dig up and write the stories of twelve grassroots initiatives and/or movements around affordable and safe housing in twentieth-century Budapest. In this project, dissemination was of key importance as the main goal was to raise awareness about these traditions both in and outside of the current housing movement. We held a series of workshops in different social settings from night shelters through family support centers to cultural centers and we also designed an outdoor exhibition, which was featured for more than a year in the poorest district of Budapest. To address those who are not directly affected by the housing crisis, but may play the important role of allies, we also collaborated with the Kassák Museum in Budapest to create a temporary indoor exhibition, which turned out to be the most visited exhibit in the museum thus far.

The most recent participatory action research project that I was involved in lasted from 2016 to 2018. In this one, a group of physically disabled people and their allies engaged in research about the necessary social, physical and economic conditions of independent living for physically disabled people (for more details, see Balázs et al. 2019). As earlier, members of the research team were recruited via an open call and co-researchers received a small monthly stipend for 12 months. In this case, the accessibility of the research was of utmost concern to us, which meant that the activist center where our meetings took place had to be retrofitted to build an elevator and accessible bathrooms (this was financed through a crowd-funding project). We also had a personal assistant on the research team whose main job was to give all the necessary support to disabled researchers in the weekly meetings. In addition to building heavily on the experiences of participants, we conducted a survey among disabled people and service-providers, made interviews about people's personal histories of housing and collected public data and statistical information. In addition to publishing our findings in a booklet that we have been disseminating for free, our group played an important role in the successful struggle to make Metro Line 3 in Budapest wheelchair accessible. Finally, an even more significant and long-term outcome of the project was the birth of a new advocacy organization. As it turned out, the common research experience and the knowledge we had collectively gained was so powerful that members of the research group decided to stay together as a collective and establish a grassroots advocacy group. Today, the group is led directly by disabled people and focuses on the education of both the general public and disabled people about independent living and accessibility.

Conclusions

The above experiences have reinforced my belief that critical participatory action research is a very powerful form of political education for everyone involved regardless of their social position and educational background. In each of the above cases, both my co-researchers and I were deeply transformed by our common learning experiences. For example, I learnt to put the slogan of participation in actual practice when homeless researchers challenged me to change my original research questions and I realized both the limits of my own knowledge and my own freedom of movement from members of the Living independently group. On the other hand, I had the chance to witness how a homeless co-researchers started to recover from his alcoholism after he 'started to use his brain again', as he put it, in our research process. I was also amazed to see how a mother of five living in poverty and with little formal education became an expert in archival research and was greeted with the greatest warmth by the librarians in the official archives of the city of Budapest. The PAR process in the Living independently group empowered one of the co-researchers to move to a wheelchair accessible apartment after 50 years of living on the third floor of a building without an elevator.

While short-term trainings in political education are perfect for honing existing skills and providing inspiration for further action, participatory action research is a thorough and in-depth process that not only produces new knowledge but also helps to transform all of us at a much deeper political and personal level. For this to happen, it is very important that this process is equitable and that academically trained researchers are as fully open to this process as co-researchers who are directly affected by the issues we study. PAR can be a very effective approach to the development of an active civil society whose members are capable of reflecting critically not only on social processes and structures, but also on themselves and are committed to social interventions based on a collective identification of problems and thorough grassroots research. While this kind of critical consciousness is essential everywhere, it is especially relevant in the context of Hungary where paternalism is highly institutionalized in academia and where the state is a leading player in the objectification and oppression of human beings.

Disclosure statement

No potential conflict of interest was reported by the author.

References

Appadurai, A. 2006. "The Right to Research." *Globalisation, Societies and Education* 4 (2): 167–177.

Balázs, P., A. Csengei, I. P. Czégé, V. Gulyás, E. Hruskó, Cs Kiss, V. Kovács, et al. 2019. "Önállóan lakni – közösségben élni." In *A kutatás felszabadító ereje. A részvételi akciókutatás elmélete és gyakorlata*, edited by ÉT Udvarhelyi and M. Dósa, 189–215. Budapest: Napvilág Kiadó – Közélet Iskolája.

Billies, M. 2010. "PAR Method: Journey to a Participatory Conscientization." *International Review of Qualitative Research* 3 (3): 355–376.

Csécsei, I., A. Csengei, M. Dósa, I. Kleiner, M. Palotai, I. T. Szakmáry, Z. Sziráki, et al. 2017. "When is it Time to Act if Not Now?!" Participatory Action Research about Housing Movements in Hungary. http://kovasz.uni-corvinus.hu/2017/2017-1-4.php

Han, H. 2014. *How Organizations Develop Activists. Civic Associations and Leadership in the 21st Century*. New York: Oxford University Press.

Pataki, G., and A. Vári, eds. 2011. *Részvétel – akció – kutatás. Magyarországi tapasztalatok a részvételi-, akció- és kooperatív kutatásokból*. Budapest: MTA Szociológiai Kutatóintézete.

Rahman, A. 2008. "Some Trends in the Praxis of Participatory Action Research." In *The Sage Handbook of Action Research: Participative Inquiry and Practice*, edited by P. Reason and H. Bradbury, 49–62. Los Angeles, CA: Sage.

Torre, M. E., M. Fine, B. G. Stoudt, and M. Fox. 2012. "Critical Participatory Action Research as Public Science." In *APA Handbook of Research Methods in Psychology*, Vol. 2, edited by H. Cooper, P. M. Camic, D. L. Long, A. T. Panter, D. Rindskopf, and K. J. Sher, 171–184. Washington, DC: American Psychological Association.

Trehan, K., and M. Pedler. 2016. "Critical Action Learning." In *Gower Handbook of Leadership and Management*, edited by J. Gold, R. Thorpe, and A. Mumford, 405–422. London: Routledge.

Udvarhelyi, ÉT. 2014. *Az igazság az utcán hever. Válaszok a magyarországi lakhatási válságra*. Budapest: Napvilág Kiadó.

Udvarhelyi, ÉT, and M. Dósa, eds. 2019. *A kutatás felszabadító ereje. A részvételi akciókutatás elmélete és gyakorlata*. Budapest: Napvilág Kiadó – Közélet Iskolája.

Udvarhelyi, ÉT, and Á Török. 2006. "The Dirty Residents of a Clean City." *Anthropology News*, February: 60.

The transformative potential of action learning in community-based research for social action

Ortrun Zuber-Skerritt 🆔 and Lesley Wood

ABSTRACT

Action learning within community-based research is a powerful capacitator of social action. Here, we consider three aspects of action learning that are vital to enable this: (i) developing self-directed and lifelong action learning; (ii) generating local and theoretical knowledge through action research and reflection on learning; and (iii) identifying the key principles and processes of action learning as an integrated concept within the participatory action learning and action research (PALAR) paradigm. We argue that action learning has to be developed in a systematic, educational way to enable people to take responsibility for improving their life circumstances. Examples from university partnerships with communities in South Africa and Australia demonstrate how action learning, within a PALAR process, can inspire and enable individuals and whole communities to learn and develop skills, attitudes, values, and understandings to engage in social action most effective for their particular needs and contexts. In this way, people become self-directed learners, creators of knowledge and activists able to challenge and disrupt dominant power relationships and traditional ways of conducting research. These case examples illustrate how action learning, as part of a PALAR process, enables the university to partner with community for social action towards a more just society.

Introduction

One of the problems in community-based research is that most practitioners are usually not interested in research, which they conceive as the realm of specialist academic researchers. Instead, they are interested in 'doing' and experimenting by trial and error, discussion and reflection in, on and after action, in a classical spiral of cycles of planning, acting, observing and reflecting. Therefore, a partnership between communities and universities can be very effective if the concepts and practices of action learning (AL) and action research (AR) are integrated (as ALAR) and focused on inclusion, collaboration and participation by both specialist researchers and community practitioners into the fairly new notion of 'participatory action learning and action research' or PALAR.

In the social sciences literature, action learning is variously located in the paradigm of experiential learning (Kolb 1984), lifelong learning (Jackson 2011) and lifelong action learning (Zuber-Skerritt and Teare 2013), as well as PALAR (Wood 2020; Zuber-Skerritt and Wood 2019). However, from our perspective, action research is normally conceived as being more complex than action learning because of the stringent quality criteria concerning the research process and the need to produce findings that make a contribution to knowledge. A PALAR process enables research skills to be introduced gradually over time, almost as a by-product in an action learning project. Based on our experience and research, we argue that if the characteristics of action learning are clarified, learned and practised systematically and strategically in the beginning of a collaborative team project, the potential for positive social action through action research will increase. The main aim of this article is to take a fresh look at the role of action learning as an important precursor and integrated component of community-based action research in the over-arching paradigm of learning, research and knowledge creation.

Our methods of achieving these aims in the following sections are (1) identifying and defining the principles and processes of action learning that are mutual and essential for maximizing the success of PALAR projects; and (2) illustrating the successes and possible pitfalls by case examples from community-based PALAR projects in South Africa and Australia. The significance of this article concerns the important contribution of action learning to community-based research for social action and change.

Action learning as an integral component of the action research process

Action learning (Revans 1982) and action research (Lewin 1946) were initially developed as separate and independent concepts, practices, processes and methods. Action learning was used mainly in management, business and organization development and action research in community development, education and higher education. It was only in the late 1980s that action researchers realized the close relationship between AL and AR in practice, theory and paradigm. In 1990 at the 'First World Congress on Action Learning, Action Research and Process Management' in Australia, AL and AR were integrated, and in 1991 an international network association, the Action Learning and Action Research Association (ALARA), was founded.

From then on, action researchers recognized clearly that creation of knowledge in the modern age needs an action-oriented research and development approach that is inclusive, participatory and collaborative, **with** and **for** people as 'participants' and 'co-researchers', in a project of mutual interest. This shift in paradigm in the human and social sciences was (1) to create practical, personal (tacit) and shared local knowledge; (2) to focus on urgent, complex problems or issues of concern to a community of practice for the common good (rather than the researcher's own interests and hypotheses); and, (3) to practise and live by common values, such as inclusion, participation, collaboration, team/relationship building, openness to new ideas, and trust to enhance mutual understanding through communication, debate, discussion, conversation, story-telling, and other participatory methods.

In sum, within the alternative paradigm in the social sciences, PALAR requires a new type of researcher/facilitator who is a knowledge expert and is not only clever, but also wise (Revans 1991). That is, a researcher who is willing and able to (1) understand the lived realities of others; and (2) support these people to meet their needs and priorities, providing an enabling environment for them to develop their skills and ability to

achieve positive change in their workplace or community. This requires PALAR practitioners to embody specific philosophical principles in their relationship with their co-
researchers, as we discuss in the next section.

Key principles of PALAR: 7Cs and 3Rs

The key principles of PALAR are grounded in democratic, life-enhancing values that accept
that all people, irrespective of their social, educational or class status, are able to take
action to improve their own lives, if facilitated to do so (Wood 2019). Zuber-Skerritt
(2018) summarizes the key features of PALAR as the 7Cs and the 3Rs. By embodying
and modeling these key features and principles, the researcher is able to create a safe
space for critical reflection and dialogue to occur. Such reflexive dialogue acts as the catalyst for participants' personal and professional transformation. We briefly summarize
these key principles below, first the 7Cs.

Communication

Within an action learning set in a PALAR process, communication is inclusive and dialogical. Members of the action learning set learn to 'listen with the heart' (Lazarus 2018, 56)
through practising active listening skills that take note of verbal, non-verbal and emotional
cues, in line with the PALAR paradigm that views learning as a cognitive, social and
affective process (Fletcher 2015). This kind of listening precludes interpreting what
others say through personal lenses, and encourages openness to,

> … both rational and intuitive understandings, to explore both 'scientific' and 'spiritual' under-
> standings of the world and to trust … intuitive understanding of a situation or of what is being
> expressed. It is not about separating the mind from the heart, but rather recognizing that the
> heart and mind together lead one to wisdom. (Lazarus 2018, 56–57)

Learning to communicate in this way is the basis for developing trusting, caring relationships where people learn to embrace action for positive change.

Commitment

Participation in an action learning set helps build participants' commitment to the change
project, as they begin to realize they are a valuable part of a team and that their absence
would impact negatively on the collective goals. This requires them to accept personal
responsibility for contributing to project aims.

Competence

Competence is built gradually within the action learning set, as part of the PALAR process
(see Figure 1). Building confidence involves helping people to identify their learning needs
and finding ways to help them develop new skills and competences, using talent within
the learning set or bringing in expert help. The personal competences built within a
PALAR project typically include problem-solving, communication, empathy, critical thinking and confidence, as well as technical skills (Wood 2019).

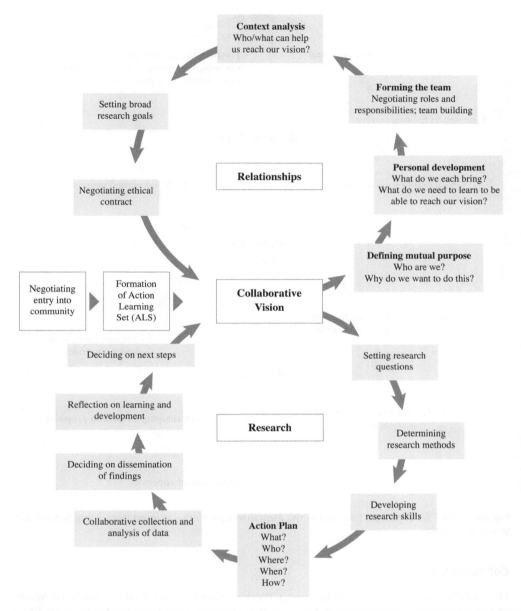

Figure 1. The PALAR process followed in the South African case study (adapted from Zuber-Skerritt and Wood 2019, 200). Notes: Figures 1 and 2 are adapted and Figure 3 reproduced here with permission from the publishers.

Compromise

Compromise was not one of Zuber-Skerritt's (2011) original Cs, but was added by Wood and Zuber-Skerritt (2013), on recognizing that it is a vital component in collaborating with others. Compromise refers to the ability to make personal sacrifices for the greater benefit of the project.

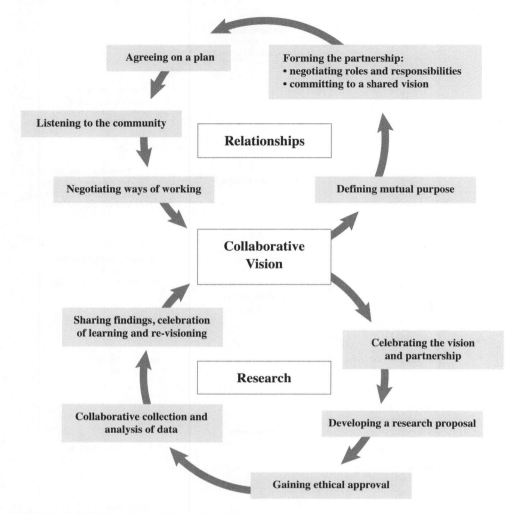

Figure 2. The PALAR process followed in the Australian case study (adapted from Zuber-Skerritt and Wood 2019, 200).

Collaboration

This principle goes almost without saying. Working together to attain the common vision of the group is of course essential in a participatory process. Here leadership is fluid to accommodate different needs and competences at different times in the project. The academic researcher must therefore be open to stepping back and encouraging other group members to facilitate when needed.

Critical self-reflection

As in all forms of action research, critical self-reflection is a key principle, and the basis of all learning. In a participatory process, it is important to be critically aware of not only your own learning, but also how you may be influencing the group process.

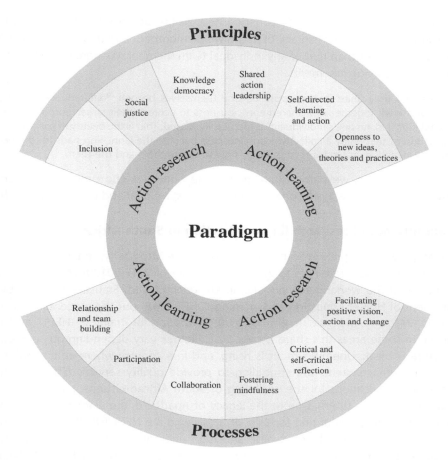

Figure 3. AL/AR paradigm, main principles and process (reproduced from Zuber-Skerritt and Wood 2019, 218).

Coaching

As relationships develop within the action learning set, members can coach each other supportively, sharing skills and expertise for the good of the project. As Wood (2020) suggests, group members take on the role of critical friends, to gently and sensitively help each other to grow and develop according to individual needs and abilities.

These key principles are operationalized by core processes, known as the 3 Rs. Kearney, Wood, and Zuber-Skerritt (2013, 125) explain these as 'the development of democratic, authentic, trusting and supportive *relationships*; continual critical *reflection* in a collaborative learning context; and *recognition* of the achievements of all participants'. A community of action learners is an unstructured network of relationships, built on shared values of collaboration, cooperation and work for the common good. In our various PALAR projects, we continually observe team members shift beyond individual consciousness at the beginning of the process, to more expansive ways of thinking, acting, being and knowing that we call 'collective consciousness' (Savary and Berne 2017, 55), i.e. thinking as one cohesive unit whose members acknowledge and pursue their shared interests collectively and have and give access to the consciousness of the others. This collective entity is necessarily more complex than any of its individual members, and their shared consciousness becomes richer than that of any individual team member. We agree with Savary and Berne's (2017, 54–55) statement:

> People who truly unite for a purpose beyond themselves become "differentiated" as they unite and work together in a shared consciousness to achieve their larger purpose. ... In a true relationship, no one's individuality is lost. It is increased. That is the beauty of connections. These unions that enjoy a collective consciousness become the launching pads for the next stage of evolution, as we learn consciously how to create them and use them.

In the next sections, we demonstrate how these principles and processes can enable action for social change at personal, professional, institutional and community levels.

Community-based research for social action in South Africa

The unemployment figures in South Africa in 2019 (see https://www.fin24.com/Economy/just-in-unemployment-rate-rises-to-276-in-first-quarter-of-2019-20190514) indicate over one-quarter of the working-age population are unemployed. Statistics released by the Department of Higher Education and Training (DHET 2018) put the percentage of youth (aged 15–24) who are not in employment, education or training (NEET) at 31.2%. However, in some areas this share is over 50%. Figures vary depending on sources, but the picture is bleak. Unemployment is rising, and in a country where education, health and social welfare systems are struggling to provide quality services (Ebersöhn 2017), this has dire implications for the wellbeing of South African citizens, particularly youth who are the nation's future. Due to the legacy of Apartheid, the Black population bears the highest burden, accounting for 84% of those who are NEET (DHET 2018). Given the extent of poverty, a very low tax base and high unemployment, improvement in the near future is unlikely. It is therefore imperative, in our opinion, that people learn to improve their own lives, as they see fit. Thus our choice of PALAR, an educative, emancipatory and political process through which people learn how to attain positive personal and technical outcomes (Wood 2020).

Educative, emancipatory and political outcomes of PALAR

PALAR, as a form of participatory action research or PAR (Fals Borda and Rahman 1991; Stern 2019), enables transformational engagement (Bowen, Newenham-Kahindi, and Herremans 2010), positioning community partners as full participants in all aspects of the research process. In a context where the legacy of colonization, Apartheid and persistent poverty has robbed people of their agency, dignity and freedom to control their own lives, such an approach is vital to raise the consciousness of people about the value of their contextual knowledge and experience and their agentic potential. In our experience of conducting PALAR projects with people who initially have little hope of change, the value from integrating an explicit action learning process into a participatory action research design is immensurable. As Freire (1970, 2007) stated, the point of education is to help people flourish and, time and again, we have seen this happen when people learn how to become self-directed, lifelong learners through action learning in a safe, dialogical space.

The process of PALAR is *educative* in and of itself, because of the explicit focus on action learning in the first phases of any project. Action learning continues throughout the process, but in the *relationship* phase (see Figure 1) the participants develop self-knowledge and begin to explore their potential. They set personal goals and determine what they need to learn to attain these goals. They practise self-reflection and collective reflection; they learn experientially to collaborate, communicate clearly, and critique constructively within a safe space. The time it takes for participants to become self-directed, reflective learners, able to dialogue with others, depends on many factors, especially the starting point. In one project, working with unemployed youth to improve their employability and capacity for helping their peers to do so, participants were involved for almost a year before they were ready to actually begin the research (see Wood 2020); when working with school children (see Mathikithela and Wood 2019) who were trying to make their school a more enabling space, several sessions were needed, but because of their existing relationships with each other and with the teacher/researcher, they could progress to the research phase within a few weeks.

This educative process within the action learning set in PALAR helps people to recognize and *emancipate* themselves from self-imposed limits, enabling them to begin to appreciate their own agentic potential to change/inform the development of policies and practices that impact on their lives. The action learning that participants experience in the PALAR process thus fosters action leadership (Zuber-Skerritt 2011), as they learn how to take responsibility for changing their own circumstances and to influence others to do the same (*political* outcome).

In this case study, we do not have space to document evidence of all the outcomes of projects we have facilitated. Instead, we present an instructive example of a project (mentioned above) that aimed to enable youth classified as NEET to learn how to make themselves more employable, and how to educate other youth to do the same. Since the participants in this study were all living in poverty, with little hope of employment, they initially felt hopeless (e.g. *I am always lazy. I don't feel like doing things. I have mood swings sometimes and I don't talk to people. Sometime you feel like you don't live on purpose, you just live because you have to live Y4.*). So it was imperative to spend time within the relationship cycle of PALAR, helping enable participants to build their self-esteem and self-belief, and develop a sense of purpose and agency. The few quotes in Table 1 illustrate the benefits of this action learning process to enable educative, emancipatory and political outcomes. We worked together through the stages of the relationship-building phase of PALAR by meeting in regular action learning sessions for a year, before participants moved on to research the needs of unemployed youth in their area as a basis for developing and presenting workshops, entrepreneurship programs and social media information sharing platforms to improve youth employability. Of course, there is overlap between educative, emancipatory and political outcomes; here we have tried to separate them for this discussion.

This example illustrates how participants have learnt to take action to improve their lives in one project. Many examples of other projects of similar outcomes do likewise, for example, so-called vulnerable learners in a rural school were successful in getting the teachers and school management to develop and implement policies to make their school safer and more health-promoting (Mathikithela 2020); students with disabilities who successfully advocated for management to craft a policy and initiate other

Table 1. PALAR outcomes to enable social action.

OUTCOMES		
Educative	Emancipatory	Political
Personal development: growth in self-confidence, self-belief, optimism and sense of purpose, ability to communicate, etc.	**Belief in own agency; seeing the bigger picture; aware of self-limiting thinking, renewed hope, etc.**	**Ability to network, organize, mobilize resources, talk to peers and influence change in others.**
Technical skills: presentation, facilitation, computer literacy, entrepreneurship, 3D printing, etc.	*Ever since I have been in this program, I have been exposed to so many things. I had a huge confidence boost and the other thing is that I have learned about the problems in my area. I have learned to work better with people. I talk a lot, so I learned to give others time to talk. Y1*	*I now have a platform to mobilize our resources and the 'how to' to do so. MM*
I have learned self-respect and personal growth. What I mean with self-respect is that sometimes you don't actually believe in yourself that you will be able to make it and I was that person, I never had that self-respect for myself. I believe that this program is about helping others, but before you can do so you should start with yourself before you can help others. The thing that I have also learned is the need for patience. I am not patient at all and I should start changing that. Y5		*I can do something about the drugs. I can talk to the youth and try to change their mentality, or even mobilize them to join the program so that they have something to do and so that they can leave the drugs. Y1*
	It made me a better person because I learn every day. I feel like there is a future, I feel like there is something that I will be able to achieve at the end of the day. It has given me a bit of direction. Y2	*It is possible for me as a young individual to try and change the problems. Y4*
To be reliable, I keep my promises. Before I wasn't comfortable with working in a team but now I am able to work in a group. I wasn't able to communicate with others but now I am able to talk in a group. Y3	*Think big – as you work with people who can see things outside of our experience, you learn to think big like them, realize that many of the limits come from your own thinking. MM*	

changes to make the academic and social spaces in their college more inclusive (Luthuli 2019); teachers who created structures to ensure at-risk learners received necessary psycho-social support to enable learning (Setlhare and Wood 2019); community parents and teachers who collaborated to develop a program for parents to provide support to their primary school children (Wood and McAteer 2017). Wood (2020) presents many more examples of how participants in community-based projects were able to move to action, based on the capabilities they developed from the process of action learning. Certainly, PALAR may present challenges, stemming from personal problems, institutional processes/demands, and social and structural inequalities. Yet we can conclude that participatory action learning, coupled with action research, is a most useful process to empower people living in socially unjust contexts to move towards social action to bring about positive change.

Community-based research for social action in Australia

This case study is located in Logan City, a local government area in southeast Queensland, Australia. In some areas of the city, there is a significant level of disadvantage relative to other areas of Queensland. A particular concern has been a higher proportion of children who are developmentally vulnerable at five years of age when transitioning to school and are therefore less likely to achieve learning, development and well-being outcomes in later years (Australian Government 2019). Therefore, a key goal for the community has been to encourage families to use quality early education services such as kindergarten[1] to encourage all children's successful transition to school. This seemed particularly important for

Samoan families, who are highly represented in Logan City, yet are under-represented as users of early education services.

The community collaboration discussed in this case study involved members from three not-for-profit community organizations. One organization provided early learning services nationally. Its services were highly concentrated in less advantaged areas and particularly focussed on enhancing outcomes for children in vulnerable circumstances. Another organization was a church community, which provided spiritual support for its strong membership of Samoan families residing in the city. This organization provided a variety of culturally appropriate outreach service for members. The remaining organization engaged and empowered members of the Logan community to work collaboratively for the common good and had encouraged collaboration between the other two organizations.

Teams from two universities were also involved. Both teams were based locally at campuses that valued community engagement and prioritized social inclusion. Collectively, the academics committed to the research collaboration, represented interest and expertise in areas that included early childhood education, applied linguistics and community engagement, and had worked collaboratively with the church community on earlier projects.

As shown in Figure 2, our PALAR process started with crafting a collaborative vision. To achieve this vision, representatives of the three organizations and the two universities met as a community of action learners. Participants were explicitly aware of their involvement in an action learning process.

Over the course of two or three meetings they *defined their purpose* and *formed a partnership*. This involved *negotiating roles and responsibilities, ways of working* and *committing to a shared vision* to ensure authentic participation of all participants in designing, implementing and evaluating the project. At times, this involved compromise on the part of individuals as they discussed their organizations' different operating principles and practices. Once members had *agreed on a plan,* they set about implementing the first step in that plan: *listening to the community*. This consultative process was undertaken and confirmed that many Samoan families chose not to use early childhood education services as they believed these services did not provide their children a culturally safe experience, that is, a space where children's sense of cultural identity was respected rather than challenged. The group reflected on what such a space might look like and designed their vision for a culturally safe kindergarten. This process involved several community consultations with Samoan families.

The community's shared *vision and partnership for the kindergarten were recognized and celebrated* through a traditional 'ava[2] ceremony hosted by the Samoan church community. This ceremony acknowledged the community's valuing of the partnership and its members' collaborative vision. Two months later, the kindergarten, hosted by the early learning organization, accepted its first intake of students. By that stage, the action learning group had continued meeting and had *developed a research proposal* guided by three questions:

(1) How does the kindergarten support Samoan language and culture?
(2) How does the kindergarten build a positive Samoan identity in a culturally safe space?
(3) How does the kindergarten experience enhance children's school readiness?

Ethical clearance was gained before *data collection and analysis* over a seven-month period. Data collection involved systematic observations at the kindergarten, with video, photographs and field notes, as children engaged with educators and with each other. The group used *talanoa*, a conversational method endorsed by Pacific Island researchers (Taleni et al. 2018), to gain perspectives of families and educators.

Findings indicated that families' experience of this kindergarten had influenced use of Samoan as a heritage language in homes. Where Samoan was spoken at home, the children's familiarity with Samoan songs and prayers strengthened the family's use of the heritage language. Parents who had lost their heritage language when shifting to English as they migrated or grew up, talked about Samoan language being revived in the home where, in some cases, children were teaching their parents. In Samoan culture, core cultural values include obedience, respect, love, and service (Va'a 2009). These values were well evidenced in the educators' interactions with children, and among the children. The kindergarten provided a culturally safe space for the children where their heritage language was valued. Findings also revealed important aspects of school readiness such as enhanced confidence and a developing sense of identity and belonging. As one Samoan educator commented:

> ... by surrounding them [the children] with culture, surrounding them with language, that helps because they need to know who they can identify with and they need to know where they belong, and their sense of belonging is key for supporting them through their whole journey in life. (Talanoa 3)

A final and important step in the PALAR process was an opportunity to *share findings* and to *celebrate learning for the group*, so members from all participating organizations came together to reflect critically on the findings and the learning that had occurred. The group is now in the process of *re-crafting* a collaborative vision to focus on ongoing collaboration.

Discussion

In this article, we have focused on the transformative potential of action learning in community-based research for social action, justice and positive change. This is particularly relevant in today's world of increasing violence, youth unemployment, mental health problems and ecological disasters. We have argued that action learning – developed systematically as lifelong, self-directed, collaborative learning, from and with others, to address important issues of mutual concern for the common good – can be a valuable introduction to and powerful capacitator for social action, especially in combination with participatory action research. In PALAR, action learning and action research share the same philosophy of learning and R&D when it comes to epistemology (theories of 'knowing'), ontology (theories of 'being') and methodology (theories of 'doing' research).

We have discussed two case studies to illustrate how PALAR can be used in community-based research: (1) in South Africa to address youth unemployment, and (2) in Australia to improve the life chances of pre-school children from Pacific Islander communities.

In summary, Figure 3 illustrates the essential theoretical and practical characteristics of action learning as an integral part of participatory action research, as discussed in the two case studies.

Conclusion

Reflecting on this article, including the two case studies it explores, we affirm here that the 7Cs and 3Rs of action learning and action research are rooted in the 3 Ps: Paradigm, Principles and Process. In both case studies, the focus is on developing participants' entrepreneurial mindset and personal characteristics such as self-directedness, creativity, independent and (self) critical thinking; the ability to collaborate and communicate with others in diverse contexts; a strong sense of self and purpose; and values that enable action for the common good, such as integrity and care for the human and non-human environment.

In this twenty-first century, it is more important than ever to adjust to increasingly rapid change in technology, ecology, economy and global politics and to explore all kinds of learning, research and development that are progressive, effective, diplomatic, communicative, transformational and ethical for all people and all other life on this planet. As this article makes clear, action learning is well placed to contribute to further development of such a transformational paradigm and principles in community-based research.

Notes

1. In Queensland, kindergarten (or kindy) is a part-time educational program provided in the year before children start school. Children attending kindergarten are at least 4 years old by 30 June in the year they are enrolled.
2. This ceremony is an important custom for Samoan people involving oratory, preparation of 'ava and the formal drinking of 'ava.

Acknowledgements

Parts of this article were enabled by research funded by the National Research Foundation in South Africa. Any opinion, findings or conclusions are those of the authors and the NRF cannot be held liable thereto.

Disclosure statement

No potential conflict of interest was reported by the authors.

ORCID

Ortrun Zuber-Skerritt ⓘ http://orcid.org/0000-0002-0816-9308

References

Australian Government. 2019. *Is Your Child Ready for Big School?* https://www.learningpotential.gov.
au/is-your-child-ready-for-big-school.
Bowen, F., A. Newenham-Kahindi, and I. Herremans. 2010. "When Suits Meets Roots: The Antecedents
and Consequences of Community Engagement Strategies." *Journal of Business Ethics* 95: 297–318.
DHET (Department of Higher Education and Training). 2018. *Fact Sheet on NEETs*. Pretoria:
Department of Higher Education and Training.
Ebersöhn, L. 2017. "A Resilience, Health and Well-Being Lens for Education and Poverty." *South
African Journal of Education* 37 (1): 1–9.
Fals Borda, O., and M. A. Rahman, eds. 1991. *Action and Knowledge: Breaking the Monopoly with
Participatory Action Research*. New York: Apex Press.
Fletcher, M. 2015. "Professional Learning." In *Professional Learning in Higher Education and
Communities: Towards a New Vision for Action Research*, edited by O. Zuber-Skerritt, M. Fletcher,
and J. Kearney, 41–75. London: Palgrave Macmillan.
Freire, P. 2007. *Pedagogy of the Oppressed*. New York: The Continuum International Publishing Group.
Jackson, S. 2011. "Lifelong Learning and Social Justice." *International Journal of Lifelong Learning* 30
(4): 431–436.
Kearney, J., and M. Todhunter, eds. 2015. *Lifelong Action Learning and Research: A Tribute to the Life
and Pioneering Work of Ortrun Zuber-Skerritt*. Rotterdam: Sense.
Kearney, J., L. Wood, and O. Zuber-Skerritt. 2013. "Community-University Partnerships Using
Participatory Action Learning and Action Research." *Gateways: International Journal of
Community Research and Engagement* 6: 113–130.
Kolb, D. 1984. *Experiential Learning: Experience as the Source of Learning and Development*. New
Jersey: Prentice Hall.
Lazarus, S. 2018. *Power and Identity in the Struggle for Social Justice. Reflections on Community
Psychology Practice*. Chamonix, CH: Springer Nature.
Lewin, K. 1946. "Action Research and Minority Problems." In *Resolving Social Conflicts: Selected Papers
on Group Dynamics*, edited by K. Lewin, 201–216. New York: Harper and Row.
Luthuli, A. 2019. "Advocating for Social and Academic Inclusion for Students with Disabilities in an
Institution for Higher Learning." PhD diss., Port Elizabeth: Nelson Mandela University.
Mathikithela, M. 2020. "Vulnerable Youth as Agents of Change: A YPAR Approach to Making Schools
Enabling Spaces for Learners." PhD diss., Potchefstrom: North-West University.
Mathikithela, M., and L. Wood. 2019. "Youth as Agents of Change: First Cycle of a YPAR Process to
Make School a More Enabling Space." *Educational Research for Social Change* 16 (2): 77–95.

Revans, R. 1982. *The Origins and Growth of Action Learning*. Bromley: Chartwell-Bratt.

Revans, R. 1991. *Action Learning: Reg Revans in Australia* [Video Series Produced by Ortrun Zuber-Skerritt (Now on DVD)]. Brisbane: Video Vision, University of Queensland. https://www.alarassociation.org/?q=about-al-and-ar/reg-revans-and-action-learning

Savary, L., and P. Berne. 2017. *Teilhard de Chardin on Love: Evolving Human Relationships*. Mahwah, NJ: Paulist Press.

Setlhare, R., and L. Wood. 2019. "A Collaboratively Constructed Action Leadership Framework for Sustainable Learner Support in Contexts of Adversity." *Educational Action Research*: 1–15. doi:10.1080/09650792.2018.1559070.

Stern, T. 2019. "Participatory Action Research and the Challenges of Knowledge Democracy." *Educational Action Research* 27 (3): 435–451.

Taleni, T. O., A. H. Macfarlane, S. Macfarlane, and J. Fletcher. 2018. "O le tautai matapalapala: Leadership Strategies for Supporting Pasifika Students in New Zealand Schools." *Journal of Educational Leadership, Policy and Practice* 32 (2): 16–32.

Va'a, U. 2009. "Samoan Custom and Human Rights: An Indigenous View." *The Victoria University of Wellington Law Review* 40: 237–250.

Wood, L. 2019. "PALAR: Participatory Action Learning and Action Research for Community Engagement." In *Action Learning and Action Research: Genres and Approaches*, edited by O. Zuber-Skerritt and L. Wood, 193–206. Bingley, UK: Emerald.

Wood, L. 2020. *Participatory Action Learning and Action Research: Theory, Practice and Process*. Abingdon, UK: Routledge.

Wood, L., and M. McAteer. 2017. "Levelling the Playing Fields in PAR: The Intricacies of Power, Privilege, and Participation in a University–Community–School Partnership." *Adult Education Quarterly* 67 (4): 251–265.

Wood, L., and O. Zuber-Skerritt. 2013. "PALAR as a Methodology for Community Engagement by Faculties of Education." *South African Journal of Education* 33 (4): 1–15.

Zuber-Skerritt, O. 2011. *Action Leadership: Towards a Participatory Paradigm*. Dordrecht, NL: Springer Science & Business Media.

Zuber-Skerritt, O. 2018. "An Educational Framework for Participatory Action Learning and Action Research (PALAR)." *Educational Action Research* 26 (4): 513–532.

Zuber-Skerritt, O., and R. Teare. 2013. *Lifelong Action Learning for Community Development: Learning and Development for a Better World*. Rotterdam: Sense.

Zuber-Skerritt, O., and L. Wood, eds. 2019. *Action Learning and Action Research: Genres and Approaches*. Bingley, UK: Emerald.

Action learning & Action research to alleviate poverty

George Boak, Jeff Gold and David Devins

ABSTRACT

The purpose of this paper is to examine the role played by action learning in a collaborative action research project to alleviate poverty in a city region in the UK. Researchers from two universities worked with 12 large anchor organisations to investigate procurement and employment practices that positively impacted inclusive growth within the city region, and therefore had a positive effect on poverty, and spread those practices more widely. A core group of representatives from the 12 participating organisations met in action learning sets to share the results of their investigations, to design a model of good practice, and to develop and support action plans. The paper summarises the results of the project, examines the different methodologies that were employed, and reviews the contribution made by action learning.

Introduction

Action learning and action research were used in a collaborative project funded by the Joseph Rowntree Foundation to alleviate poverty in the Leeds City Region through the identification and spread of good practices in employment and procurement by large local organisations. Researchers from York St John University and Leeds Beckett University worked in partnership with representatives from 12 large organisations based in the City Region to explore employment and procurement practices that can have a positive effect on poverty and to take action to spread these practices more widely.

The action research took an Appreciative Inquiry approach, with representatives of the 12 organisations seeking examples of good practices in their own organisation and in their supply chains, and then planning how to spread the practices more widely. Action learning was used within meetings of the representatives who, together with the university researchers, formed a 'core group' to analyse and share findings and to make plans to progress the project (Gold 2014).

The information on which this paper is based was gathered by the researchers throughout the life of the project, and beyond its official conclusion. Representatives of the 12 organisations contributed notes of their findings, and data from their organisations. The university researchers took detailed notes of meetings during the project, and of interviews with the participants at the project's end.

This paper discusses how the employment and procurement practices of large organisations as anchor institutions can impact poverty in a region and uses lessons from the project to suggest how action learning and action research may be used to achieve collaborative efforts to alleviate poverty.

Anchor institutions and their potential

Large organisations that are committed to a location have become known as 'anchor institutions'. By virtue of their size, they exercise an economic impact on the location, largely through their employment and purchasing practices. Examples include local authorities, hospitals, housing associations, universities and further education colleges. Private sector organisations with headquarters in a locality may also be anchor institutions. Private sector organisations in the US that act as anchor institutions in social projects include media and utility companies, large corporations such as pharmaceutical and technological companies, and sports franchises (NCP 2008). Anchor institutions in the US have initiated regenerative ventures such as Evergreen Cooperatives in Cleveland, Ohio (Howard, Kuri, and Lee 2010), the Chicago Anchors for a Strong Economy (JRF 2016), and the Anchors in Newark procurement scheme (Zeuli, Ferguson, and Nijhuis 2014). In the UK projects include the West Midlands Procurement Framework (2010), projects with anchor institutions in Birmingham (CLES 2018) and Preston (CLES 2017, 2019), and work with and a range of case studies reported from the Cooperative Councils Innovation Network (2019).

Anchor institutions are ideally situated to use 'place-based' mechanisms (Breeze et al. 2013) working in alliances to achieve social value (Ehlenz, Birth, and Agness 2014) and boosting their local economy by using their large procurement expenditures to benefit local businesses, invest in deprived areas, and increase local employment (CLES 2017; Jackson 2015; Macfarlane 2014). The purchasing power of anchor institutions can be directed towards local businesses, or local benefits can be included in contracts that are placed with businesses located elsewhere. In this way, procurement can be used to boost the local economy, to generate inclusive growth (RSA 2017; LCC 2018) and to increase local employment.

Gaining employment and progressing in work is consistently identified as a significant factor contributing to inclusive growth and reducing poverty. However, a body of research shows that entering employment does not provide a sustainable route out of poverty if the quality of the work is not also addressed (Brewer et al. 2012; OECD 2015). The continued prevalence of low-skilled, low-paid work in the economy, and employment where there is little chance for entry-level workers to move into better-quality jobs, contribute to the existence of in-work poverty (Lloyd, Mason, and Mayhew 2008). Jobs with few formal skills requirements, which offer little or no training, act as dead ends rather than pathways to progression. The concept of a 'good job' or 'good work' is closely associated with 'job quality' (Coats and Lekhi 2008; Parker and Bevan 2011).

Sweeney (2014) identified the characteristics of a 'good job' as relating to:

- Effort and reward: a person's effort is reflected in the rewards they receive, and reward structures are transparent.
- Skills training: there are opportunities to use and to develop skills.

- Safe and secure: employees do not fear imminent job loss or a loss of job status.
- Autonomy and choice: employees have a degree of control over their work.
- Fairness and trust: employees are treated fairly, and employers act to build trust at work.
- Relationships: there are opportunities to build and maintain good relationships.
- Voice: employees have the right to be heard and to express their views.

Whilst anchor institutions might be expected to ensure the quality of jobs for the majority of employees, areas for improvement can concern workers in the lowest pay bands and part-time, agency or temporary workers. Workers in the supply chains of anchor institutions may not experience 'good jobs' and there is a potential for anchor institutions to influence this through ethical trading policies and contract requirements.

Establishing the project

The Leeds City Region is the largest of all UK core city regions outside London in terms of output and population: economic output was £62 billion in 2016, generating 5% of England's output (LCREP 2016). There are more than 70 large anchors in the Leeds City Region, employing more than 200,000 people, and controlling expenditures of over £11 billion.

The university research team recruited 12 anchor institutions to take part in the project: four local authorities, two healthcare organisations, two further education colleges, one university, two third sector organisations and one private sector company (Boak et al. 2016; Devins et al. 2017). In each case, the chief executive (or equivalent) was briefed on the project and agreed that the organisation would participate. Private sector organisations have participated in inclusive growth projects in the US, and attempts were made to engage more private sector organisations in this project, but without success. A regional economic strategy emphasising inclusive growth, or 'good growth' (LCREP 2016) – growth that benefits a wide range of people in the locality – together with individual institutional drivers to achieve social benefits attracted the 12 anchor institutions to the project (Devins et al. 2017).

A short 'statement of intent' was sought from the executive team of each organisation, setting out what the organisation aimed to achieve through participation in the project. Common themes within these statements of intent concerned self-assessment of current actions to reduce poverty, and improved performance in this respect, including through learning from good practice elsewhere. A senior manager from each organisation – either a member of the top management team or someone who reported directly to that level, was sought to as a representative to the core group of the project.

The original plan was for the representatives to form two action learning sets to meet in groups of six, in Leeds and York, but following the launch event, where all the representatives met together, the anchor institution members asked that all future meetings should include both learning sets in a single session, the better to share good practice widely. Half-day meetings were scheduled every 5–6 weeks.

The issue of the alleviation of poverty can be seen as falling into the category of 'wickedness' where there are complex underlying causes, difficulties in finding simple solutions and little agreement on how to address what are considered as enduring and intractable difficulties (Spicker 2016). There cannot be quick solutions for such a difficulty; however, there is scope for progressive improvements. In seeking to respond to this challenge, we drew up approaches to collaborative engagement between academe and practice by use of what are called action modes of research (Raelin 2015). Such approaches place value on collective reflection in tackling complex and difficult issues such as poverty and the potential for producing knowledge which is considered useful and can be applied in practice and in doing so can create change. We advocated a combination of action research with action learning and the use of Appreciative Inquiry (Cooperrider and Whitney 2005).

Appreciative Inquiry is an approach to bringing about change that seeks examples of good practice and considers how they can be spread more widely, rather than identifying problems and attempting to solve them. After an area for research into change has been identified, the first stage of Appreciative Inquiry is to explore examples of good practice, to analyse what enabled them to work well, and to consider what can be learned from them. The following stages of the process concern imagining, where learning is shared collectively and re-organised thematically. This allows the consideration of possible changes as an image for a preferred future, followed by planning how to spread parts or all of the practice more widely. Using principles of Appreciative Inquiry, the core group members interviewed up to four people within their organisation or its supply chain. The university researchers summarised published examples of good practices in anchor institutions elsewhere to provide more information for the core group.

Action learning took place in sets of 4–6 members within the core group, as members discussed their progress with gathering information and considered how the good practices they had identified could be spread more widely. The sets were facilitated by university researchers with long experience of action learning. This activity comprised the bulk of the time spent at the core group meetings. At the second and third meetings of the group, a model of factors that enabled good practice was developed from common themes across the examples. At the fourth meeting of the core group, members were asked to work in the action learning sets to develop and discuss individual action plans for their own organisation for the next six months and undertook to discuss these plans with their senior management team.

The action learning sets also discussed how learning derived from the project might be implemented more widely. For example, one discussion revisited the model of factors that enabled good practice and considered:

- What might motivate an organisation to implement the model in relation to procurement
- Different ways in which the model might be implemented to contribute to tackling poverty
- Which organisations in the Leeds City region could be encouraged to use the model
- How the model could be connected to existing sectoral networks

There were nine meetings of the core group in total. Guest speakers with expertise in aspects of social investment, payment of a living wage, and social change were invited to share ideas and experiences with the core group for three of the four final meetings, and these presentations formed a preface to discussions in the action learning sets.

Outcomes

Outcomes achieved in the course of the project included the identification of a number of good practices within the participating organisations and their supply chains; the development of a model of core components of an effective anchor intervention; some collaborative projects between participating organisations; the extension of good practices in the anchor institutions; and some reported personal development on the part of core group members.

Examples of good practices

Appreciative inquiry interviews found a number of practical measures to assist local small- and medium-sized enterprises in the supply chain, such as creating smaller lots within invitations to tender in order to increase opportunities for smaller businesses; providing technical assistance and training relating to procurement processes; providing training on diversity issues to enable smaller businesses to meet tendering criteria.

The core group found some social requirements were included in invitations to tender. For example, tenders that require suppliers to create apprenticeships are reasonably common in construction contracts. One anchor institution issued an equality and diversity questionnaire with all invitations to tender: the responses were scored and this factor could comprise up to 10% of the overall score. That organisation also provided free equality and diversity training to suppliers and stated a clear expectation of requirements relating to diversity at both the tendering stage and during contract delivery, with an assessment of performance forming an integral part of the annual review of the contract.

Two of the local authority anchors provided examples of how they implement the Ethical Care Charter (Unison 2015) which highlights the importance of good terms and conditions and the allocation of the same homecare worker(s) wherever possible for the delivery of quality homecare services. The Charter emphasises the importance of employee benefits such as the payment of statutory sick pay, travel time, travel costs and other necessary expenses such as mobile phones.

One collaborative intervention between anchor institutions sought to reconnect people most at risk of exclusion from the labour market with employment opportunities. The organisations arranged for the provision of advice, guidance and support by a dedicated worker. Services provided by relevant intermediary bodies were coordinated to meet a variety of social, economic and health-related issues. The anchors participating in the project offered work placements to help the long term unemployed back into work. In-work mentoring was made available to support individuals through periods of difficulty and to ensure continuity of employment.

Core group members also identified a number of capacity-building initiatives and meet-the-buyer events designed to encourage the wider use of apprenticeships, payment of the living wage, and other aspects of good work in the supply chain.

The model

The model developed by the core group (Figure 1) identifies the key components of an effective anchor institution intervention in employment or procurement practice. The

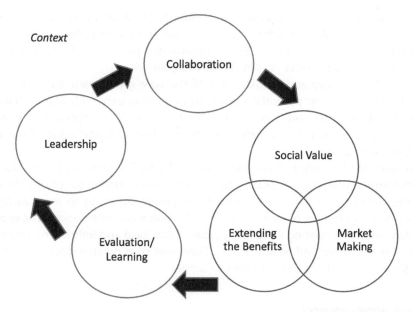

Figure 1. Core components of an effective anchor institution intervention in employment or procurement practice.

model is based on more than 30 examples of good practice identified by core group participants in the initial stages of the project. The examples of good practice in Leeds City Region organisations were supplemented by case study evidence, gathered by the research team, of successful anchor institution interventions elsewhere. The examples were introduced and discussed in action learning sets, and the model was developed through collaborative discourse and thematic analysis.

Leadership: leadership is needed at all levels in order to identify opportunities to promote inclusive growth and social value, and to align people and resources to achieve results.

Collaboration: developing and using partnership working across departmental, organisational and sectoral boundaries to design and deliver interventions. Collective action is a powerful means of achieving inclusive growth.

Shared value: three overlapping elements of shared value are: *Social value* – identifying and acting on opportunities to achieve social as well as economic value; *Market making* – supporting local businesses to identify and take advantage of procurement opportunities; *Extending the benefits* – supporting inclusive growth through good jobs in the organisation and in the supply chain.

Testing and learning: monitoring and carrying out constructive evaluations of interventions, adjusting where necessary, and spreading knowledge of good practice.

Collaborative projects

The potential to realise shared value though collaboration manifested itself in several ways during the project. For example, following discussions in the core group, three organisations co-operated in a Help the Aged initiative in West Yorkshire that focused on reducing loneliness. Two participating organisations collaborated to set up an in-project second-ment, linked to the West Yorkshire Low Pay Charter. One organisation also set up a cross-city conference to raise awareness of opportunities for other stakeholders to use procurement to encourage better jobs in the City Region.

At the end of the project, almost a half of the core group participants reported an increased awareness of the potential and added value associated with wider collaboration. One core group member said that their CEO had been initially sceptical of the scope for collaboration across such diverse organisations, but had seen the value of the exercise and became supportive of it.

The project was thought to have built a legacy for further cross-anchor institution collaborations and developments. Six core group members continued to collaborate after the end of the project through a 'procurement sub-group', agreeing to meet as an action learning group on a regular basis to review practice and share experiences. The group considered key questions relating to keeping expenditure local and influencing other groups in the local government and health sectors. There was considerable discussion on how to include social value criteria in invitations to tender.

Extending good practices

One of the original aims of the research project was to facilitate the adoption of new practices to encourage anchor institutions to make a stronger contribution to the local economy, and a majority of core group participants reported one or more outcomes associated with this aim. The Appreciative Inquiry, examples of good practice, action learning sets, and core group discussions all played a role in knowledge exchange and in helping to build a commitment to change. Some relevant project outcomes identified by core group participants included:

- Better awareness of the potential for achieving social value as a result of the Appreciative Inquiry mapping of policies and practice. The mapping of procurement expenditure was seen by some core group members as crucial in raising awareness among senior managers of the potential for using procurement to leverage greater local social and economic impact.
- Increased awareness of the potential for differentiating recruitment, pay and benefit structures to better reflect the needs of workers in low paid, entry-level jobs. By the end of the project, several anchor institutions were considering introducing or extending the targeted recruitment of workers in entry-level positions. One organisation had come to recognise the scope for differentiating recruitment marketing; another was proposing a review of support staff non-wage benefits to explore how to optimise the value of the employment package to lower paid employees. Two anchors had introduced a commitment to pay the living wage for their own staff during the course of the project; for one this was a direct result of the Appreciative Inquiry conducted during the project. Two other organisations were exploring the opportunities to redesign jobs to reflect higher pay and progression opportunities for those entering lower paid jobs.
- Raised aspirations in the organisation to engage with social value concepts and to use them to promote better work. At least two anchors were using knowledge acquired

through the project to inform strategic reviews, and another was using it to inform the refreshment of corporate strategy, where early discussions on realising wider social objectives through procurement had started with stakeholders. Others had seen a stronger connection between strategy, human resources and procurement around 'good work', which was reported to have built confidence in challenging 'the ways things are usually done within individual directorates'.

• The project was reported to have stretched senior manager thinking by providing the framework for 'good jobs' to reconsider their expectations of procurement. In four organisations, there had been an introduction of social value requirements in modified or new procurement practices, with one of these stipulating that all suppliers of outsourcing and other contracts would be required to pay the living wage and provide evidence to that effect as a condition of contracting. One organisation had introduced a social value question into their Pre-qualification Questionnaire, and in another organisation a requirement was introduced embracing the Unison Code of Ethical Practice in parts of their social care contracting.

Personal development

Personal outcomes were reported by nearly half of the core group participants and centred on greater confidence from a wider understanding of the issues and better practice, and from making contributions to knowledge exchange. Some felt their confidence had increased in tackling specific development needs around, for example, procurement, including a better understanding of legal and compliance constraints. Confidence gains also related to having widened their experience in multi-partner projects, with one core group member saying they were now better placed to play a more active role in co-creation with other anchor institutions in the city region and in other external networks.

Discussion

Action modes of research through Appreciative Inquiry within action research were methodologies for achieving the positive outcomes of this project, and action learning provided the vehicle for the delivery of a process. In action learning sets of representatives from anchor institutions, participants were able to work with the methods involved in Appreciative Inquiry to provide data for shared learning and the creation of knowledge that is actionable, as shown in Figure 1. Crucially, we hope that the model can become of value and use to others. Poverty is not an easy fix as recent reports have found. For example, Barr, Magrini, and Meghnagi (2019) highlight how national averages hide the high levels of economic inactivity with respect to employment and payment in various regions and cities in the UK. It therefore becomes essential to take a longer view to tackle poverty in such regions. This project makes a start, but only a start.

The efforts required to engage participants were to some extent underestimated by the research team during the design of the project. In most instances, multiple meetings and conversations were required in each organisation to engage internal champions and the senior leadership team. In several instances, the university researchers were unable to navigate organisational gatekeepers and start a dialogue with the senior leadership team. Champions were necessary to 'sell' the project to multiple internal stakeholders, and they often required direct support from the research team to clearly articulate the nature of action research and its benefits. The prevailing context of austerity, where economic justifications for the allocation of resources and finding the space for 'yet another change initiative' were key factors influencing the propensity of organisations to commit to engage. In addition, the open-ended nature of the outcomes of action research did not sit easily with assessments of value based on the achievement of clear, predetermined project outputs and return on investment which appear to be prevalent in many large organisations. Nevertheless, 12 organisations were willing to embrace the opportunity and make commitments to the project, establish a statement of intent, contribute to the core action research group, and make progress towards taking learning forward in the organisation.

In sustaining such an effort, collaboration must underpin the way forward which implies, based the Latin origin of the term, the working together for some agreed purpose. Wood and Gray (1991, 146) suggest that 'collaboration occurs when a group of autonomous stakeholders of a problem do engage in an interactive process, using shared rules, norms, and structures, to act or decide on issues related to that domain'. Such a process requires a degree of facilitation and given the likelihood of participants holding differing concerns and interests, collaboration must allow a convenor to bring people together to help create mutuality.

Collaboration based on the action modes of research, which was convened by the team from the universities and the core group representatives through action learning, uncovered and shared examples of good practices in employment and procurement from the anchor institutions in the Leeds City Region and elsewhere. These examples were then used to identify potential aims and outcomes that could be achieved from further action, and some evaluation of these further actions had already been carried out by the end of the project, as described in the previous section.

The collaborative nature of the research, and the expectation that good practices would be shared by participants, may have been an obstacle to recruiting more private sector organisations to the project. Discussions were undertaken with two anchor institutions in the retail sector, but issues about revealing competitively sensitive information were a factor in them deciding not to take part.

An original aim of the university researchers was to help the core group representatives and the senior management teams of the participating anchor institutions to establish project groups within each organisation, which would work along action learning principles, to progress the plans drawn up by core group representatives. The establishment of a core group drawing organisations together from a range of sectors and geographical locations was an ambitious element of the project. Those that engaged shared an aspiration to build relationships across sectors and spatial areas and to share practice. However, rivalries between localities, commercial sensitivities, tensions between organisations both cooperating and competing in the same and different spaces all surfaced in the core group discussions and provided an insight into some of the complexities at play in seeking to develop a collaborative approach to poverty alleviation. The notion of 'good work' and its social, economic and health-related benefits was a concept around which the core group could coalesce in pursuit of solutions to the wicked problem of poverty.

The project design envisaged active, systematic implementation spreading into all 12 participating organisations. In the event, progress was achieved in more organic and pie-cemeal ways, with awareness being raised within the organisations, and some actions being undertaken by those with responsibility for aspects of employment and procure-ment. Some new organisational arrangements came into being, with the creation of cross-institutional collaborations, but the ambition of creating project groups to drive change within each participating institution was not generally realised. This was due to a number of complex and interrelated socio-economic, cultural and project-related factors. For example, two organisations found their initial statements of intent relatively simplistic and over-ambitious. One of these organisations refined the goals but the other ostensibly withdrew from the project reflecting afterwards that 'with hindsight we did not really get to grips with it'. Others noted timing-related issues, where action-oriented developments associated with the project were contingent on influential organ-isational and regional strategies still in development. Others drew attention to the resource-based and cultural challenges of working across boundaries at different levels both within and between large organisations. Most participants reflected that whilst the early project focus on setting intent, Appreciative Inquiry and good practice had provided some momentum and pressure on participants to respond in a relatively short timeframe, translating what was learnt from the process required considerably more time than initially envisaged, especially in the multi-layered and complex organisations participating in the project. A frequent early outcome was recognition of the added value of collaboration across the region associated with poverty-related intervention. During the project time-frame several of the participants in the core group modified their procurement practices including selection guidance and evaluation criteria and worked towards harmonising procurement processes.

The action research is thought to have built a legacy for intra-organisational collabor-ations and reinforced the value of co-production in initiatives to promote good work and innovation to achieve greater social value. Tangible outcomes emerged beyond the project timeframe for several of the participating organisations in areas of procurement and employment and a Leeds Anchor Network has been established to maximise the local benefits of their procurement and employment policies (Leeds Anchor Network 2019). Several participants in the core group subsequently collaborated on the develop-ment of employment to support good work and promote inclusive growth in the region, and this resulted in a number of changes to policies and practices (Devins, Watson, and Turner 2019).

Action learning was a central part of the design of the project. Within the action learn-ing sets in the core group, participants shared information, discussed meanings and impli-cations, and supported and challenged one another in making plans for further actions. The process worked well, facilitated good exchanges of ideas and information, and pro-voked participants to consider new ways in which their organisation could address issues relating to poverty.

The action learning processes did encounter challenges, however, in particular concern-ing the stability of group membership in the second half of the project. Levels of motiv-ation over the course of the project varied. For a number of participants, this had intensified through the focus on action research and increased senior management atten-tion as the results of the project became tangible. However, just over half of the participants found it difficult to sustain attendance at core group meetings. For most this was not an issue of diminishing interest but of intense personal work pressures, delegation, or consequences of re-organisation of responsibilities. The volume and range of work pressures on such senior managers as made up the core group were considerable. In some models of action learning the propensity to withdraw is seen as a legitimate and at times inevitable outcome to be accepted by the facilitators. However, in this instance, the facilitator actively encouraged continued engagement. One-to-one updates, briefings and clear communications were important elements of project management that sought to encourage continued engagement, with varying degrees of success. One participant noted that non-attendance at the core group 'was down to us, other work pressures and staffing … ..I can't see what more the project could have done to keep us involved'. From the fifth meeting onwards, some core group members were replaced by alternate organisational representatives and, as Edmonstone and Flanagan (2007) found in their project, there can be a loss of focus and momentum when new members of action learning sets need to be included into an established group.

In addition to action learning set discussions, the core group meetings were also used by the university researchers to provide information from elsewhere of relevant activities of anchor institutions and cross-organisational action to reduce poverty, and to feed back to the group members aggregated information from their organisations. These inputs were designed to be informative for group members, and also energising – surfacing information and ideas about progress and potential, and engaging the whole group in discussions.

This project sought to tackle the complex issue of poverty through a collaborative underpinning, the use of action modes of research, and delivery through action learning. The knowledge generated in this project leads us to offer the following recommendations for anchor institutions:

- map procurement spending to assess how much remains within the region and how much goes outside of it;
- consider shifting 5 to 10% of current expenditure on the procurement of goods and services to competitive suppliers in the region: in the case of the anchor institutions in this project, such a shift could add hundreds of millions of pounds to the regional economy each year;
- test the framework set out in Figure 1 to embed social value into procurement and employment activities;
- increase the supply of apprenticeships by securing one apprenticeship for every £1 million of expenditure;
- send collective market signals relating to the importance of good work;
- collaborate with local suppliers to build capacity to bid for public procurement opportunities.

Conclusion

Anchor institutions in a region can have an impact on poverty by virtue of their size, their expenditure on goods and services, and the number of people they employ. Where anchor institutions have a social purpose as part of their mission – such as is found in local authorities, healthcare organisations, educational establishments and third sector organisations – they have institutional drivers to collaborate to explore and expand good practices. Where private sector organisations have a sense of social responsibility for a locality – as was the case with the transport company that took part in this project – they may also be motivated to join such a collaboration.

This project focused on alleviating poverty, an issue championed over many years by its sponsor, the Joseph Rowntree Foundation. However, a similar approach could be taken to tackling other complex and difficult social issues. This project aimed to take action within a particular region and was aligned with activity elsewhere that is designed to build inclusive growth in a locality, but similar processes could be used to bring together participants from much wider geographies.

Change in large, complex organisations is challenging and commitment to a collaborative project such as this is best achieved with the backing of the most senior managers in the organisation, who are in a position to provide leadership and initiate new actions. Collaboration might seem from the outside as easier than is actually the case and it often takes considerable time and perseverance for new ideas to take root and provide a platform for action and embedding practice.

An Appreciative Inquiry approach to collaborative action research can discover good practices that are enlightening, thought-provoking and uplifting. In this project, the members of the core group learned from good practices from within the participating organisations and elsewhere.

Action learning offers a positive, supportive dynamic to this kind of collaborative research, enabling researchers to share, reflect, create, and develop ways in which to make progress.

Disclosure statement

No potential conflict of interest was reported by the authors.

Funding

This research project was funded by the Joseph Rowntree Foundation, York.

References

Barr, J., E. Magrini, and M. Meghnagi. 2019. *Trends in Economic Inactivity Across the OECD: The Importance of the Local Dimension and a Spotlight on the United Kingdom*. OECD Local Economic and Employment Development (LEED). Working Papers, No. 2019/09, Paris: OECD Publishing.

Boak, G., P. Watt, J. Gold, D. Devins, and R. Garvey. 2016. "Procuring a Sustainable Future: an Action Learning Approach to the Development and Modelling of Ethical and Sustainable Procurement Practices." *Action Learning: Research and Practice* 13 (3): 204–218.

Breeze, J., C. Cummins, M. Jackson, N. McInroy, and A. Nolan. 2013. *Addressing Poverty Through Local Governance*. York: Joseph Rowntree Foundation. Accessed October 7, 2019. https://www.jrf.org.uk/report/addressing-poverty-through-local-governance.

Brewer, M., A. Dickerson, L. Gambin, A. Green, R. Joyce, and R. Wilson. 2012. *Poverty and Inequality in 2020: Impact of Changes in the Structure of Employment*. York: Joseph Rowntree Foundation.

CLES. 2017. *Community Wealth Building Through Anchor Institutions*. Manchester: Centre for Local Economic Strategies. Accessed November, 18 2019. https://cles.org.uk/wp-content/uploads/2017/02/Community-Wealth-Building-through-Anchor-Institutions_01_02_17.pdf.

CLES. 2018. *Local Wealth Building in Birmingham and Beyond: A New Economic Mainstream*. Manchester: Centre for Local Economic Strategies. Accessed November 18, 2019. https://cles.org.uk/publications/local-wealth-building-in-birmingham-and-beyond/.

CLES. 2019. *How We Built Community Wealth in Preston*. Manchester: Centre for Local Economic Strategies. Accessed November 18, 2019. https://cles.org.uk/wp-content/uploads/2019/07/CLES_Preston-Document_WEB-AW.pdf.

Coats, D., and R. Lekhi. 2008. *'Good Work': Job Quality in a Changing Economy*. London: The Work Foundation.

Cooperative Councils Innovation Network. 2019. Accessed October 7, 2019. https://www.councils.coop/case-studies/.

Cooperrider, D. L., and D. Whitney. 2005. *A Positive Revolution in Change: Appreciative Inquiry*. San Francisco, CA: Berrett-Koehler.

Devins, D., J. Gold, G. Boak, R. Garvey, and P. Willis. 2017. *Maximising the Local Impact of Anchor Institutions: a Case Study of Leeds City Region*. York: Joseph Rowntree Foundation.

Devins, D., A. Watson, and P. Turner. 2019. "Evidence Based Change in a UK Public Sector Organisation." In *Evidence Based Initiatives for Organizational Change and Development*, edited by R. G. Hamlin, A. D. Ellinger, and J. Jones, 398–404. Hershey, PA: IGI Global.

Edmonstone, J., and H. Flanagan. 2007. "A Flexible Friend: Action Learning in the Context of a Multiagency Organisation Development Programme." *Action Learning: Research and Practice* 4 (2): 199–209.

Ehlenz, M.M., E.L. Birth, and B. Agness. 2014. *The Power of Eds & Meds Urban Universities Investing in Neighborhood Revitalization & Innovation Districts*. Accessed October 7, 2019. http://penniur.upenn.edu/uploads/media/Anchor-Institutions-PRAI-2014.pdf.

Gold, J. 2014. "Revans Reversed: Focusing on the Positive for a Change." *Action Learning: Research and Practice* 11 (3): 264–277.

Howard, T., L. Kuri, and I. P. Lee. 2010. *The Evergreen Cooperative Initiative of Cleveland, Ohio: Writing the Next Chapter for Anchor-Based Redevelopment Initiatives*. Minneapolis, MN: The Cleveland Foundation.

Jackson, M. 2015. *Building a New Local Economy: Lessons from the United States*. Manchester: Centre for Local Economic Strategies. Accessed November 18, 2019. https://cles.org.uk/wp-content/uploads/2016/10/Lessons-from-the-United-States.pdf.

JRF. 2016. *Chicago Anchors for Strong Economy*. Accessed October 13, 2019. https://www.jrf.org.uk/case-study/chicago-anchors-strong-economy-case.

LCC. 2018. *Leeds Inclusive Growth Strategy*. Leeds: Leeds City Council. Accessed November 18, 2019. http://www.leedsgrowthstrategy.co.uk/wp-content/uploads/2018/06/Leeds-Inclusive-Growth-Strategy-FINAL.pdf.

LCREP. 2016. *Leeds City Region Strategic Economic Plan 2016-2036*. Accessed October 8, 2019. www.the-lep.com.

Leeds Anchor Network. 2019. Accessed October 13, 2019. http://www.leedsgrowthstrategy.co.uk/anchor-institutions/.

Lloyd, C., G. Mason, and K. Mayhew. 2008. *Low-Wage Work in the United Kingdom*. New York: Russell Sage Foundation.

Macfarlane, R. and Anthony Collins Solicitors LLP. 2014. *Tackling Poverty Through Public Procurement*. York: Joseph Rowntree Foundation. Accessed October 7, 2019. https://www.jrf.org.uk/report/tackling-poverty-through-public-procurement.

NCP. 2008. *Anchor Institutions Toolkit: A Guide for Neighborhood Revitalization*. Philadelphia, PA: Netter Center for Community Partnerships, University of Pennsylvania. Accessed November 18, 2019. https://community-wealth.org/content/anchor-institutions-toolkit-guide-neighborhood-revitalization.

OECD. 2015. "Making Inclusive Growth Happen." Accessed October 7, 2019. http://www.oecd.org/economy/all-on-board-9789264218512-en.htm.

Parker, L., and S. Bevan. 2011. *Good Work and Our Times: Report of the Good Work Commission*. London: The Work Foundation.

Raelin, J. 2015. "Action Modes of Research." In *A Guide to Professional Doctorates in Business & Management*, edited by L. Anderson, J. Gold, J. Stewart, and R. Thorpe, 57–76. London: Sage.

RSA. 2017. *Inclusive Growth Commission. Making our Economy Work for Everyone*. London: Royal Society for the encouragement of Arts, Manufactures and Commerce. Accessed November 18, 2019. https://www.thersa.org/discover/publications-and-articles/reports/final-report-of-the-inclusive-growth-commission.

Spicker, P. 2016. *Poverty as a Wicked Problem*. Berge: CROP (Comparative Research Programme on Poverty) Poverty Brief.

Sweeney, E. 2014. *Making Work Better: An Agenda for Government*. London: The Smith Institute. Accessed October 11, 2019. http://www.smith-institute.org.uk/wp-content/uploads/2015/09/Making-work-better-an-agenda-for-government.pdf.

Unison. 2015. "Unison Ethical Care Charter." Accessed October 11, 2019. https://www.unison.org.uk/content/uploads/2013/11/On-line-Catalogue220142.pdf.

West Midlands Procurement Framework. 2010. Accessed October 10, 2019. https://www.birmingham.gov.uk/site_search/results/?q=west+midlands+procurement+framework.

Wood, D., and B. Gray. 1991. "Toward a Comprehensive Theory of Collaboration." *Journal of Applied Behavioural Science* 27 (2): 139–162.

Zeuli, K., L. Ferguson, and A. Nijhuis. 2014. *Creating an Anchored Local Economy in Newark Recommendations for Implementing a Comprehensive Local Procurement Strategy*. Accessed October 14, 2019. http://icic.org/wp-content/uploads/2016/04/ICIC_NEWARK_rprt_REV.pdf.

Carbon management and community-based action learning: a theory to work experience

Annie Booth, Kyle Aben, Todd Corrigall & Barbara Otter

ABSTRACT
We discuss an innovative action-learning course co-developed by the University of Northern British Columbia, the Prince George Chamber of Commerce (Canada) and local businesses. The Carbon and Energy Management course is an undergraduate/graduate course initiated by the Chamber to address an interest in climate change amongst local businesses/non-profits. Growing awareness of climate change and the need to better manage carbon has led to businesses eager to reduce greenhouse gases. Students, seeking to create a more sustainable world while gaining practical skills, create carbon footprint analyses for business clients. We discuss the course impacts on students as an action learning initiative.

Introduction

Here we present the lessons learned from creating an innovative university course incorporating action learning, developed in partnership between the University of Northern British Columbia (UNBC) (Canada), the Prince George Chamber of Commerce (PGCOC) and Prince George, BC businesses and non-profits. UNBC's 3rd year undergraduate/graduate course, Carbon and Energy Management (CEM), was co-created in response to a request by the Chamber to address a growing interest in climate change on the part of local businesses wishing to reduce their greenhouse gas emissions but lacking the knowledge to so do. UNBC professors, in turn, recognized that students working on sustainability initiatives are interested in gaining marketable skills, particularly outside of the classroom. The CEM course was designed to meet the needs of all participants. UNBC students develop practical skills through investigating a business's functions and activities and then creating real carbon footprint analyses for these real life clients. The businesses increase their understanding of their carbon management practices, receive practical ideas for reducing their emissions and, if they wish, assistance in implementing these reductions from an affiliated student intern. Through this work, the PGCOC provides an important service to its members while the primary PGCOC funder, CN Rail, has an opportunity to constructively invest in communities in which it operates. The CEM has been highly successful since its start in January 2015: 46 businesses and non-profits have partnered with over 30 students and 5 summer interns. The PGCOC has shared its experiences with the course at provincial and national Chamber events and, as of 2019, are rolling out the program for Chambers nation-wide interested in similar action learning partnerships, while the university instructors are sharing the lessons from the partnership through conferences and publications.

We present the lessons learned through integrating action learning into the community from multiple perspectives. Key lessons for practitioners include the need for action learning to meet the needs of all partners, particularly through developing and maintaining genuine community partnerships through focussing upon a genuine community need. It is also important to ensure that there is clear support for the action learning activity at all levels. Finally, there is a need to be alert to opportunities and to not be afraid to take a chance.

This paper utilizes two sources of data: the five years of experiences and reflections of the authors, and the reflections of students who have taken the course or worked as the Carbon intern. All persons quoted are identified by name and position/role with permission.

The principles of action learning

The CEM course is grounded within the concepts of action learning and public pedagogy. Public pedagogy defines a community as a living classroom, moving 'beyond institutiona-lized spaces and roles' (Sandlin, O'Malley, and Burdick 2011, 361). Action learning is based on doing, where students engage in learning that allows them to 'apply their skills to auth-entic or "real-world" problems that would enable them to challenge their intellect while becoming adapt at both technical and process skills needed after graduation' (Favaloro, Ball, and Lipschutz 2019, 92). Hands-on experience offers significant advantages in post-graduation job searches; however, it is in the testing of ideas that such experience creates a better student (and citizen):

> Students [in action learning coursework] report being confronted – sometimes for the first time in their degree – with the need to think carefully about whether or not particular theories or claims made in the literature can actually be applied or used … They point out that they have never really thought about how to determine what makes research more or less (or not at all) useful in the 'real world'. (Levac 2019, 5)

Such real-world experience offers significant advantages in post-graduation job searches, and can create a more thoughtful graduate.

Action learning and public pedagogy are particularly useful for addressing sustainability problems (Suskevics, Hahn, and Rodela 2019). Universities have important roles in contri-buting to both understanding the need for, and co-creating, sustainability solutions within their local and regional environments (Filho et al. 2019). Sustainability is a significant concern today, and post-secondary institutions have important roles in contributing to both understanding the need for and the co-creation of sustainability solutions to chal-lenges within an institution's local and regional environment. One way to do this is through action learning courses and experiences co-created between universities and communities, but much as with sustainability initiatives in general, such courses and experiences need to be complex in nature:

> [In sustainability education] students and graduates need more than simple, disciplinary education: they should also be prepared to go beyond their specialization and attain holistic and system-level understanding in order to effectively tackle the challenges of becoming sustainable. This is where 'experiential learning for sustainability' can play a critical role: teaching students how to think about complex and wicked environmental, ecological and social challenges, and providing them with the opportunities to address these really-existing problems and projects. (Favaloro, Ball, and Lipschutz 2019, 93)

As Schnitzler (2019, 2) notes, a shift in how we educate is needed, 'from learning how to understand to learning how to act and transform', key principles within action learning initiatives.

One such 'wicked' environmental problem is climate change and the resultant need for carbon management. The CEM course addresses climate change, a significant global challenge. Addressing climate change requires the reduction of carbon emissions produced through the release and burning of greenhouse gasses, both to mitigate climate change and to adapt to existing impacts. The International Panel on Climate Change states that global greenhouse gas (GHG) emissions must decrease by 85% by 2050 to stabilize the global climate (McGlade and Ekins 2015), although such timelines appear to shrink with every new study. One organizational response is carbon management, the process of measuring and reducing an organization's carbon emissions. To succeed, businesses and organizations must mobilize to adopt carbon management practices (Seles et al. 2018, 764), while taking advantage of the business opportunities that such actions generate. However, most businesses lack the knowledge and techniques necessary (Lister 2018). A carbon footprint analysis can be used to identify energy consumption and to realistically set informed energy goals and processes (Giama and Papadopoulos 2018). The CEM course does precisely this for participating businesses.

The carbon and energy management course case study

The CEM course embodied action learning and public pedagogy principles from its beginning, as it was co-created to address an explicit community need, as former PGCOC Executive Director Christie Ray notes:

> In 2014 the PGCOC was looking for ways to bring the business community value in areas related to environmental responsibility. There was appetite for programming on the broad topic, but little organized community effort. After discussing with Annie Booth possible programming on the reduction of carbon footprints in the business community, the Chamber went searching for funding. CN Rail agreed to financially support such programming for one year, providing the business community with dedicated assistance on carbon reduction. This was what was needed by businesses, as the majority were small with limited resources or expertise in executing such objectives.

At UNBC, Annie Booth was actively looking for hands on experiences for her Environmental and Sustainability Studies students:

> I have two courses that utilize community projects. Environmental and Sustainability Studies courses really require hands-on action learning as these students want to make a difference in

the world. But they also want real tools that can be used both for finding employment and making that difference. When I received a call from the PGCOC in late November 2014 saying they had funding and wanted to run a project on carbon management, I had to tell them it was too late for my existing classes, but then thought, this is too great an opportunity to let go. In three weeks, I created a course, found an instructor willing to try, and convinced students to try a new course. The student response over the last several years encouraged me to change the CEM course into a permanent course.

Such action learning opportunities do support the role of the university within the community, as UNBC's Provost Dan Ryan notes:

Courses that include opportunities for experiential learning provide an uncontrolled environment where students can engage in critical thinking, team work, problem solving, and communication skills and can apply knowledge and skills in real-world settings. There is no substitute for experience in the development of these skills, and the interactions within industry, the community and with professionals in a student's intended area of work, should aid in the development of confidence and leadership, but also understanding, humility and empathy for the complexity and challenges of effecting change.

The course explicitly aims to meet the students' needs for the skills Ryan identifies, in particular critical thinking, real-world problem-solving and communication through utilizing a mix of classroom taught theory and hands-on community engagement with businesses and non-profits looking for carbon management strategies. Critically, the students learn equally from the instructor, the PGCOC and the business/non-profit partners. Over the months leading up to the course, for example, the PGCOC Grants Administrator recruits businesses/non-profits as course partners. They are briefed on the course requirements (providing certain data, hosting students, and being willing to discussing their interests in carbon management). The PGCOC plays a critical role in recruiting businesses/non-profits, coordinating data collection, and facilitating the relationships between the students and businesses/non-profits. The PGCOC acts as the trusted broker, providing the security that the community partners need to come into the project, while also providing an education to the students on creating partnerships. In class, students learn the fundamentals of carbon management, its importance for business and how to gather the necessary data to calculate a carbon footprint and to theorize about potential redress. The rest of the course involves working one-on-one with interested businesses/non-profits.

The action learning opportunities begins early in the semester when students meet their businesses/non-profits at a group meet and greet and then meet later with their partners to identify their needs. A considerable portion of the course is spent one-on-one with the community partner. During these on-going series of meetings, the students visit each partner's site, tour the actual facilities and discuss with staff how the business/non-profit actually operates to determine all sources of greenhouse gas emissions. They then undertake research on alternate practices that are specific to the needs of their partner and may do follow-up discussions to ensure possible alternatives are appropriate to the partner. This hands-on process requires developing professional communication skills as well as critical thinking to undertake site analysis and solution identification. At the end of the course, the findings and recommendations are formally presented to the partner (and the instructor and PGCOC Grants Administrator) and a written report with recommendations is turned over (both are considered confidential). During the summer, a separately funded intern, working out of the PGCOC and supervised by the instructor, offers the partners support in implementing the recommendations and undertaking footprints for additional partners.

The action learning aspect is precisely what students eventually find appealing although the approach is initially confounding, as instructor Kyle Aben discusses:

> The first CEM class of the year is always interesting. Many of the students show a high level of concern after reviewing the syllabus for the first time. More than one student has admitted they considered dropping the course after the first day but were extremely glad they did not. Why are some students so intimidated? The CEM course is true experiential learning where students are taught theory and then act on it by working with local businesses. The students are required to learn some climate science and understand the different radiant forcing's and global warming potentials of each greenhouse gas, they must understand business structure and details around leasing agreements, and they must understand climate policy and the different requirements demanded by civic, provincial, federal and international policies.
>
> From an instructor's perspective, the most enjoyable classes are the working labs where students end up teaching students. Seeing the pride on a student's face when they successfully transfer new knowledge to another peer is priceless. The course seems to elevate the confidence of all the students who have participated. They express a great sense of accomplishment and feel it is actual work experience that rarely happens in a university class. I treat the students more like colleagues during the course, knowing they must learn carbon accounting, practice it and then apply it all within four months. I cannot teach them all they need to know during this time and their interactions with each business are done by themselves. The students have experienced unique situations and have asked me questions I may not have ever run into otherwise and this only adds to the collegial feeling developed within the class. I have had keen students correct my answer keys, suggest appropriate methods of calculations when others were not available and present materials in a way I continue to replicate in my professional consulting career.

Such circular learning, from the classroom, out to the community/partner, and back in to the classroom, is a hallmark of the opportunities that action learning processes facilitate over conventional in-class instruction, as Sinead Earley, who will be inheriting the course in 2020, suggests:

> In the classroom it is apparent that students engaging in climate change issues are fatigued by conceptual discussions of the problem and are wanting greater opportunities for action. The carbon footprints measured by the CEM students have led to real GHG reductions, and carbon neutrality in some cases. The businesses that have followed through with operational changes are now exemplary climate change leaders in Prince George.

Thus, as hoped for within action learning theory, the outcomes are practical, applied and real-world in application.

In turn, the students' value multiple aspects related to the action learning aspect of the course. Nathan Malcom (student) argues that the CEM course,

> empowers students with the knowledge and skillset necessary to take leadership in the fore of climate change. Instead of talking about the often abstract science of atmospheric physics and global emissions, we were given the opportunity to engage climate solutions in real time. No other class in my undergraduate or graduate career has given me as much autonomy to take over the reins in making a meaningful community impact during time already dedicated for learning.

Hannah Renaud (student/summer intern) feels that,

> the Chamber Carbon Action Plan has been a key part of my studies and work. In 2019 I had the pleasure of taking the CEM course in which myself and peers got to work directly with businesses. This is a unique and amazing opportunity offered in that we get to interact and work alongside business professionals. It not only showed us the value of business people in the community, it was also a way to engage with the community in a more professional manner but still work under the student mindset. I was able to join the team at the PGCOC as the 2019 Carbon Intern. I believe that university involvement in the community is essential in creating the balance between the businesses and the students and negating the wall between those two 'worlds.'

Louisa Hadley (graduate student/summer intern), who worked with another student, Rachelle Linde, on these changes, documents the real-world skills obtained from the CEM course:

> I learned how to communicate with businesses in a professional manner, how to problem solve and adapt when given data that differs from the 'perfect' textbook example, and how to present a business case for carbon reduction recommendations and more sustainable business operations. This project is likely to be important for other students as it bridges the gap between course theory and the practical application of that theory in the workplace. The practical work experience is only made possible because of the engagement of UNBC with the community.

The CEM course thus provides the students and the community with valuable work, meeting real-world needs and increasing understanding of solutions to climate change, a real-world 'wicked' societal and planetary challenge. The reflections of Rachelle Linde (student) are most indicative of the opportunities that action learning opportunities such as the CEM course allow in explicitly translating her hands-on experience in to actual practice in a subsequent professional position:

> The CEM course allowed me to take lessons learned in the classroom and apply them almost immediately within my community. Something unexpected that I took away from the opportunity was a new connection to members of the Prince George community. I moved to Prince George at 21, and submerged myself into the university culture, but I didn't start to explore outside of that university bubble until later. The course was an important part of that change, and I made connections with potential employers, project sponsors, and community organizations.
>
> The CEM course has certainly shaped my career so far at The Exploration Place, (a Museum & Science Centre). When I moved into my current role as Public Programs Coordinator, I had the opportunity to apply the same critical eye to the consumptive nature of my position as I had done in the CEM course. Since then, I've changed our outreach programming to be nearly zero-waste, prioritized the use of recycled materials, and have encouraged staff participation in community initiatives like Go by Bike Week. Last fall, I also had the opportunity to facilitate the participation of The Exploration Place in the Chamber's Carbon Action Plan. With another CEM student, I experienced the project from the participating organization's point of view and helped collect the necessary data on our organization's consumption. Getting to see the project from both sides was a really interesting experience, and helped me to understand better why organizations take on these projects, and what making changes to reduce emissions really entails.

Discussion and conclusions

What students and partners identify as critical aspects in the CEM course are (a) the partnership around the course, (b) the highly applied skills learned and practiced in a real-world setting and (c) the meaningful application of the course in creating bonds between the university, the students and the community the university operates within. In reflecting upon the CEM course as an action learning practice, we agree that these are the lessons we would take from the course.

The genuine partnership between UNBC and the PGCOC is one key reason the course has succeeded. The university essentially acted on an opportunity proposed by the Chamber, but could not have created that opportunity on its own. Too often, in our experience, it is universities telling communities what is needed or what will happen. In this case it was the community directing the university towards a self-identified, and therefore prioritized, need with which the university could assist. Neither partner can operate the course independently; they must always be aware of and respect the needs, goals and aspirations of the other while sharing equitably in the outcomes.

Developing such partnerships takes work. In this case it also took the willingness and ability of the first two participants, Ray and Booth, to recognize and value a unique opportunity, to be willing to move on the opportunity at short notice and at some cost of time and effort, and to commit to the long term opportunity without everything being laid out in stone. Without that initial leap of faith by both partners a valuable action learning opportunity would have been lost. While not always possible, particularly given the inflexibility of academic institutions, those committed to expanding action learning must be willing to take such a leap when an opportunity presents itself.

It is perhaps self-evident that action learning should involve hands-on learning. Where the CEM course succeeds, according to students and the current instructor, is in the opportunity for clear application of the skills learned and multiple opportunities to apply them in different settings through work with different types of businesses/non-profits, ensuring that the skill set is broadly understood. They learn to move beyond rote, such as when data is not as they were taught, and to solve problems in the field and on the fly. Such real-world practice becomes critical to building student confidence in their abilities, particularly when thinking through to their entry into full-time employment with real projects and problems to solve.

The CEM course redefines the partners' understanding of learning and of the nature of action learning and sustainability-directed partnerships. It becomes clear that the skills the CEM course teaches must be valued by all participants. The students and one instructor note how important peer-to-peer instruction is in this context, which in turn sets the students up to learn from the other non-traditional instructors such as businesses/non-profit operator/owners or Chamber staff. In turn, the students, as they acquire expertise, serve as instructors in sharing back the knowledge and skills gained outside of both a classroom and university setting back in to that university. Such practices set up the students to continue to be innovative learners/instructors in their future careers and to share within their workplaces, as one student demonstrated in taking the skills into her workplace and then back in to the community. It changes significantly how instructors think about teaching in general and in action learning initiatives in specific.

Finally, the CEM course breaks down the walls between classroom and community, for both students and community members. UNBC professors are well aware that while the Prince George community is proud of their university, it is also quite tentative in their relationship with it. They might send their children 'up the hill' to get a degree, but hesitate to venture up themselves. Seeing students in their shops and factory floors, working collaboratively to address a challenge, creates a different, more productive relationship between 'town and gown' in an innovative fashion. As Ray notes,

> Equally important to the PGCOC in seeing this project come to fruition was the opportunity to work on the relationship between the Prince George business community and UNBC – a connection that had enormous potential but mixed reviews and much room for improvement. To be able to link UNBC students directly with businesses in the community would potentially allow for further opportunity to collaborate and hire UNBC students as employees. It would also demonstrate UNBC's desire to align with the business community and ability to provide useful resources on relevant business issues and challenges. Moreover, it would allow UNBC to better realize what an opportunity existed in tapping into the Prince George business community. From experiential learning and Co-op placements to collaboration with academic researchers looking for industry applications, the potential seemed endless.

By no means, however, has the offering of the course been easy. On the PGCOC side, they have struggled with recruiting sufficient businesses/non-profits. Some have been withdrawn when they failed to provide the required data. Much of this has reflected a learning process, as the PGCOC Grants Administrator refines her approach and as businesses become more fully aware of what is needed to participate. A second struggle has been in encouraging partnering businesses and non-profits to act on the recommendations that the students have developed for reducing greenhouse gas emissions. While a few partners have used the students' work to gain and maintain carbon neutrality (and gained certification for this), the majority have not. No one is certain as to the reasons partners fail to carry through, although future research is planned on this, but it is a failure no one anticipated. Action learning should create, well, action, but the course itself has not been sufficient to assure this outcome. We should have planned more carefully for follow-though which is, five years in, difficult to add in with currently limited resources.

On the UNBC side, the struggle has revolved around student recruitment and administrative support for an oddball course. Until 2019, the CEM course was offered as an ad-hoc 400-level course. This meant that it was often difficult to convince students to take the course (it was new, and did not meet existing degree requirements). We have learned that for students, new is not always welcome, especially if it looks like work! Now a required regular course for two degrees, core enrollment is no longer a yearly struggle, but recognizing student hesitation over what seems like a tailor-made opportunity to learn about a useful skill might have been better anticipated.

The other challenge has been convincing university administrators that this was a course worth funding. For the first year, Kyle Aben took on the role as the instructor as part of his other work. For subsequent years, however, it was important to find salary funding. Some administrators simply did not see the value in funding a course with necessarily small enrollments. Only intense persistence and argument every year kept the salary money appearing. While it was troubling to discover just how little value the university saw in a community-based action learning course if it was going to cost, persistence has led to an on-going commitment to the course through a full-time faculty position. One last lesson is that community-based action learning can be more valued in theory than in practice, and persistence is necessary to set solutions in motion.

As Sinead Earley concludes,

> The actors included in our active learning partnership (post-secondary institution, Chambers of Commerce, and businesses/non-profits) are eager to engage in climate action in

municipalities across Canada, and we see the potential to develop the model for adoption by Chambers and post-secondary institutions elsewhere. Our project is an example of place-based, community-led climate change solutions, but we see its' further reach. As a 'community of communities', the model could act as a sharable, viable, hands-on sustainability solution that strengthens university-community relations elsewhere – provincially, federally, and internationally.

The course teaches that the utility of a 'technological fix' (i.e. a practical tool like carbon foot-printing) will increase if situated within a broader, socially and politically informed adaptation strategy. It is becoming increasingly important to recognize transitions not solely as technical and infrastructural change, but to acknowledge (and act upon) the social relations that govern access and distribution of carbon reduction knowledge and techniques.

As an innovative action learning based practice, the CEM course has been highly successful, engaging university students, community businesses and non-profits, the local government (that now awards letters to those businesses and non-profits that became carbon neutral through the C^2AP) and the Prince George Chamber of Commerce. But it has only been through the on-going commitment of those involved that such success has happened.

Disclosure statement

No potential conflict of interest was reported by the authors.

Using Participatory Action Learning to Empower the Active Citizenship of Young People

Anna Jarkiewicz

ABSTRACT

This article aims to presents the effects of participatory action learning (PAL) as a method of work to Empower the Active Citizenship of young people in schools. The author of the article was involved in an educational project called Future Youth School – Forums (FYS-FORUMS). The basic aim was to create a model of schooling that promotes the idea of active citizenship with the use of a Youth Forum. This study describes the effects of the PAL method on young people in two British schools. The qualitative approach was used to collect data in the study, based on focus group interviews with the youth involved in the project. The impact of the PAL method was identified in a number of areas: (1) the first one concerned the sense of developing the soft/transversal skills and competences; (2) the second one was connected with perceiving oneself as an acting entity; (3) the third one involved improvement of the relationships between students and teachers; and (4) the last effect concerned the evolution of the students' attitude towards active citizenship, which was reflected in their way of thinking about social actions and the need to get involved in them.

Introduction

This paper provides some findings about the use of participatory action learning (PAL) in the EU Erasmus+ funded educational project called Future Youth School – Forums (FYS-FORUMS) running from 2015 to 2018. FYS-FORUMS took place in Cyprus, Italy, Lithuania, England, and Poland. The FYS-FORUMS partners were persons connected with the following institutions: University of Lodz (Poland), OXFAM GB (Great Britain), OXFAM ITALIA (Italy), Jaunimo karjeros centras (Lithuania) and Centre for Advancement of Research and Development in Education Technology LTD CARDET (Cyprus), but also representatives of fourteen schools, both teachers and students from middle schools and high schools, as full participants able to co-decide about the future direction of the project development.

The basic aim of the project was to create a model of schooling that would promote the idea of active citizenship with the use of a Youth Forum. Promoting empowerment, participation and active citizenship of young people was our main objective. We wished to reach this goal through establishing in the school space the institution of a youth forum with students acting as participants and, at the same time, organisers. The youth forum was defined in the project as an event organised by students and the creation of a place for expressing opinions and presenting ideas for actions coinciding with the democratic decision-making process was its priority. Thanks to the organisation of and participation in the forum, students were supposed to shape their skills of aware action-taking based on social equality in the school, local and global environment. In the project creators' opinion, it was extremely important to grant the forum the status of an institution co-deciding on matters connected with the activities undertaken by the school, so that students were able to experience the real consequences of their decisions. Owing to the above, their sense of empowerment, value and decisiveness were to be strengthened. The above was the element distinguishing 'our' forum from other similar ones established in various schools in different parts of the world.

The perception of the current educational system as an ineffective one was the first stimulus for the attempts to establish the youth forum institution in schools. In most European countries educational programmes are focused on equipping students with theoretical knowledge and not transversal skills and competencies (also known as soft or generic skills or graduate attributes), such as communication or organisational skills, the usefulness of which young people could see for themselves relatively soon in their private and, later on, professional life (see e.g. Pereira and Costa [2017]; Tam and Trzmiel [2018]; Mesquita, Lima, Sousa and Flores [2009] on transversal skills.) The recognition of problems concerning democracy, participation and youth involvement in local and global matters as essential and important for the development of an aware and active citizen was the second crucial argument. The project organisers noticed in the curricula a shortage of subjects which might promote the issues mentioned above efficiently. According to Birdwell and Bani (2014), the deficit in the focus in this scope directly translates into the approach to social involvement issues taken by young people. According to the above-mentioned authors, contemporary young people become involved in civic issues in a very limited way, which is connected with the school and teachers' attitude towards subjects, during which young people learn about citizenship and they are encouraged to be socially active. Poland, Lithuania or Great Britain, in which subjects such as civics or entrepreneurship education have a significantly lower status than such subjects as mathematics or physics, may serve as examples.

The project organisers hoped that establishing in schools the institution of the youth forum with real power to make decisions on issues essential from the point of view of students would contribute to changes in fields regarded as 'neglected in educational terms'.

Perspectives on participatory action learning and youth participation

The Author deliberately uses in the text the term PAL instead of action learning, in order to emphasise active participation of all parties involved in the project, mostly including students and teachers. According to our assumptions about PAL, it integrates the methodologies of AL (see, for example, Pedler, Burgoyne and Brook [2005] on action-learning) and critical action-learning (see, for example, Rigg and Trehan [2004] on critical action-learning).

PAL, which has been defined in the project as involving young people to collaborate with teachers in each step of the learning process to make connections between their learning and work experiences, develop the need to participate in social actions, make their own decisions on issues that affect them and advocate for themselves. Students, just like in the case of AL, were supposed to take actions on real tasks or problems and the learning process was, in its turn, directly connected with the reflection on the actions taken.

There are distinguished three basic assumptions adopted with respect to PAL for the project. Firstly, as proposed by Argyris and Schon (1974), participants are encouraged to become aware of their theories-in-use. Secondly, they are encouraged to think critically, as Carr and Kemmis refer to action research: ' … a deliberate process for emancipating practitioners from the often unseen constraints of assumption, habit, precedent, coercion and ideology' (1986, 192). Thirdly, informed by Belenky et al. (1986) theories on levels of learning, 'tutors also encourage participants to value their own experience and insights; to make their own models, in other words, to create theory from practice' Rigg and Trehan (2004, 154).

We aimed at promoting and shaping active citizenship full of involvement and based on the participation and democracy principles within the framework of the FYS-FORUMS project. The co-creation of space by all of its participants, according to Granosik (2018, 80) 'meaning those who have knowledge and for whom the results might be of significance', is the basic feature of these principles. In the FYS-FORUMS context, participation involved numerous dimensions, starting from co-creating space and co-deciding on it, through attempt(s) to abolish the dichotomy within the teacher-student relations and its inherent traditional hierarchy and division of power characteristic for schools, to co-participation in the learning process. The co-participation in the learning process in the project's context meant that both students and teachers learnt during the project. Students acquired e.g. knowledge and abilities falling within the scope of transversal skills, which were gained through the organisation of and participation in the forum, and teachers learnt to work with the youth with the help of PAL. In this case it often meant that teachers tried to refrain from their usual form of behaviour in the student-teacher relation and, instead, to be with young people and support them when they were asked for support only. Thus, the definition of the teacher's and the student's role had to be changed in the project. The teacher was perceived as the facilitator supporting learners as they learnt to assess evidence, negotiate, make informed decisions, solve problems and work both independently and with others. The student, in turn, was an active co-participant of the learning process taking responsibility for the process, listening to opinions expressed by other participants and trying to acquire knowledge and skills through experiencing.

Assuming that school is a space mostly created by its adult representatives, in the project we decided to support and enhance the position of students by extending their possibilities of cooperation and getting involved in the issues that are of significance from their perspective. With regard to this, we were inspired by the critical youth studies approach, and particularly the work of such researchers as Sibley (1995), Austin and Willard (1998), Herr (1999), Johnson (2001), Schwartzman (2001), Vadeboncoeur and Stevens (2005), O'Kane (2008), and Quijada Cerecer, Cahil, and Bradley (2013). The authors mentioned call for a change of the paradigm of thinking about young people as full and acting entities, and not objects of somebody else's educational measures. As noticed by Quijada Cerecer, Cahill and Bradley, 'young people and their actions need to be treated seriously and in compliance with the adopted assumption that the youth are citizens, and not citizens in the making' (2013, 221).

According to critical trends supporters, suggesting changes in this field demonstrates care for democratisation of young people and their participation in the social life.

The FYS-FORUMS project's organisers, similarly to the representatives of the critical trends, opposed the objectification of the youth by adults and the resulting deprivation of young people of their rights to decide and participate in the social life. They offered to replace the traditional school order based on the *working for youth* approach with the pursuit of the participatory approach and *working with youth*, thus recognising young people's rights to co-decide and take action in the social environment.

Future youth schools forums in practice

During the three years' period of the project fourteen schools were involved in its implementation. Two youth forums were organised in each school at the local level (in the school, in which students learnt) and one joint forum was held at the international level (organised in one of the schools taking part in the project, to which students and teachers from other countries involved in the project implementation came). The forum topics were democratically chosen by the youth and concerned the possibility to become involved in help for people forced to flee[1] (the topic of the first forum) and the issue of gender inequality (the topic of the second forum). During each forum students made decisions on the direction of actions and possibilities of students' participation within the scope of the discussed topic. The above tasks were fulfilled in all of the schools. However, it does not mean that the project was similarly implemented or achieved a similar effect in terms of the desired areas of changes in each of the schools.

Due to the fact that the Author of the text was responsible within the FYS-FORUMS project for the preparation of the concept of research involving students and teachers as well as for the analysis of empirical materials, whose conclusions were, most of all, to help with setting an appropriate direction[2] (compliant with the PAL assumptions) of the project activities, and for monitoring of correctness of the actions taken in terms of their compliance with the adopted methods of work, including the examination of the impact of the project activities on persons involved in the project, the next part of the text presents the impact of the PAL method of work in two British schools. Their choice was determined by a different way of implementing this method of work in the similar baseline situation. Both the similarities and the differences in the presented schools were noticed during the analysis of the empirical material.

The conclusions are based on the analysis of group interviews conducted with young people,[3] and are presented below.[4]

Method

The qualitative approach was used to collect data in the study, based on focus group interviews (FGI) with the youth involved in the project, and it was adopted to receive in-depth responses. In order to conduct focus groups with the participants, the fourteen selected schools in four countries (England, Italy, Lithuania and Cyprus) were visited twice between January and April 2016 and 2018. The interviews were conducted by two moderators: one person asked questions, while the other was responsible for making field notes and producing transcripts. The first moderator also posed follow-up questions to each FGI to facilitate the expansion of the groups' ideas. This allowed for unanticipated perspectives and other information not solicited by the planned questions (Miles and Huberman 1994; Patton 2002). The study took place in two rounds. The first round of the study was held before the relevant actions were taken in schools (one in each partner country), and its generally formulated objective was to understand the current needs of young people in the educational context with particular consideration being given to the research participants' need and possibility to make decisions and act within the school space. The next study took place after the project activity finished (in two or three schools in each partner country) and it was aimed at getting to know the impact of the project activities on the project participants, including, in particular, the impact on the students' need for social involvement and participation. All of the FGI were kept small (four-six participants), and they took the form of informal discussions. It was important to conduct interviews in both rounds with the same groups of people. Students who had completed the workshops cycle developed within the project and who were participants of the Forum itself took part in the focus group interviews. The data from FGI discussions was analysed in the following way: the data was subject to initial and preliminary coding in order to identify key categories; based on the coding, the researchers produced each focus group's responses to the research questions. Each participant's response was identified and compared with other participants' responses across the FGI (Corbin and Strauss 1990).

Findings

In one of the schools, the teachers, from the very beginning of their participation in the project, assumed the role of facilitators, whose help depended on young people's needs. In that school, students invented their own desired structure of the forum and, later on, distributed tasks among themselves and fulfilled them consistently. The situation looked different in the other school, where teachers were not able to abandon the role of the teacher-expert-organiser and, thus, they followed a typical pattern of behaviour based on the top-down distribution of work and selection of students, who, in teachers' opinion, guaranteed success in the pursuit of actions. In this school students were not able to voluntarily participate in the forum because it was the teachers who granted the consent.

In both schools students' initial opinions on the need for participation and involvement in civic issues did not indicate their high interest in these matters. The analysis of the first round of interviews conducted with the youth in two schools showed that involvement was considered by them in terms of a school duty fulfilled by them during classes dealing with the society. Students responding in such a way were called 'the Learning-Oriented' category. Difficulties in defining participation and determining the importance of the ability to be an active citizen was characteristic of this group of students. Nevertheless, 'the Learning-Oriented' students were able to list some issues of importance related to being active and having a possibility to decide about things related to themselves. The following words spoken by one of the students may serve as an illustration of the above:

1: Yes, we learn that at school. We've recently discussed poverty, climate changes, etc. That's a normal subject at school, maybe a little easier than maths (laugh).[5]

The importance of involvement in the areas mentioned above was, however, measured with the help of potential benefits gained thanks to their activity at school. Such students usually became involved in social issues directly connected with the school and assessed at school. It did not need to be directly connected with the grade each time, sometimes informal forms of reward, e.g. recognition by the teacher, a better image at school, etc. were sufficient. The following statement made by one of the students may serve as an empirical example:

C: I was recently involved in a project concerning the LGBT, which was connected with a subject and, owing to this, I improved my grade a little.

It was characteristic of the members of this group to describe their involvement in developing skills in a similar way: in terms of improving their position in the school and, in general, in their future life. Their arguments developed this way seemed to us, in a number of places, to be in opposition to the idea of human solidarity and other norms and values stressed by the global citizenship perspective. The first round of FGI exposed the fact that young people generally showed a limited understanding of participation and the need to be involved in the process of decision making, but, at the same time, they showed some interest and wish to take part in it.[6]

Effects of work with the help of the PAL method

The analysis of the empirical material from the second round of FGI revealed significant differences in responses of the students from the two schools presented above. The differences are likely to be connected with the process of the forum organisation, including, in particular, the role assumed by teachers.

Just like in the first round, two categories of responses were successfully generated.

Students from the first school belong to the first category called 'the Active Participants'. The characteristic feature of this category is that its representatives were involved in the whole Forum process. It could be seen from their responses that the Forum was not only another extra-curricular activity offered by the school, but it became their own space. Below is a response of one of the participants:

5: We were meant to have three weeks but there was the holiday, so that was out of our control. It would have been helpful if we had had that time. (…) I hope, next year we will have the time because we can plan it 6 months ahead.

Although certain organisational problems are described in the response mentioned above, I believe that attention ought to be, most of all, paid to the way of its formulation. The active role of students reflected by the use of pronouns 'I' and 'we' is emphasised in this answer.

It can be seen from this answer that students attending this school had much more freedom.

Teachers stayed withdrawn, which probably had a positive effect on students, who started to feel responsible for the Forum. Owing to that, they gained much more experience in participation. The participants from this category indicated what they wanted to change and modify in the organisation of the Forum in the future, to make it more effective and involve more students.

> 4: We need to improve planning skills, the planning was rushed and we had a lot of ideas but we were confused. We were confused about what we should and what we shouldn't do.

Students from this school declared that they experienced the effects of the PAL method in a number of areas: (1) the first one concerned the sense of developing the transversal skills and competences; (2) the second one was connected with perceiving oneself as an acting entity; (3) the third one involved improvement of the relationships between students and teachers; and (4) the last effect concerned the evolution of the students' attitude towards active citizenship, which was reflected in their way of thinking about social actions and the need to get involved in them. The answers given by the students from this school did not reveal any considerable differences in the way of thinking about participation in FYS-FORUMS or any differences arising out of new forms of experiencing the effects of work. On the contrary, each answer seemed to complement the previous one.

(1) Students from this school frequently mentioned the development of soft/transversal skills and competences, which they attributed directly to their participation in FYS-FORUMS. In particular, they paid attention to an increase in organisational, planning and communication or even social (interpersonal) skills. Here are some of the students' answers:

> 1: I think we did have timing and organization skills (…) and I don't think I was very good with that before and now I am a bit better

> 2: You gain a social skill and you meet new people, and when you meet new people you find out different things.

The students also emphasised improved competence in public speaking, which was expressed as follows:

> 2: The Forum helped with public speaking and standing in front of an audience. (..) You feel more comfortable around people.

> 3: For me public speaking. I used to get scared when I had to speak in public before. I used to get pretty nervous so this boosted my confidence as well. (…) Now I am way more confident than I used to be.

Another skill, the acquiring of which was attributed by students to the project, was connected with leadership.

> 1: I also think leadership skills. Some people have got to host an activity and I think being a leader is something powerful and makes them feel good about themselves.

The students emphasised that the development of these skills would be impossible in traditional lessons, which was expressed by one of the girls interviewed as follows:

> 2: It's a good opportunity to develop skills like that as you can't do that in class where you mainly listen to teachers.

(2) The effects of work using the PAL method were experienced by students as a change in the way they perceived themselves as acting agents who were able to do something.

In their answers, they emphasised that taking part in the project empowered them to act, at the same time making them more self-confident. For example, one of the students gave the following answer to the question: 'How did you realise that you made an impact?':

3: *When you have the attitude that we are going to make a change it actually makes you believe that it actually did make a change. It makes you feel that you can change all things. If I can make a change you can make any change you want.*

(3) The use of PAL as a method for working with students improved their relationships with teachers. The teachers claimed that thanks to FYS-FORUMS they could test a different method of working with students, thus viewing them from a different perspective – as acting persons, who are well-organised, offer interesting insights, and have much to say. Thanks to this, they became more open and more willing to share their experiences. The students also noted this effect, which is proved by the following two statements:

1: *We definitely got to get closer, we didn't have that fear of asking questions. This boosted our confidence in asking questions as we used to be scared. Because we got to them more I am definitely not scared now.*

3: *We got to understand more from them about inequality as teachers shared how they and their family have faced inequality and their own views. It got to develop a bond to understand more about them.*

(4) The last of the effects identified concerns a change in the students' attitude towards active citizenship. All participants of the interview emphasised that they were considering involvement in social actions or that they were already taking part in some. The interviewees attributed this change directly to their participation in the project. Many of them openly said that the organisation of and participation in the forum inspired them to be more active in the future.

1: *I thought about it but I never did it. But definitely because of the forum I have that thought and I might start.*

During the interview, also specific ideas for action were given:

3: *"We could write a letter, make a presentation or just tell them"* (this refers to a possibility of wielding influence on the decision-makers in countries which violate the human rights – Author's note).

The structure of the students' discussion following the above statement resembled a brainstorm. Each participant tried to add a new idea for action or improve the idea of the preceding person. For example, the students started to discuss possible ways of convincing teachers to their ideas and how to get more people – young people and/or adults – from other schools, the whole city or even the whole country involved in the action.

Apart from thinking about involvement, the students provided numerous examples of specific actions they performed after taking part in the project.

2: *Before the forum I was not one that would take risks and go to many different clubs, but after joining it, I started to join clubs and I have also recently started volunteering because of that. (…) The forum has inspired me.*

4: For the action after the forum, we are going to go to a primary school to raise more awareness so that's going to benefit the wider community in (name of the city - Author) *and I think, in terms of school we probably raised more awareness.*

All interview participants mentioned talking to their families or friends about the subject of the forum. Here is a statement of one of the students:

1: I definitely talked to mum about this, before she didn't think it was such a big thing (gender inequality –Autor's note) *but she knows now.*

The students agreed that continuing work using the PAL method and organising another forum were things they wanted and needed. Thus, they declared that they would take appropriate steps in the future.

Taking into consideration students' answers, it can be claimed that the implementation of the PAL method in this school has had the desired effect.

The second category of participants represented by students from the second school, was called 'the Currently Focused on Learning'. The students classified this way evaluated the participation in the forum as an interesting extra-curricular school activity, during which it was possible for them to learn something new. The following voice of one of the students may be representative of this category:

A: I learnt how to develop my skills of how I work with different people, especially people from the other towns who don't go to our school. This school has a style of doing things, so it's good to learn to be flexible and learn how other people do things.

The educational aspect was stressed in the responses. These participants appreciated the fact that they were able to participate in the Forum and gain new skills and knowledge, which might be used by them if they wished to. They also emphasised that the methods of learning used during the Forum had been prepared in an interesting way. Below are some of their responses:

C: Gender Equality has always been a word that you hear, and what I wanted to do was not just say it but make more examples of what it is. I wanted to stop talking about gender equality and make it more concrete.

B: Not many people like to pay attention in class but if we do it in a funny way, some people might engage and really like it.

In spite of the fact that students from this school recognised the social involvement issue as an important one, they did not express their wish to continue or voluntarily participate in any action of this kind. Teachers stuck to their usual role and, as a result, young people continued to play the role they had played before the Forum started (the role of pupils) and they tried to meet the expectations related to that role, i.e. learning.

Conclusions

The key purpose of this research was to assess how the PAL approach may empower active citizenship of young people. Analysis of FGI suggests that implementation of this approach in schools based on the assumptions made has an effect on the development of a civic attitude in young people and on an increase in the sense of agency and self-esteem of the agent. Moreover, work employing the PAL method allows to trigger an authentic need for social action, which is proven by the attitude of students from the first of the schools presented, who got involved in different activities after the project and emphasised that they were motivated to do this by their participation in FYS-FORUMS. The effects of work based on the PAL method change as soon as teachers start modifying it. For example, they interfere in students' activities, control them or even take over the role of the leader, which brings the whole experience closer to the traditional division of school roles. In such a situation, work based on the PAL method may not bring about all the desired effects. Students will definitely appreciate a different form of education and learn many interesting things, however, it is hard to expect them to treat it differently from other subjects and view it as a general principle behind social life that can be used at their age at school and outside it. An empirical example of a failure to use the PAL method in full is the second of the schools I presented.

PAL offers teachers in schools, but also practitioners working with young people in different institutions, a number of opportunities: it can be used to teach such subjects as civics or entrepreneurship, but it can also be employed in other classes as a method supporting the development of transversal skills. The PAL method can be used as part of extracurricular activities with young people, initiated by the youth. In institutions such as community centres, the whole work or its part can be based on the assumptions of the PAL method.

There is no doubt that before it is applied, one should ask oneself a question about the extent to which it can be used so that it is not too distorted and the participation is not only symbolic or tokenic (see, for example, Arnstein [1969]). In case there are any doubts about this, it is perhaps worth starting with methods that are less invasive with regard to the relationships and hierarchy of power.

Notes

1. The first forum took place in 2016, when numerous European countries were experiencing the so-called 'migration crisis'. Arguing the need to focus the discussion on this topic, young people raised such issues as: the sense of security, the media hype, sympathy, fear and the need to discuss this topic with others.
2. This, in particular, concerns the conclusions from the first round of the study.
3. Detailed research conclusions from the focus group interviews with teachers may be found in the following publication: Leek (2019)
4. More research conclusions may be found, e.g. in the following publications: Jarkiewicz (2019).
5. Italics are used when referring to the statements made by the youth. Numbers and letters preceding the statements are assigned to the students taking part in a given interview. In the first school, the interview was conducted with 5 girls aged 13. In the second school, there were 4 participants (2 boys and 2 girls) aged 14.
6. The category of students described as 'the Learning-Oriented' was opposed to the category called 'the Experience-Oriented' whose members 'are involved in a wide range of community activities. They are involved in volunteer work. Their responses reflect their personal (direct or indirect) experience and (…) have a much deeper and greater understanding of the importance of participation, but it needs to be pointed out that this group was much smaller than the second one.' (Jarkiewicz 2019, 29). More information on this topic may be found in the quoted article.

Disclosure statement

No potential conflict of interest was reported by the author.

Funding

The author(s) disclosed the receipt of the following financial support for the research, authorship, and/or publication of this article: 'The inspiration to write this article came from the research work I undertook as a part of the international Future Youth School Forums project led by Oxfam UK and financed by the European Commission (Grant Number 2015-1-UK01-KA201-013456), as well as the Ministry of Science and Higher Education Republic of Poland (Grant Number 3558/ ERASMUS +/2016/2).'

References

Argyris, Chris, and Donald A Schon. 1974. *Theory in Practice –Increasing Professional Effectiveness.* San Francisco: Jossey-Bass Inc. doi.org/10.1002/bs.3830390308.

Arnstein, Sherry. 1969. "A Ladder of Citizen Participation." *Journal of the American Planning Association* 35 (4): 216–224. doi:10.1080/01944366908977225.

Austin, Joe, and Michael Willard. 1998. *Generations of Youth: Youth Cultures and History in Twentieth-Century America.* New York: University Press.

Belenky, Mary F., Blythe M. Clinchy, Nancy R. Golderger, and Jill M. Tarube. 1986. *Women's Ways of Knowing: The Development of Self, Voice and Mind.* New York: Basic Books.

Birdwell, Jonathan, and Mona Bani. 2014. *Introducing Generation Citizen.* London: Demos.

Carr, Wilfred, and Stephen Kemmis. 1986. *Becoming Critical: Education Knowledge and Action Research.* London: Falmer Press.

Corbin, Juliet, and Anselm Strauss. 1990. "Grounded Theory Research: Procedures, Canons, and Evaluative Criteria." *Qualitative Sociology* 13 (1): 3–21.

Granosik, Mariusz. 2018. "Participatory Action Research in Social Work: Towards Critical Reframing." *Pensée Plurielle* 48 (n° 48): 77–90. doi:10.3917/pp.048.0077.

Herr, Kathryn. 1999. "The Symbolic Uses of Participation: Co-Opting Change." *Theory Into Practice* 38 (4): 235–240. doi.org/10.1080/00405849909543859.

Jarkiewicz, Anna. 2019. "Empowering Youth At-Risk in School Through Participatory Methods of Work Developed Within the FYS-Forums Project - Research Findings." *Czech and Slovak Social Work* 19 (1): 23–34. http://www.socialniprace.cz/eng/index.php?sekce=2&podsekce=&ukol= 1&id=101.

Johnson, Heather. 2001. "From the Chicago School to the new Sociology of Children: The Sociology of Children and Childhood in the United States, 1900–1999." In *Children at the Millennium. Where Have we Come from, Where are we Going?* edited by Sandra Hofferth, and Timothy Owens, 53–93. New York: Elsevier Science Ltd.

Leek, Joanna. 2019. "Teachers Perceptions about Supporting Youth Participation in Schools: Experiences from Schools in England, Italy and Lithuania." *Improving Schools* 22 (2): 173–190. doi:10.1177/136548021984050.

Mesquita, Diana, Rui M. Lima, Sousa Rui M., and Maria Assunção Flores. 2009. "The Connection between Project Learning Approaches and the Industrial Demand for Transversal Competencies." Paper presented at the 2nd International Research Symposium on PBL, Melbourne, Australia December 3–4.

Miles, Matthew B., and Michael, A. Huberman. 1994. *Qualitative Data Analysis: An Expanded Sourcebook.* Thousand Oaks, CA: SAGE.

O'Kane, Claire. 2008. "The Development of Participatory Techniques: Facilitating Children's Views about Decisions That Affect Them." In *Research with Children: Perspectives and Practices*, edited by Pia Pia Christensen, and Allison James, 125–155. New York: Routledge.

Patton, Michael Q. 2002. *Qualitative Research and Evaluation Methods*. Thousand Oaks, CA: SAGE.

Pedler, Mark, John Burgoyne, and Cheryl Brook. 2005. "What has Action Learning Learnedto Become?" *Action Learning: Research and Practice* 2 (1): 49–68. doi:10.1080/14767330500041251.

Pereira Orlando, Petiz, and Alberto A.T Costa. 2017. "The Importance of Soft Skills in the University Academic Curriculum: The Perceptions of the Students in the new Society of Knowledge." *International Journal of Business and Social Research* 07 (03): 25–34. doi:10.18533/ijbsr.v7i6.1052.

Quijada Cerecer, David, Caitlin Cahil, and Matt Bradley. 2013. "Toward a Critical Youth Policy Praxis: Critical Youth Studies and Participatory Action Research." *Theory Into Practice* 52 (3): 216–223. doi:10.1080/00405841.2013.804316.

Rigg, Clare, and Kiran Trehan. 2004. "Reflections on Working with Critical Action Learning." *Action Learning: Research and Practice* 1 (2): 149–165. doi:10.1080/1476733042000264128.

Schwartzman, Helen. 2001. "Introduction: Questions and Challenges for 21st-Century Anthropology of Children." In *Children and Anthropology. Perspectives for 21st Century*, edited by Helen Schwartzman, 1–37. Westport: Bergin and Garvey.

Sibley, David. 1995. *Geographies of Exclusion: Society and Difference in the West*. New York: Routledge.

Tam, Antony, and Barbara Trzmiel. 2018. "Transversal Skills as a Missing Link Between School and Work: Experiences From the Asia-Pacific Region." In *Transitions to Post-School Life,. Responsiveness to Individual, Social and Economic Needs*, edited by Margarita Pavlova, John Chi-Kin Lee, and Rupert Maclean, 35–49. Singapore: Springer Nature Singapore Pte Ltd.

Vadeboncoeur, J. A., and L. Stevens. 2005. *(Re)Constructing "the Adolescent": Sign, Symbol, and Body*. New York: Peter Lang.

Social Action Learning: Applicability to Comrades in Adversity in Nigeria

Adrian Ogun & Jeff Gold

ABSTRACT
The paper considers the learning of former abductees in Nigeria who enrolled on the New Foundation School University Preparatory (NFSUP) programme at the American University of Nigeria (AUN). The research question is: Can action learning enable a holistic evaluation of the student learning experiences of former terrorist abductees on a university preparatory programme at the AUN? The methodology employed is based on the praxeology of action learning, combined with grounded theory. Literature relating to abduction, stigmatisation and exclusion are considered along with coverage of the Boko Haram abduction of Chibok school girls in Nigeria. Findings show action learning enables student engagement, promotes confidence, encourages social and emotional learning and provides a forum for feedback from NFSUP students. This paper could also be relevant for preparatory and transformational courses in a wider community that includes refugees, internally displaced persons, child soldiers, teenage victims of trafficking and sexual grooming. Action learning probably enables a more holistic evaluation of student learning than Course Experience Questionnaires. A hybrid of both approaches should be considered by educational institutions as an assessment tool.

1. Introduction

Since 2013, over 1000 teenage girls and boys have been abducted by terrorists in Northern Nigeria (UNICEF 2018). Many abductees when released or rescued enrol on university preparatory programmes in educational institutions in Nigeria. To assess the impact of these preparatory programmes, educational institutions generally make use of Course Experience Questionnaires (CEQs). CEQs are the traditional tool used by educational institutions for the assessment of student engagement, course delivery and design (Munns and Woodward 2006; Ramsden 1991). CEQs have been criticised for not adopting a holistic approach to the assessment of student learning experiences outside the class room, especially in diverse cultural settings (Griffen et al. 2003). Where course evaluation is not based on a holistic approach, the data collected does not fully capture the contextual, cognitive, social and emotional learning experiences of students. Consequently, improvements to student performance, course delivery and design may be limited and sub-optimal. This paper seeks to answer the research question: Can action learning enable a holistic evaluation of the student learning experiences of former terrorist abductees on a university preparatory programme at the American University of Nigeria (AUN)?

To answer this question, we employ an action learning methodology, inspired by Revans (1971) and expounded upon by Coughlan and Coughlan (2010), that when combined with grounded theory (GT) may generate actionable knowledge, which addresses the research question (cf. Pauleen, Corbitt, and Yoong 2007). Two action learning sets (consisting of four former terrorist abductees) met on three occasions in April and May 2019 to discuss learning problems and proffer remedial actions. Furthermore, action learning set members, through the medium of a focus group (held in October 2019), were used reflexively (Alvesson and Skoldberg 2009) in the interpretation of data and the validation of working hypotheses and GTs. We start by briefly considering the circumstances surrounding abduction, stigmatisation and exclusion of victims of social conflict. Then, we explore action learning in education, student engagement and the utility of CEQs. We further outline the background to the study with reference to Boko Haram terrorist activities in Nigeria and the methodology employed in this study, before the development of a number working hypotheses or GTs that attempt to answer the research question. We conclude with comments on how former abductees and teachers benefited from action learning sessions and how Action Learning Research, based on the learning experiences of NFSUP students, may have implications for the wider community of victims of war and social violence.

2. Literature review

2.1. Abduction stigmatisation and exclusion

There is a dearth of psychological models, in extant literature, that anticipate fully the novel circumstances, history and teaching needs of students in Nigeria, who were former terrorist abductees (Adepelumi 2018). However, the accounts of abduction experienced by young Ugandan girls during a brutal civil war in Northern Uganda (that raged on for 20 years from 1987) may provide some insight into the teaching and needs of girls abducted, more recently, in Nigeria. Following abduction by competing armies during the Ugandan civil war, many girls became sexual slaves of their abductors and approximately 30% had children for army soldiers (Allen 2005). In instances where young girls (and their children) escaped or were rescued and returned to their homelands, they were stigmatised and excluded from community life due to the legacy of their horrific experiences while in captivity. In addition, their children were discriminated against, and some were labelled as 'children of the enemy', because villagers were fearful that their fathers might return to claim them or they were afraid that male children would grow up to claim rights to village property, especially where the soldier's child was the first born male in the family (Namanya 2013). Even in cases where former abductees were accepted back into local communities, they faced immense economic challenges in supporting themselves and their children because they had missed out on completing their formal education and acquired only nascent vocational skills prior to their abduction. Owing to stigmatisation, the chances of former abductees marrying were very low, and some girls, in a bid to improve their chances of marriage, abandoned their babies (Kalla and Dixon 2010).

2.2. Action learning and education

In relation to social action learning, the definition of action learning proposed by Revans (1982) envisaged helping people resolve complex challenges in the sparsely researched fields of social conflict and education, as well as the frequently researched fields of leadership and organisational development.

In a book review of action learning in schools, based on 100 teacher case studies, Aspinwall (2011) noted that a cycle of four processes was proposed for the effective implementation of action learning in schools, especially where there was an emphasis on the professional development of teachers. The first process was 'reflection', which involved thinking through a problem. The second process was 'community' and the sharing of issues within the set and beyond. The third was 'action', which involved the exploration of ideas and actions generated. Finally, the fourth was 'feedback' from students and teachers affected by actions taken (p.173). Although 100 case studies examined in the book (Aubusson, Hoban, and Ewing 2009) highlight how action learning could enable the professional development of teachers in schools, there was no significant examination of the link between action learning, student engagement and achievement. This study attempts to shed light on this under researched area.

Educationalists argue that for students to be fully engaged in productive learning, it is essential to incorporate individual and collective student self-assessment into a teaching programme (Munns and Woodward 2006; Perry, VandeKamp, and Nordby 2002). McFadden and Munns (2002) emphasise that

> it is the students themselves who will be able to tell us that they are engaged and who will say whether education is working for them in a culturally sensitive and relevant way.

Ten proposals for action to improve student engagement are recommended by Zepke and Leach (2010, 169), namely, enhance student beliefs, encourage autonomous working, recognise that teachers are central to engagement, create collaborative and active learning, challenge students to extend their academic abilities, encourage diversity, provide support services for special needs, be adaptive to student expectations, enable students to become 'active citizens' in curriculum building and enable students to develop their social and cultural capital.

Since action learning incorporates individual and collective self-assessment, specifically for students, the process provides opportunities to engage in discourses on what they are learning (knowledge), what they are achieving (actions), teaching practices (pedagogical spaces), their view of themselves as learners (self-esteem) and their say over the direction and evaluation of learning (their voice). Furthermore, where set members, in an educational setting, are drawn from different ability levels, then action learning sessions may facilitate the transfer of knowledge between students with different ability levels and those experiencing similar challenges in different contexts (Conklin et al. 2012). Finally, action learning may promote life-long adult learning and aid students in solving work- or organisation-related problems collaboratively in their career after graduation (Zuber-Skerritt 2013).

2.3. Course Experience Questionnaires

CEQs are the traditional tool used by educational institutions for the assessment of student engagement, course delivery and design (Munns and Woodward 2006; Ramsden 1991). The CEQ attempts to collect information on the quality of teaching and courses. It assumes a strong association between the quality of student learning and student perceptions of learning. Student perceptions of teaching effectiveness in higher institutions are used to create a performance rating system for academic organisational units in different institutions – a useful benchmarking tool for funding organisations. In addition, CEQ performance indicators assist educational institutions with the internal monitoring, evaluation and improvement of course quality and delivery – a useful guide for educational organisations (Ramsden 1991). Although CEQs benefit primarily funding and educational organisations, students also receive useful information and feedback that may aid them in choosing which educational course and institution to attend through the publication of 'Good University' guides (Ashenden and Milligan 2000).

However, CEQs have been criticised for not incorporating a holistic approach to the assessment of student learning experiences and life outside the class room, especially in diverse cultural settings (Griffen et al. 2003). CEQs have also been criticised for not emphasising the assessment of social and emotional learning (Zins and Elias 2007). If course evaluation is not based on a holistic approach and data collected do not capture fully student course experiences, then improvements to student performance, course delivery and design may be limited and sub-optimal. Areas not included in traditional CEQs include the social and emotional dimensions of learning, the learning climate and intellectual environment, a contextual approach to student learning, guidance and support to boost confidence and encourage independent inquiry (Griffen et al. 2003). This paper seeks to examine how action learning might enable a holistic evaluation of student learning experiences. The following section discusses the background to the study and the methodology employed to answer the research question.

3. Background to study and methodology

This study considers the abduction of school girls from the village of Chibok in Nigeria by the Islamic State in West Africa (ISWA), commonly known as Boko Haram. Boko Haram is a jihadist terrorist organisation based in North Eastern Nigeria with tentacles active in neighbouring Chad, Niger and Cameroon. The term 'Boko Haram' has been variously translated as 'Western education is forbidden' or 'Western influence is a sin or sacrilege or fake' (Newman 2013). Boko Haram was founded as a non-violent religious organisation by Mohammed Yusuf in 2002 but was transformed into a terrorist organisation by Abubakar Shekau in 2009 and has been strategically aligned with the Islamic State of Iraq and the Levant since 2015.

On 14th April, 2014, Boko Haram abducted 276 school girls (aged 15 years and older) from the town of Chibok, Borno state, North Eastern Nigeria. Today, 112 school girls from Chibok are still missing. One hundred sixty-four school girls were either rescued or escaped captivity. One hundred thirty of those girls, who were either rescued by the Nigerian government (106) or escaped (24), enrolled (from 2014) on a predominantly government sponsored university preparatory programme at the AUN's New Foundation

School (NFS), based in Yola, the capital of Adamawa state, North Eastern Nigerian (AUN 2018). A handful of the 130 of the former abductees, who were initially enrolled at NFS, subsequently withdrew and returned to Chibok – with some taking up offers of marriage. A Boko Haram propaganda video of abductees and their children, released in 2018, featured some of the 112 missing young ladies from Chibok. A few of these, featured in the video, asserted that they no longer wished to be brought back home from captivity. The extent to which they were coerced into making propaganda statements or succumbed to the 'Stockholm Syndrome' could not be independently confirmed (Reuters 2018). The 'Stockholm Syndrome' denotes a situation where abductees form psychological alliances with their captors and in some cases express sympathy for their causes (Jameson 2010).

The methodology employed in this study is based on the praxeology of action learning outlined by Revans (1971), which identifies three interlocking systems: 'Alpha, Beta and Gamma. System Alpha is the use of information for designing objectives; System Beta is the use of information for achieving objectives and System Gamma is the use of information for adapting to experience and to change (Revans 1971, 33). In Figure 1, adapted from the study by Coughlan and Coughlan (2010, 197/198), these three

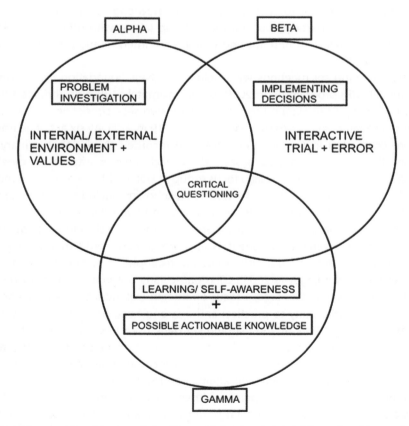

Figure 1. Action Learning Systems Alpha, Beta and Gamma (adapted from Coughlan and Coughlan 2010).

systems are depicted as 'problem investigation', 'implementing decisions' and 'learning and self-awareness'.

System Alpha focuses on diagnosis, in relation to the internal and external environment and values associated with the problem. In contrast, System Beta focuses on the interactive trial-and-error process associated with implementing actions. System Gamma focuses on learning and self-awareness and 'how thought processes … adapt to and evolve with actions directed towards solving the problem' (Coughlan and Coughlan 2010, 198). The critical questioning of power relations, politics and learning assumptions is depicted in Figure 1 as a prominent sub-section within each system. As argued by Coughlan and Coughlan: 'In action learning research, the researcher is involved in system gamma … clarity on the nature of the involvement, the interpretation of that involvement and the evaluation of the impact of that involvement underpins the presentation of the actionable knowledge' (198).

To bring clarity to researcher involvement, interpretation and evaluation of action learning data related to potentially actionable knowledge, grounded theory (Corbin and Straus 2008) was deployed in an attempt to bring rigour, transparency and reliability to the process of formulating actionable knowledge within System Gamma. The combination of GT and Action Learning to produce a Grounded Action Learning approach to actionable knowledge generation has been endorsed by Pauleen, Corbitt, and Yoong (2007) and Rand (2013). In an attempt to validate actionable knowledge generated within System Gamma, set members participated in a focus group (along with other stakeholders) to reflexively examine research findings and validate the interpretation of results (Alvesson and Skoldberg 2009).

Six action learning set meetings were held at the New Foundation School University Preparatory (NFSUP) programme in 2019 for approximately 130 girls abducted from the village of Chibok by Boko Haram terrorists in 2014. Two sets, consisting of four students, met on three separate occasions in April and May 2019 in AUN. All six action learning sessions were conducted in English and were tape recorded. A written summary of the content of the set meeting was produced by each adviser after each meeting. In October 2019 following data analysis, a focus group of stakeholders was used to reflexively validate the working hypotheses and GTs. The stakeholders included two academic and two administrative staff members, two set advisers and two other set members.

The primary role played by GT in this paper was the analysis and articulation of the experiential data discovered by set sessions. GT is not a theory but a methodology to discover theories dormant in data produced, for example, in action learning sessions (Legewie and Schervier-Legewie 2004). GT is particularly useful in situations where there is little previous research in an area; a focus on human experience and social interaction; a high degree of applicability to practice; and a strong need for cultural and contextual interpretation (Yoong 1996). Action learning set data, used in GT, is systematically gathered and analysed until concepts and dormant theories emerge during the research process through the researcher's continuous analytical interplay between analysis and data collection. The interplay between analysis and data collection ends when central themes reoccur frequently – the point of 'theoretical saturation' (Strauss and Corbin 1990). As data emerged from set meetings, these were analysed via Corbin and Straus's (2008) version of GT, involving 'open' 'axial', 'selective' and 'theoretical' coding. 'Open' coding involves 'breaking data apart and delineating concepts to stand for blocks of raw data' (Corbin and Straus 2008, 65). 'Axial' coding involves 'crosscutting or relating concepts to each other' (Corbin and Straus 2008, 195). 'Selective' coding is conducted after identifying –through an iterative process of engagement with data – the 'core variable'. The core variable attempts to make explicit the experiential learning of set members as they strive to resolve challenges related to the NFSUP programme and implement actions. 'Theoretical' codes weave together incomplete concepts into working hypotheses that attempt to form a theory that reconciles some of the concerns of participants.

In summary, this paper proposes that action learning provides an established way of discovering tacit knowledge, embedded within student programmed learning experiences, through the use of collaborative and problem-based questioning, action and reflection (Berns and Erickson 2001). GT provides a rigorous method for articulating emergent knowledge through a systematic process of abstraction, concept development and theory building. The results of action learning sessions, GT building and a reflexive focus group are presented in the next section.

4. Presentation of results

In this section, results from action learning set meetings are transformed from disparate primary data via integrative 'mind maps' (Buzan 1993) into core variables that give rise to several working hypotheses or GTs that shall be reflexively validated in a focus group involving set members. The 'mind map' below was developed from the set data (tape recordings and contemporaneous reflective notes written by advisers) taken from six meetings in April and May 2019 and attempts to facilitate the identification of codes and concepts. The concepts, derived from a review of action learning set data, are listed below. Concepts include the conflict between learning English (to advance studies) and being criticised by class mates for abandoning Chibok culture by speaking English outside the classroom, the stigma of being labelled a 'Chibok Girl', past experiences producing a negative self-image, the puzzle of managing time demands and the benefits derived from actions taken by students following set meetings (concepts are depicted in 'boxes' in Figure 2).

In Figure 2, the focus of action learning sessions was the resolution of challenges encountered by students during the NFSUP programme. For example, many students practiced speaking English to their kinswomen outside class but were criticised, by a minority, for denigrating Chibok culture – which promoted the native language of Kibaku. Figure 3 highlights four core working hypotheses or GTs as emanating from the concepts featured in Figure 2. The first working hypothesis suggests that the sessions empowered students by enabling them to voice their assessment of the NFSUP programme and share their learning experiences. The second suggests that action learning sessions and resultant actions increased student engagement and improved student performance in English, mathematics, self-assertiveness, time management and exam preparation. The third suggests that the process of 'comrades in adversity' sharing their experiences (of translating programmed course knowledge into local contextual practice) is therapeutic and beneficial in terms of social and emotional learning (Zins and Elias 2007). The fourth suggests that action learning builds student confidence, as evidenced by action learning set members enthusiastically requesting (in Appendix) for more action learning sessions to be instigated and for those sessions to be more frequent with wider student coverage.

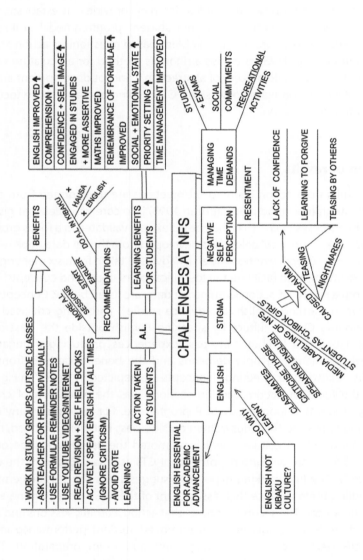

Figure 2. Themes related to concepts produced from action learning set data.

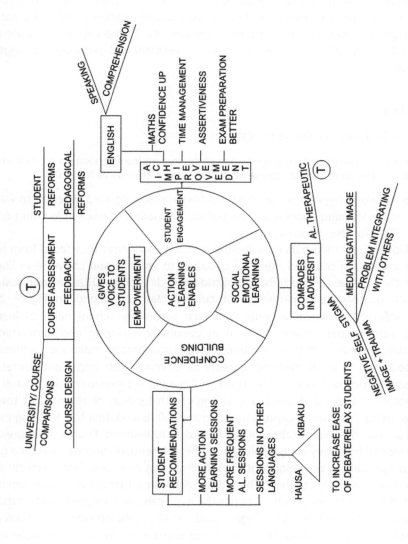

Figure 3. Action learning enables four working GTs/hypotheses.

Further research and data from additional NFSUP sponsored set sessions in the 2019/ 2020 academic year is required to further validate and refine these working hypotheses or GTs. Some GT authorities suggest that the process of data collection and analysis only ends when central themes or core hypotheses reoccur frequently – the point when 'data and theoretical saturation' is attained (Aldiabat and Le Navenec 2011)

The results of a stakeholder focus group endorsed the four central working hypotheses depicted in Figure 3. The detailed results of the focus group are presented in the Appendix. The validation of working hypotheses that suggest set sessions provide a voice for students to give a course assessment and that action learning enables social and emotional learning is significant because the hypotheses incorporate GT theoretical codes (denoted by the letter 'T' in Figure 3) about therapy, course assessment and pedagogy, as suggested by the researchers.

5. Discussion

This paper seeks answer to the key question:

> Can action learning enable a holistic evaluation of the student learning experiences of former terrorist abductees on the NFSUP course at the American University of Nigeria?

The four core working hypotheses arising from findings (see Figure 3) attempt to warrant claims that action learning enables a more holistic evaluation of student learning experiences than CEQs, for the following reasons:

First, in Figure 2, set members revealed the learning challenges they faced from fellow former abductees who criticised them for choosing to practice and converse in English, rather than their native tongue (Kibaku), outside the classroom. CEQs are not designed to illicit such poignant information about cultural clashes. Second, in Figure 2, set members confessed to wrestling with their past secondary school habit of learning material by 'rote' to pass exams rather than genuinely exploring and understanding subject matter. CEQs are not designed to encourage students to make such admissions, whereas the forum of a set meeting appears to facilitate such important confessions and the discussion of remedial action. Third, in Figure 2, set members highlighted how their psychological social and emotional struggle with feelings of resentment towards (and a desire to forgive) former captors haunted and influenced their NFS learning experience. CEQs are not capable of capturing such barriers to learning. Fourth, in Figure 2, set members revealed how they are grappling with the unintended consequences of a global media campaign that not only highlighted their plight but also speculated publicly about their maltreatment while in captivity. The unintended consequences are expressed in the reticence of NFSUP students to initially to use the main campus canteen based on the fear or perception of potential teasing by degree students about their history, as 'Chibok girls'. CEQs are not designed to reveal the unintended consequences of a viral social media campaign.

5.1. Results predicted by literature review and findings that were unexpected

The literature review predicted that the Stockholm syndrome may influence abductee behaviour. This prediction is particularly relevant in relation to the cultural conflict caused by some students wishing to practice speaking English to their kinswomen, from Chibok, outside the classroom (see Figures 2 and 3). The 'Stockholm syndrome' may offer an explanation as to the motivation of some former abductees to actively discourage fellow Chibok abductees from practicing English outside the classroom. It could be argued that a few former abductees may have unwittingly been indoctrinated during captivity into believing that 'Western influence is a sin' (Newman 2013). Consequently, attempts by the NFSUP programme or fellow Chibok kinswomen to promote the study of English outside the classroom may be seen as an affront to Chibok culture – in sympathy with Boko Haram teachings. An alternative explanation could be that those objecting to the use of English outside the class room have a natural ability to switch between languages and have difficulty understanding why their kinswomen cannot do the same.

The literature review predicts (based on the experiences of former Ugandan girl abductees) that Chibok former abductees might struggle to learn, during the NFSUP programme, while dealing with the psychological trauma of their abduction and the understandable resentment still felt against their abductors. Figure 2 highlights the dilemma faced by some former abductees. On the one hand, they resent their captors for their maltreatment, while, on the other hand, their strong Christian commitment (approximately 95% of the abductees are church-going Christians) urges them to forgive their captors and move forward to take advantage of the educational opportunities afforded by their scholarships at AUN.

It is interesting to note that the literature review did not predict the struggle NFSUP students might face to break free from a tradition of using rote learning to pass exams (their secondary school experience prior to abduction) to a pursue a genuine understanding of subjects through persistent individual self-inquiry (see Figure 2). Perhaps the most surprising revelation (not predicted by the literature review) was how former abductees might be wrestling with the unintended consequences of the global 'Bring Back Our Girls' campaign that went viral. In detail, the benefits of a viral social media campaign that exerted political pressure on governments to secure their rescue (Njoroge 2017) are juxtaposed against the stigma (see Figures 2 and 3) associated with the notoriety of their experiences in captivity that may hinder integration within the main student population at AUN, local communities and their chances of marriage (Kalla and Dixon 2010).

5.2. Comparison of findings with Ugandan study of girl abductees

A Ugandan study into the rehabilitation of girls abducted and abused during a 20-year-long war highlighted the teaching need for vocational skills to enable the returnees to sustain themselves when returning to their homeland (Namanya 2013). Set sessions at NFSUP made no mention of vocational training needs or how the young women will sustain themselves after the NFSUP course in the event that some do not proceed onto degree courses. The incidence of pregnancies highlighted in the Ugandan report of 30% is higher than those experienced by the young women from Chibok. Following the Nigerian government's rescue of 106 young women, three years after their abduction from Chibok, they were kept together in isolation from the media and the rest of the world for another year before joining the 24 escapes already studying at NFSUP, whereas the Ugandan abductees were left to find their own way back to their homelands without government support.

Although more action learning sessions are yet to be held and analysed, the initial working hypotheses, depicted in Figure 3, appear to warrant claims that action learning enables a holistic assessment of the NFSUP student learning experiences both inside and outside the classroom. Furthermore, we have tried to show how action learning research, in combination with other methods, provides an important source of data that can be analysed to produce working hypotheses and new avenues for future research that may aid the education of victims of war and social violence.

6. Conclusion

The conclusion, so far, is that action learning probably enables a more holistic evaluation of student learning experiences on the NFSUP programme than CEQs. The conclusion is based on the analysis of six action learning set meetings and the triangulation of those results with feedback from a focus group (see Appendix) of set members and teachers. However, in practice, a hybrid of both approaches to assessment should be considered by educational institutions to draw upon both the contextual (bottom-up) strengths of action learning and the universal (benchmarking) strengths of CEQs.

In addition, the underlying importance of action learning research, embodied in working hypotheses (featured in Figure 3) – indicating that action learning enables student engagement, promotes confidence, encourages social and emotional learning and enables students to voice their learning concerns – is that other victims of war and social violence may benefit from student's learning experiences. The hypotheses readily lend themselves to being applied in preparatory courses seeking to assist child soldiers, refugees, internally displaced persons and a wider community that includes the re-orientation of victims of teenage trafficking and sexual grooming circles, highlighted recently in British media.

Disclosure statement

No potential conflict of interest was reported by the authors.

References

Adepelumi, A. 2018. Psychological consequences of the Boko Haram insurgency for Nigerian children. (PhD Thesis), May 2018. Walden University. Available from http://scholarworks.waldenu.edu/cgi/viewcontent.cgi?article=6430&context=dissertations, accessed 14 October 2019.

Aldiabat, K., and C. Le Navenec. 2011. " Philosophical Roots of Classic Grounded Theory: Its Foundations in Symbolic Interactionism." *The Qualitative Report* 16 (4): 1063–1080.

Allen, T. 2005. *War and Justice in Northern Uganda: An Assessment of the International Criminal Court's Intervention*. An Independent Draft Study Report, February 2005. http://r4d.dfid.gov.uk [last accessed 14 October 2019].

Alvesson, M., and K. Skoldberg. 2009. *Reflexive Methodology: New Vistas for Qualitative Research*. 2nd ed. London: Sage.

Ashenden, D., and M. Milligan. 2000. *The Good Universities Guide: Postgraduate and Career Upgrade Courses in 2000*. Subiaco, WA: Hobson.

Aspinwall, K. 2011. "Action Learning in Schools: Reframing Teacher's Professional Development." *R. Action Learning: Research and Practice* 8 (2): 173–174.

Aubusson, P., G. Hoban, and R. Ewing. 2009. *Action Learning in Schools: Reframing Teachers' Professional Learning and Development*. London: Routledge.

AUN. 2018. "New Foundation School Marks Freedom Day for Chibok Girls", 29th May 2018. https://www.aun.edu.ng/index.php/news-events/news/new-foundation-school-marks-freedom-day-for-chibok-girls [last accessed 14 October 2019].

Berns, R., and P. Erickson. 2001. "Contextual Teaching and Learning: Preparing Students for the New Economy." The Highlight Zone: Research @ Work No. 5. http://www.nccte.com/publications/infosynthesis/index.asp#HZ.

Buzan, T. 1993. *The Mind Map Book*. London: Pearson Education Group.

Conklin, J., R. Cohen-Schneider, B. Linkewich, and E. Legault. 2012. "Enacting Change Through Action Learning: Mobilizing and Managing Power and Emotion." *Action Learning: Research and Practice* 9 (3): 275–295. Routledge, Taylor and Francis Group.

Corbin, J., and A. Straus. 2008. *Basics of Qualitative Research 3e*. Los Angeles: Sage.

Coughlan, D., and P. Coughlan. 2010. "Notes Towards a Philosophy of Action Learning Research." *Action Learning: Research and Practice* 7 (2): 193–203.

Griffen, P., H. Coates, C. Mcinnis, and R. James. 2003. "The Development of an Extended Course Experience Questionnaire." *Journal of Quality in Higher Education* 9 (3): 259–266.

Jameson, C. 2010. "A 'Short Step' from Love to Hypnosis: A Reconsideration of the Stockholm Syndrome." *Journal for Cultural Research* 14 (4): 337–355. Taylor and Francis.

Kalla, K., and P. Dixon. 2010. *Learning from TFV's Second Mandate; From Implementing Rehabilitation Assistance to Reparations,* Trust Fund for Victims, 2010, http://www.trustfundforvictims.org. Last Accessed 15th October 2019.

Legewie, H., and B. Schervier-Legewie. 2004. "Anselm Strauss: Research is Hard Work, it's Always a Bit Suffering. Therefore, on the Other Side Research Should Be Fun." Forum: Qualitative Social Research, Vol. 5. No. 3, 2004. http://www.qualitative-research.net/index.php/fqs/article/view/562 last, accessed 20th October 2019.

McFadden, M., and G. Munns. 2002. *British Journal of Sociology of Education* 23(3): 357–366. Taylor and Francis.

Munns, G., and H. Woodward. 2006. "Student Engagement and Student Self-Assessment: The REAL Framework. *Journal of Assessment in Education: Principles, Policy and Practice* 13 (2): 193–293. Taylor and Francis.

Namanya, P. G. 2013. Discussion Paper on Ugandan war Girl Abductees." Published by Consultancy Africa Intelligence's Gender Issues Unit, South Africa.

Newman, P. 2013. "The Etymology of Hausa Boko." http://www.megatchad.net/publications/Newman-2013-Etymology-of-Hausa-boko.pdf [last accessed 14 October 2019].

Njoroge, D. 2017. "Erratum to: Global Activism or Media Spectacle? An Exploration of 'Bring Back Our Girls' Campaign." *Digital Activism in the Social Media*. https://link.springer.com/chapter/10.1007/978-3-319-40949-8_16

Pauleen, D., B. Corbitt, and P. Yoong. 2007. "Discovering and Articulating What is not yet Known: Using Action Learning and Grounded Theory as a Knowledge Management Strategy." *The Learning Organization* 14 (3): 222–240.

Perry, N., K. VandeKamp, and C. Nordby. 2002. "Investigating Teacher-Student Interactions That Foster Self-Regulated Learning." *Educational Psychologist* 37 (1): 5–15.

Ramsden, P. 1991. "A Performance Indicator of Teaching Quality in Higher Education: The Course Experience Questionnaire." *Studies in Higher Education* 16 (2): 129–150. Taylor Francis.

Rand, J. 2013. "Action Learning and Constructivist Grounded Theory: Powerfully Overlapping Fields of Practice." *Action Learning: Research and Practice* 10 (3): 230–243. Taylor Francis.

Reuters. 2018. "Video Purporting to Show some of the Remaining 112 Chibok Girls Still Held in Captivity." https://www.reuters.com/article/us-nigeria-security/boko-haram-video-purports-to-show-some-kidnapped-chibok-girls-idUSKBN1F417F [last accessed 14th October 2019].

Revans, R. W. 1971. *Developing Effective Managers*. New York: Praeger.

Revans, R. W. 1982. "The Psychology of Deliberated Random." In *Origins and Growth of Action Learning*, edited by R. Revans, 718–771. Bromley: Chartwell Bratt.

Strauss, A., and J. Corbin. 1990. *Basics of Qualitative Research: Grounded Theory Procedures and Techniques*. Thousand Oaks, CA: Sage.

UNICEF. 2018. "More than 1,000 Children in North East Nigeria Abducted by Boko Haram Since 2013", Published by UNICEF. http://www.unicef.org/wca/press-release/more-1000-children-northeastern-nigeria-abducted-boko-haram-2013.

Yoong, P. 1996. "A Grounded Theory of Reflective Facilitation: Making the Transition From Traditional to GSS Facilitation." (Unpublished doctoral thesis). Victoria University, Wellington.

Zepke, N., and L. Leach. 2010. "Improving Student Engagement: Ten Proposals." *Journal of Active Learning in Higher Education* 11 (3): 167–177. Sage.

Zins, Joseph, and Maurice Elias. 2007. "Social and Emotional Learning: Promoting the Development of All Students." *Journal of Education and Psychological Consultation* 17 (2–3): 233–255. doi:10.1080/10474410701413152.

Zuber-Skerritt, O. 2013. *Professional Development in Higher Education: A Theoretical Framework for Action Research*. London: Routledge.

Appendix: Validation/Triangulation of Grounded Theory by Focus Group

Introduction

In mid-October 2019, a focus group, consisting of 4 members of staff (2 academic and 2 Administrative) and 4 students (2 set advisers and 2 set members – who participated in A.L. sessions held in April and May 2019), met to discuss the analysis of results from 6 taped action learning sessions held in April and May 2019. Each of the 6 set meetings consisted of 1 set adviser and 3 set members. Focus group topics were driven by questions derived from working hypotheses/GTs featured in Figure 3.

Focus Group Conclusion

Detailed responses to questions, from students and staff (see below), triangulated with nascent working hypotheses or grounded theory (GT) depicted in Figure 3. However, there is a future requirement to analyse and incorporate into the GT process new data from the most recent sessions held in October and planned sessions in November 2019 to enhance the validity of hypotheses.

Detailed answers that support the focus group conclusion:

Q1. Action learning (A.L.) enabling students to express challenges to learning

Set members made the following comments:

'Now I ask questions, both in and outside the classroom, to help me to understand better problem areas'.

'In between sessions I put into practice some of the recommendations from colleagues and it is improving my learning skills'.

'Following A.L. sessions my set members now request for more tutorials from teaching staff'.

'A. L. sessions are helping with confidence and helping the planning of studies throughout the new semester'.

Staff made the following observations:

'I have noticed set members' confidence and learning skills improving because they are now asking more questions and being more assertive in class'.

'Prior to A.L. sessions I noticed that a set member was experiencing challenges in learning and understanding biological terms but now she asks more questions in class to get clarification and is more confident in expressing herself in public in front of class mates'.

'A.L. has given set members a platform, outside class, to debate and discuss possible future career paths or choices'.

'I think it is good when set members ask more questions, in class'.

Q. 2 The influence of feedback from A.L. sessions on course delivery and design

'As a member of staff the A.L. sessions have given me more feedback on the problems students are having, especially with mathematics. As a result, we have instigated new and more interesting ways to make the learning of mathematics more interesting through the introduction of fun Maths quizzes and 'mathematics mania' – a new programme.'

'The feedback from set members on some of the challenges they are facing with learning English has caused the NFS to buy each student a personal dictionary to help them readily understand words and improve their vocabulary. We have also given them tutorials on how to best use the dictionary'.

'I picked up from A.L. sessions that some members where posting formulae on bedposts and placing them on furniture around their rooms to help them remember, so during my next lecture to students I recommended that other students do the same to help memorise formulae'.

Q.3 Have A.L. sessions improved engagement, achievement, performance

'I used to get angry very easily but discussing issues with A.L. set members has helped me to manage my emotions and study better'.

'I used to think that we have too many activities in a week but the A.L. sessions have helped me to set new priorities and improve my time management'.

'A. L. sessions have helped with my self-control and helped me to plan goals for the week'.

'Following A.L. sessions I now prioritise my work and assignments'.

Q4. In what ways has A.L. sessions been therapeutic?

'At the first set meeting members did not want talk very much but with each set meeting they began to talk more about issues and more freely about challenges and we were more engaged'.

'Initially my set members were shy but in later meetings they were more engaged and began discussing the planning of their studies and setting priorities'.

'As a staff member, I noticed that A.L. set members outside of meetings appeared to manage their emotions better than others classmates – especially when some of them (as well as their class mates) received disappointing news recently'.

'As a teacher in class, I noticed that A.L. set members show more belief in themselves and their ability to overcome challenges in their subjects through asking for individual help'.

Q.5. Has A.L. has improved confidence, self-assertiveness, English, SEL and discouraged rote learning?

'Following the A.L. meetings, I have more confidence to meet teachers to ask them to help me understand mathematics. Now, when I struggle to understand a maths formula, I ask the teacher to explain the formula to me, in more detail'.

'After A.L. sessions I now go to fellow students to ask them to explain to me things I don't understand – and they help me. I used to feel shy about admitting to class mates my lack of understanding but now I don't hesitate to ask for help'.

'Before I was afraid of making mistakes with my English, so I did not speak much incase people laughed at my mistakes or teased me. But after discussions in A.L. sessions about others facing similar challenges in English, I am more confident'.

'I used to be shy about speaking in English because I wanted to speak at all times correctly but now I just let it flow and 'blow' or shower my words on people freely. Of course I make mistakes but I am happy and relaxed to listen to corrections from others, so my speaking of English has improved'.

'A.L. session have taught me to socialise more to learn from how others are overcoming problems'.

'A.L. has taught me to share my problems with others'.

'The A.L. sessions there is a lot of interaction which helps set members to learn new ways of solving problems'.

'After A.L. discussions about 'rote' learning, I understand that cramming is not good. Now I try and understand words and formula in my own way rather than just cram'.

'A.L. sessions have made me understand that cramming the night before, in order to pass an exam. It is not good to cram'.

'As a teacher I have seen the performance of set members improve after A.L. sessions. In addition, I have seen fewer emotional breakdowns in set members after the sessions compare to their times before A.L.'.

'As a staff member I have witnessed set members speaking English more confidently after the A.L. sessions'.

'Students are showing more understanding of subjects and have improved their social interaction with one another'.

'Following A.L. sessions students are speaking English more confidently, being assertive asking more question in class and requesting tutorials out of class to get clarification. Their social interaction with one another has also increased after set meetings'.

Q.6. How many student recommendations have been implemented by staff?

In response to student requests, staff have increased the number of A.L. sessions this new academic year but have not been able to increase the frequency of set meetings (owing to scheduling constraints) from bi-weekly meetings arranged last academic year.

In response to student requests, A.L. sessions have begun at the beginning of the Autumn term rather than towards the end of the Summer term (last year), thereby giving students more time to implement actions and learn prior to end of term exams.

In response to student requests, staff have scheduled the Autumn term A.L. sessions in their first language spoken in Chibok (Kibaku) or second language spoken in Northern Nigeria (Hausa) rather than their third language used for all studies at AUN and the NFS course (English). The reason for doing so was to encourage students to speak more easily, freely and articulate more precisely their social and emotional feelings in language which they think in, rather than have to translate into English before expressing.

Action Learning in the Service of Food Security and Poverty Alleviation in Mozambique

Armando Machevo Ussivane and Paul Ellwood

ABSTRACT

We report the use of action learning within a state-owned enterprise charged with delivering a large food security and poverty alleviation program in Mozambique. Successful management of the program requires the co-ordination of a wide variety of different stakeholders including both commercial and subsistence farmers, community leaders and international private investors. Organizational issues arose within the program as efforts to foster cooperation were hindered by apparently intractable differences in the agendas of autonomous stakeholders. When the stakeholder conflicts could not be resolved with traditional project management techniques, an action learning practice was developed in order to more thoroughly explore the barriers to cooperation. In describing the challenges of adopting action learning in this context of social action, we draw attention to three particular elements of the practices developed: an unusually large and diverse action learning set; fostering critical reflection within a culture that does not question seniors; and having a set facilitator who identifies as a scholar-practitioner.

Introduction

This paper reports on the use of action learning within a Mozambican State-owned enterprise (RBL) with management responsibility for a food security and poverty alleviation program known as the 'Baixo Limpopo Irrigation Scheme' (hereafter the 'Scheme'). RBL is the critical intermediary for a complex network of social action that includes management responsibility for: (i) the Scheme's land use rights and license for river water abstraction; (ii) acting as the intermediary for local farmers with investors, suppliers and service providers; (iii) the management of water and irrigation infrastructure; and (iv) assisting local farmers to improve their production and productivity. In short, the Scheme is constituted of the value chains of complex co-operation projects, involving private investors, local farmers, community leaders, agricultural service providers, and banks. Each of these stakeholders have their own concerns and interests within the Scheme which sees them trying to contribute to the whole whilst optimising their own stake. In this article, we report on the action learning approach that has been adopted within RBL as a means of empowering its management to tackle the complex problems of co-ordinating the activities of a diverse array of autonomous stakeholders.

The Scheme started in 1951 during the colonial period, and continued operation for a number of years after Mozambican independence, only to be abandoned in 2000. A renewed impetus followed the completion of the Massingir Dam rehabilitation project (2003–2009) which brought important institutional and infrastructure development. During the same period (2007) a 'Twining Agreement' between Governments of Hubei (China) and Gaza (Mozambique), allocated 300 hectares of arable land in the Baixo Limpopo to grow rice and other crops in partnership with Chinese Investors (Chichava et al. 2013). RBL was established in 2011 to rejuvenate the Scheme, attract further investment and coordinate stakeholders in the building of local value chains. The objectives of the Scheme were redefined at this point as 'to contribute to poverty reduction through increased value addition and provision of climate resilient infrastructure for increased agricultural productivity' (African Development Bank Group 2012).

In the early years (2011) of the RBL stewardship of the Scheme, multiple interests and expectations hindered efforts to co-ordinate the activities of different stakeholders. For instance, there was a perception in some local communities of a violation of their land-use rights and this prompted them to resist the agricultural change agenda. These communities demanded access to the newly-developed land as a form of compensation after their grazing land had been allocated to the new investors. Granting such access meant the local people being trained by private investors in the new crop-growing practices. However, there was a high likelihood of production losses during the training period, which the private investors viewed as a significant financial risk. RBL are charged with resolving such apparently intractable issues and this involves their managers in a range of social action projects within the broad umbrella of the whole Scheme. These organizational challenges are complex and RBL's traditional project management approach was increasingly judged unequal to the task. Action Learning was introduced to RBL by its Chairman Armando Ussivane as an alternative way of making organizational improvements during his participation on the DBA Programme at the University of Liverpool. Paul Ellwood was Armando's DBA supervisor and their research collaboration continued following graduation (Ussivane and Ellwood 2019). This paper is a product of an on-going conversation about action learning practices in this context. The paper is structured as follows. The next section explains the rationale for introducing action learning. The way in which AL has been instituted is described along with the difficulties encountered with its adoption. The following section then offers an illustration of the way in which action learning has come to be used in pursuit of RBL's social change agendas. A Discussion section reflects upon the adoption of AL in this challenging context.

Introducing action learning in this context

The established routine of project management at RBL involved 12 senior people (three board members, three area managers, six heads of departments) participating in weekly meetings facilitated by the chairman. Each area manager, accompanied by their heads of departments, would present a report to describe progress in implementing the annual work plan. The discussion at such meetings would revolve around problems that were perceived by the managers to be hindering the implementation of the plan. People in the meeting would ask questions of clarification and suggest corrective measures to improve the performance. There was a focus on potential solutions with limited exploration of the organizational problems themselves.

As RBL encountered resistance to the implementation of their strategic plan (alluded to in the introduction above) it become evident that the traditional project management discussions were failing to resolve the issues at the heart of objections to the plan. At this point, RBL Chairman Armando Ussivane took the decision to place an action learning routine at the core of RBL's management of the Scheme. Initially, the suggestion that the traditional RBL project management meeting should be replaced by another approach was met with skepticism. In an effort to minimize confusion the new process was introduced without recourse to explanations about its origins, and initially, the very term 'action learning' was not used. Rather the new project review forum was simply described, and the principle stated that no proposal for allocation of resources would appear on the RBL Board agenda unless it has first gone through discussions at the forum.

Armando's approach was to make a virtue of diversity: in his own words 'to treat diversity as a resource, not as a way of categorising differences'. The new forum included (apart from the 12 senior managers involved in the previous project reviews) everybody in RBL with a higher degree: this made for a total of 22 participants. Together the group covers all functions in the company, has a wealth of experience both within the scheme and within the agricultural sector more generally. In addition, some of the new participants come from families in the local communities of the Scheme; and thereby have an engagement with the aspirations of the Scheme that was not only professional. A meeting of this forum lasts on average three hours and convenes every two weeks. The normal routine is that a participant shares a problem with other members. Through a process of questioning, the aim is to challenge and support the participant with the objective of helping them to take action. By doing so they help the participant better understand the problem faced, especially in situations where there were no clear answers. By these means, alternative framings of the problem and possible solutions are generated. The normal procedure is for minutes to be taken and actions agreed. Such actions often involve generating more information about the problem, and a further meeting held to reflect on progress. As appropriate a decision will be taken within this AL set to elevate decisions to the Board (e.g. in cases of significant investment).

Whilst conventional in many respects, the successful adoption of this action learning routine had to confront a number of obstacles in this context. Questioning your superiors is a behavior not acceptable in Mozambican society. Participants in the action learning group (as the forum has become known within RBL) initially understood that they were there to suggest solutions to problems rather than questioning others about the nature of the issue itself. Participants also tended to avoid questioning more senior colleagues or a problem owner from the same department. Questioning others in the Mozambican culture in some circumstances is regarded as impolite and challenging someone higher up in the hierarchy is especially difficult. At first, the AL participants tended to avoid challenging or disagreeing with each other for fear of causing someone to 'lose face'. For some participants the whole process appeared unnecessary: why should managers not simply come to these meetings and present what they had achieved from planned activities? For these reasons, it became crucial to establish ground rules that were understood and agreed by all members. The following work rules were presented in the first action learning session: the participants needed to maintain confidentiality, respect others in the group, be open to ideas and listen, and feel free to challenge others' ideas. It was found through experience that refinements were required. For example, in regards to challenging others' ideas, the facilitation practices evolved to allow the facilitator (Armando Ussivane) not to remain removed from the discussion, but to allow his own (DBA) scholarly research to contribute to the AL meeting (the challenges of facilitation are taken up in the Discussion section).

The wicked problem of ensuring RBL's sustainability through farmer payments

The following section includes an illustration of action learning being used at the RBL more recently and shows the contexts of social action in which they operate. The State corporate sector in Mozambique is (since early 2019) undergoing a re-structuring exercise that requires all State companies to become financially viable, and generate their own revenues; thereby eliminating dependence on the State budget. This policy implies radical changes in RBL's practices, and relationships with Scheme stakeholders, including smallholder (subsistence) farmers. This problem was initially presented to the action learning group by an area manager of the Works and Maintenance department of RBL and framed as one of farmers unwilling to pay for services provided by RBL. Traditional practice in the smallholder farming systems required that RBL provided a full package of equipment maintenance support at a subsidized price. When farmers could not pay even such a cost, the Government would allocate funds for RBL to provide the full service. The requirement for RBL to be self-financing put at risk its performance and legitimacy amongst its poorest stakeholders. Finding a new way in which subsistence farmers could continue to benefit from RBL's Scheme stewardship under the new public financing constraints, appeared to be a 'wicked problem' (Churchman 1967) with no immediately-obvious solution.

The understanding of this problem was opened up by the action learning group through a process of questioning. In 45 min the set members offered several questions to the area manager: How was this problem manifest in the fields? How widespread was this unwillingness to pay? What has prevented the problem from being resolved up to that point? What efforts have previously been attempted? What was the position of the local Government regarding this problem? How could RBL preserve its current legitimacy and image in the region? What were the consequence of losing such legitimacy and image? Why is it so important to preserve such an image and legitimacy given the new restructuring change in the State corporate sector? To whom are RBL now accountable and what are its targets? What is your personal feeling on the situation? Were the farmers aware of the Government cuts to RBL's budget? In this manner, the problem space was opened up by the diverse perspectives of the AL group.

The discussions in response to this questioning served to enrich the understanding of the problem by surfacing particular assumptions about the working relationship with farmers. In turn, this enabled the identification of new possibilities for action. The area manager in his response to the AL group realized that, to some extent, this problem was as much to do with the way his team had communicated with the farmers. Actions agreed for this first cycle included follow on meetings with the farmers, community leaders, and local government in order to share with them the actual resources limitations that RBL was experiencing; and to sensitize the farmers to contribute fuel for the machinery made available by RBL.

One of the first organized meetings with the farmers aimed to analyse the challenges of the smallholder farming system, particularly the maintenance of their irrigation and drainage infrastructure, and identify solutions to resolve them. It was facilitated by a public official, the administrator of Chongoene District. Such meetings are typically loud affairs with angry people shouting their objections, and arguments breaking out between participants. The meeting witnessed the participation of 51 people including the representatives of the smallholder farmers, local community leaders, district government officials and RBL managers. One notable outcome of the meeting was the agreement on the part of the 23 Farmers' Associations within the Scheme to collect money from farmers to contribute to the operation of equipment within their constituencies. RBL was tasked with the responsibility for helping in the assessment of the work and fuel requirements. A local commission was elected comprised of six representatives of the farmers and technicians from RBL who would be interacting and working on a continuous basis on the problem. It was also agreed that monthly meetings should be held to monitor the process.

A group of RBL people – comprising of the chairman, one RBL board member, the area manager and head of department of works and maintenance, and a technician for community mobilization – were present at the stakeholder meeting. Through this group, the experiences and outputs of the stakeholder meeting (including the work of the local government commission) were conveyed back to the AL group which then functioned as a forum for the evaluation of progress on the problem, and reflection on organizational learning for RBL. This on-going participation of the AL group and their experience of the wider Scheme allowed them to offer suggestions that the local commission might not have otherwise considered. For example, rather than farmers bringing their own fuel to put into the machinery, arrangement could be made to allow them to make payment for fuel and oil at the local petrol station (this was subsequently agreed and adopted by the local commission).

In comparison with the form of meetings before the creation of the AL group then, whilst some questioning from Board members would have been normal, the extent of problem exploration and range of insights would have been less than that provided by the whole company AL group. Rather, RBL's new action learning practice is institutionalising the notion that good ideas do not only originate at Board level, and that solutions to wicked problems are best found by making use of experience throughout the organization. In its encouragement of delegation, adoption of less defensive attitudes and improved ability to take criticism, this AL practice has challenged assumptions within RBL about how decisions relating to wicked problems should be arrived at.

A couple of brief examples of other problems tackled by the action learning set are offered here in concluding this section. Firstly, a problem arose in a cooperation area involving the local farmers and Chinese private investors when the minimum acceptable rice yield was not achieved: one that had been agreed as part of a risk-sharing agreement with RBL and Chinese investors. The farmers were contemplating zero income for that season and wanted a revision to how risk was shared. Possible developments in the agreement were explored in the AL group and tested in negotiation with farmers and investors. The subsequently revised agreement sees farmers having a guaranteed income in poor seasons, with a commitment from them to share a proportion of their profits in bumper seasons with stakeholders who supported them through the difficult seasons.

A second example concerns the on-going, highly-emotive issue of land use rights. A conflict arose over land allocated within the Scheme to cattle grazing. Smallholder farmers outside of the Scheme invaded this land and used it for their own subsistence rain-fed farming; thereby reducing the available land for cattle grazing. The AL group evaluated a proposal from the cattle farmers to build a fence. The conclusion was that such a fence would simply be knocked down, and proposed digging an irrigation and drainage canal instead. This approach would both provide a boundary that would be harder to breach and enhance the subsistence farmers' infrastructure compared with their rain-fed watering techniques.

Discussion

This section offers reflections about how the new practices were introduced at RBL and the ways in which their operational context influences the approach to action learning. In many respects, the classic approach (Revans 1998) to action learning is evident in this case: there was an inquiry orientation towards the problem under consideration; a rigorous evaluation of solutions through action and reflection; a quality of interaction between AL participants which enables individual critical reflection, and ultimately the learning. However, the complexity of the contexts in which RBL operates, allied to a complete absence of familiarity with this mode of learning required some adaptations of classic models. Difficulties for the learning organization, according to Revans, happen because there is lack of readiness, of willing participants with good problems and issues to tackle, and of commitment from the top. The last two of these were actually present at RBL, with the most significant adoption issue being one of lack of readiness, born of unease of questioning colleagues; particularly senior ones. In reflecting upon how this potential barrier was addressed we would like to draw attention to three particular aspects of the action learning practices developed at RBL: the wide diversity and size of the learning set; the nature of critical reflection demanded of participants; and the learning set facilitator consciousness.

A key concern with the traditional mode of project meeting at RBL was that they did not allow sufficient space for problem exploration. Whilst having a range of expertize to foster problem exploration in AL groups might be expected, having 22 participants in the AL group is a departure from conventional practice which might advocate only 6–8 AL set members (Marquardt and Waddill 2004). The size of AL group at RBL ensured that the diversity of the wider organization was represented in terms of departmental function, position in the organization, social background, age, and gender. It may also have contributed to the diffusion of the very idea of learning through action. However, initially at least, the size accentuated difficulties prompted through power dynamics (Ely and Thomas 2001) such as avoiding asking questions to more senior colleagues. Over time inhibitions prompted by power differences within the set eased with the understanding of how each participant could provide a unique contribution to the set; one that not only helped to broaden the learning capacity of others, but also enabled the learning set to generate new insights on very complex workplace problems.

The statement 'I am part of the problem, the problem is part of me' (Pedler 2008, 11) is one of the fundamental premises for engagement in the AL set. It suggests people in a learning set must develop a capacity for critical reflection on their own practice and how this impinges upon the problem at hand. The facilitator's approach at RBL of encouraging participants to engage in a deeper questioning of their own taken-for-granted assumptions appeared initially ambiguous and confusing to the participants. They would have preferred more conventional sessions in which each department came to report progress against plan, rather than the more exploratory discussions that were encouraged through the new forum. Most Mozambican public sector workers have built their experience within a system that prizes humility, as employees look to their superior to see what he/she wants them to do instead of using their own good sense and critical thinking: to appear to question that behavioral norm and view senior colleagues as equals goes contrary to one's training and lived experience. However, according to Freire (1970), it is precisely this process of problematization that such practitioners must engage in reaching critical consciousness.

The fact that the facilitator (AU) sought in his wider leadership of the company to act as a scholarly-practitioner (Ellwood 2018) created personal tensions. On some occasions, he very often felt bound to follow Revans' principles that limit facilitators to the encouragement of set members to share ideas and concerns with each other, and to develop the set as a learning system (Pedler 2008). At other times, as an insider to the organization, the facilitator had experiential knowledge of the Scheme and its stakeholders, and had developed his own perspective on the organizational change. Indeed, he had findings generated through his own scholarly research undertaken with the Scheme's stakeholders. These additional perspectives held the potential to contribute to the AL group discussions, but created a personal conflict in relation to the traditional role of AL set facilitator. The resolution to this conflict was to adopt the approach of Torbert and Associates (2004) that combines inquiry with advocacy by placing in front of the learning set specific suggestions, inferences, and assumptions in order to subject them to critique and testing.

An example of how the facilitator managed to contribute more actively to the AL group in this way was evident in a discussion about the role of Chinese investors in the scheme. During the course of this particular AL group meeting, he made use of his research findings to offer a counter-intuitive viewpoint. As he asked in a form of provocation during discussions in the learning set, ' … why are we seeing the Chinese investors of our scheme as a public partner like RBL and not as private entity whose concern is running a profitable business?' This research finding (but expressed in the form of question) surfaced a general problem underlying the cooperation projects with China: the question of how to manage in these projects the combination of a profitable business (Chinese investors), with the transfer of farming technology and skills which by nature are an aid-to-development motivated by Chinese solidarity to Africa. With this provocation, the facilitator did not intend to directly apply his research finding as a suggestion to address the problem in discussion. Rather the provocation aimed to create dissonances in the minds of the set participants (Ellwood 2018), lead to a paradigmatic shift in understanding of the nature of the Chinese partner, and thereby prepare them for previously unconsidered avenues of change.

Concluding remarks

In this article, we have illustrated how the co-author AU institutionalized an action learning practice in his organization, in order to improve their delivery of a food security and poverty alleviation Scheme. We have discussed how the action learning empowers participating managers take responsibility for and control of their own learning, and ultimately contribute to social action within the overarching Scheme. This action learning practice represented a significant departure in the established project management routines within the company, in which people were not used to challenges, and avoided exploring problems in the rush to propose solutions. Initially difficulties were experienced in adopting action learning because questioning senior managers, and thinking critically around ideas within an environment of open communication are not conventional in Mozambican organizational culture. As a result of adopting this action learning practice, RBL has enhanced its capacity for tackling the wicked problems associated with food security and poverty alleviation in an emerging nation.

Disclosure statement

No potential conflict of interest was reported by the authors.

References

African Development Bank Group. 2012. Project: Baixo Limpopo Irrigation and Climate Resilience Project. Project Appraisal Report, Mozambique.
Chichava, S., J. Duran, L. Cabral, A. Shankland, L. Buckley, T. Lixia, and Z. Yue. 2013. "Brazil and China in Mozambican Agriculture: Emerging Insights from the Field." *IDS Bulletin* 44 (4): 101–115.
Churchman, C. W. 1967. "Wicked Problems." *Management Science* 14 (4): 141–142.
Ellwood, P. 2018. "Categorical Entanglements of Scholarly Practice – Re-connecting "L", "P" and "Q" in New Ways." *Action Learning: Research and Practice* 15 (3): 249–257.
Ely, R. J., and D. A. Thomas. 2001. "Cultural Diversity at Work: The Effects of Diversity Perspectives on Work Group Processes and Outcomes." *Administrative Science Quarterly* 46 (2): 229–273.
Freire, P. 1970. "Pedagogy of the Oppressed." The Continuum Publishing Company. Penguin Classics Edition.
Marquardt, M., and D. Waddill. 2004. "The Power of Learning in Action Learning: a Conceptual Analysis of how the Five Schools of Adult Learning Theories Are Incorporated Within the Practice of Action Learning." *Action Learning: Research & Practice* 1 (2): 185–202.
Pedler, M. 2008. *Action Learning for Managers*. Aldershot: Gower Publishing Ltd.
Revans, R. 1998. *ABC of Action Learning*. London: Lemos and Crane.
Torbert, W. R., and Associates. 2004. *Action Inquiry*. San Francisco, CA: Berret-Koehler Publishers.
Ussivane, A. M., and P. Ellwood. 2019. "Using Action Research to Organize Technology Transfer in Complex Innovation Contexts." *Technology Innovation Management Review* 9 (4): 51–60.

Developing the Circular Economy in Tasmania

Genevieve Cother

ABSTRACT
This paper adds to the body of evidence demonstrating the efficacy of action learning to achieve measurable progress toward sustainability goals. It supports prior assertions that action and reflection develop the conditions of *awareness*, *agency* and *association* required to develop the circular economy. The early outcomes of a Business Resource Efficiency Program delivered in Tasmania, Australia, are presented and prompt us to revisit the true place of Questioning in Revans' Learning Equation. The findings add new insights to observations on the capabilities required for radical innovation to meet the challenges of disruptive times, and compel us to question the legitimacy of higher education as the solution to the really big problems of our age.

Introduction

The Tasmanian response to climate change

In 2017, the Tasmanian government published *Climate Action 21: Tasmania's Climate Change Action Plan 2017–2021* (Climate Action 21); a 5-year agenda for Tasmania to participate in the global response to climate change (Tasmanian Climate Change Office 2017). Climate Action 21 comprises a series of actions under six priority areas. Under Priority 4, there are nine actions to be completed by 2021, including Action 4.3: 'Undertake a business resource efficiency programme to assist small and medium-sized businesses to reduce their emissions and costs'.

The stated Objectives of the Business Resource Efficiency Program (BREP) were to:

- Help Tasmanian SMEs reduce their consumption of resources and minimise waste streams;
- Reduce operating costs and drive productivity gains for SMEs; and
- Provide SMEs with practical and tailored information regarding ways to improve their resource efficiency.

The specification for BREP stipulated that the programme design should complement an existing action learning programme, designed specifically to meet the needs of small businesses in Tasmania. Business Action Learning Tasmania (BALT) was successful in a bid to deliver BREP, which subsequently commenced in March 2018. BALT is an

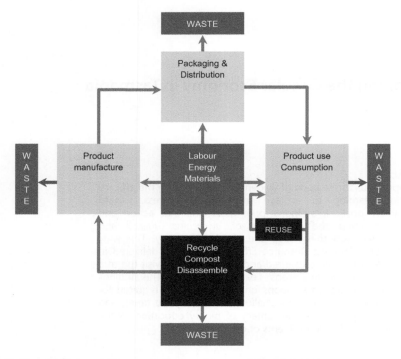

Figure 1. Product lifecycle – labour, energy, materials use (Edwards 2009).

industry-based organisation established to advance education by promoting action learning to businesses, education institutions and the community (Cother and Cother 2017).

Resource efficiency

The European Commission defines resource efficiency as 'using the Earth's limited resources in a sustainable manner while minimising impacts on the environment. It allows us to create more with less to deliver greater value with less input' (European Commission, n.d.).

Resource efficiency considers an entire product lifecycle from manufacture to end-of-life disposal. At each stage of the product lifecycle, inputs are measured in terms of materials, labour and energy, and outputs are measured in terms of: the value added to the product itself, the waste created in the value-adding step, and the waste created at end-of-life. We seek to become more resource efficient by reducing the resources lost to 'waste' streams and ultimately *closing the loop* to retain the resources as value within the process (Figure 1).

The circular economy

From the beginning of the industrial revolution, we have been operating in a linear economic system, which can be described as *take, make, use* and *dispose* (Figures 2 and 3).

Figure 2. The linear economic model.

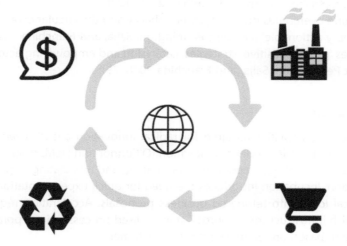

Figure 3. The circular economic model.

A circular economy is

an alternative to a traditional linear economy, in which we keep resources in use for as long as possible, extract the maximum value from them whilst in use, then recover and regenerate products and materials at the end of each service life. (European Commission, n.d.)

Organisations around the world are pursuing new business models and exploring ways to participate in the circular economy. Progress is slow and a raft of wicked problems have emerged, not least the deep institutional embeddedness of linear economic models and the need for radical innovation across the entire product lifecycle.

Relevant literature

Action learning and the circular economy

Action learning is promoted by recognised thought leaders in circular economy theory, as a method for developing the circular economy (Ellen Macarthur Foundation 2019). An Action Learning Set Toolkit, has been created specifically for this purpose.

Action and reflection are a 'vital process' for developing the three conditions needed to transition to a circular economy (Ballard 2005), that is:

1. **Awareness** (contextual, theoretical and conceptual understanding of circular economy)

2. **Agency** (individual and organisational purpose, motivation, drive and skills to lead and manifest circular economy ideas)
3. **Association** (networks, alliances, collaborators and peers)

Business must 'unlearn their reductive 'business-only-and-only-profiteering' reasoning, as a precursor to increasing awareness of sustainability and changing mental models through action learning. Reflective practice develops emotional intelligence and counteracts the perception that a lack of emotional involvement in social issues 'facilitates precise decision-making' (Krishnamurthy and Pradhan 2018, 122).

Action learning overcomes the gap between theory and the circular economy in action by 'making theory actionable' (Lambert-Pennington, Saija, and Franchina 2018). Learning by doing creates 'power sensitive' strategies, catalysing and empowering actors in priority areas (Lambert-Pennington, Saija, and Franchina 2018, 79).

Radical innovation

The organisational capabilities required for radical innovation are *discovery*, *incubation*, and *acceleration*, or the DIA model of innovation (O'Connor and DeMartino 2006). Discovery requires skills in 'creating, recognizing, elaborating, and articulating opportunities' for radical innovation. Incubation introduces the need for quick experimentation to test and articulate radical ideas into tempered business proposals. Acceleration requires investment to establish infrastructure, resources, standardised processes, incorporating continual improvement, based on feedback from the customer.

Organisations need to improve experimental capabilities and Startup thinking to achieve radical innovation to meet the urgent and imminent challenges of sustainable development (Weissbrod and Bocken 2017). Startup activities require policy and budget allowances for capital expenditure that fall outside typical limits and/or time constraints for return on investment (O'Connor and DeMartino 2006). It is the consideration of time sensitivity that reveals the gravity of organisational deficiency in experimentation. The current pace of innovation is insufficient to achieve established sustainability goals and avert catastrophic climate change (Doyle 2019).

Education for sustainable development (ESD)

Roobeek and de Ritter's (2016) survey of sustainability leaders in global corporations identifies the need for business education design to address disruptive change, such as the circular economy, digital transformation and big data. They assert that business schools bear responsibility for educating 'the leaders and knowledge workers of tomorrow' to face the real and imminent problems of humanity.

There are two dangerous assumptions in Roobeek and de Ritter's research; (1) that the requisite knowledge, to be transferred to the individual for application in the real world, must already exist or first be created by 'experts', and (2) the requisite skills, to apply this knowledge in the real world, can be developed in the class room. This assumption is evident across higher education. In particular, it has inspired activism within economics education. Rethinking Economics, the UK Manifesto for Curriculum Reform in Economics, prepared by students in representative universities across the UK, asserts that economics education has become 'increasingly narrow and detached from the world'. It cites a lack of critical thinking, alternative perspectives, real world application, and ethical and political context, as creating a 'mental straightjacket' for economic experts (Rethinking Economics, n.d., 5). It states that: 'seminars ask students to memorise and regurgitate academic theory' and to 'solve abstract equations rather than engaging critically with the actual economy and real-world economic problems' (Rethinking Economics, n.d., 2).

Such gaps between knowledge creation and its application could be overcome by a reconnection of education to the real world, through action learning. Experiential learning has been shown to be effective in a range of contexts, using a variety of delivery methods, to promote sustainability principles (Ballard 2005; Gatti, Ulrich, and Seele 2019; Kirchherr and Piscicelli 2019; Krishnamurthy and Pradhan 2018; Williams et al. 2018).

Williams et al. (2018) present a collaboration between a university and external organisation, in which students had an opportunity to apply circular economy thinking to the real world problems of a water supply and waste water treatment company. Mutual benefits reported include the applicability of student recommendations, the desire from the industry partner to continue the collaboration, positive feedback from all parties, and the quality of the exercise as a vehicle for learning. Other examples cite benefits of experiential learning as raising awareness of sustainability principles, developing emotional intelligence, generating cognitive and affective learning, improving critical thinking skills, increasing motivation, etc. (Gatti, Ulrich, and Seele 2019; Kirchherr and Piscicelli 2019; Ormazabal et al. 2017). However, these other examples fall short of action learning by limiting the scope of application to simulations and contrived scenarios, safe within the confines of the academic community. This represents a lost opportunity, not only to achieve tangible progress toward sustainability goals, but also for learning.

Methodology

BREP included a programme mapping and gap analysis, a public seminar series, an introductory workshop series, action learning set meetings, and one-on-one mentoring sessions. The action learning programme concludes with a review forum in early December 2019. A range of educational resources will be developed for publication including case studies for each project, and tools to assist SMEs to improve their resource efficiency.

Participant recruitment

Participants were recruited through an extended promotion and recruitment programme, including a public seminar series to introduce concepts of resource efficiency. Eligibility for participation was limited to small- to medium-sized businesses, defined as having less than 200 full-time equivalent employees, located in Tasmania. The programme was funded by the Tasmanian government and businesses were required to pay a subsidised fee of AUD750 to participate.

Two regions of Tasmania were targeted; the Northern and North-western regions and the introductory seminars were presented in both regions. The topics covered included:

- applying Lean principles for sustainability outcomes,
- the Circular Economy,

- Supply chain optimisation, and
- industrial composting.

Attendance for the seminars was low, particularly in the North-west, and some attendees were not eligible for BREP participation.

Following the seminar series, a second round of promotion offered waste audits as a precursor to the action learning programme. The facilitator undertook more targeted activities, including personal emails to qualified leads and face to face meetings to explain the programme and determine eligibility.

Set formation

Sets were formed based on geographic location. Three action learning sets were formed, two in the North and one in the North-west of Tasmania.

Participants were required to sign an agreement, protecting the confidentiality of set members and consenting to the use of information collected as the basis for a case study.

Project selection and planning for action

Projects were co-designed with set members and/or senior management of each business, based on opportunities identified during the waste audit. Measurable objectives and targets were established, which reflected the overarching objectives of BREP.

Workshop series

During the introductory workshop sessions, set members created a problem statement, brainstormed potential solutions for exploration and developed an action plan, as a starting point for action learning. The first workshop was devoted to explaining the action learning process, understanding and accepting the Values and Beliefs of Action Learning (Bourner 2011) and developing ground rules for set management. Revans formula for learning (Pedler and Abbott 2013, 18) was presented and the importance of questioning was emphasised.

Set meetings, site visits and mentoring sessions

Six action learning set meetings occurred over six months between June and November 2019. Between each meeting, the facilitator met with set members individually, face to face or by phone, to assist them to prepare for the next set meeting. This usually included reflecting on progress made against the actions from the previous meeting, lessons learnt that might be shared with the set, and questions that might be put to the set.

The North-western Set chose to hold their workshops and set meetings at each other's sites, on a rotating basis. This provided an opportunity to view the results of implemented actions first-hand and over time, as each site hosted at least two sessions, creating a 'before' and 'after' effect.

The Northern sets chose to meet concurrently, to share learning and maintain connection across both sets. This worked well as, if one or two set members were unable to attend, the sets could combine and achieve sufficient numbers to operate effectively. An added benefit was the random introduction of relatively 'fresh eyes' to the set, bringing new ways of thinking. Some set members hosted site visits prior to the workshops and some set meetings were hosted on-site. It was difficult for all set members to visit sites outside the metropolitan area and hosting on-site sessions was limited to those with premises that could accommodate the combined cohort.

Site visits to other external organisations were conducted before or after set meetings and set members across both geographical regions were invited. Sites visited included landfills with industrial composting facilities, materials recycling facilities, and a vertically integrated plastics recycling and manufacturing facility.

Set members reflected on each site visit and shared their observations at the beginning of the following set meeting.

Data collection

Workshops and set meetings were recorded as video or audio recordings and transcribed into session notes, which were distributed to set members following each meeting. Outputs of the workshops, in the form of storyboards and notes collected on butchers' paper, were collected and typed up in the notes. Images, business records and documents, and other outputs of participant activities between sessions were collected and shared in online team spaces.

The early outcomes of the action learning programme presented here are summarised from facilitator observations and personal reflections of participants in the final action learning set meetings, conducted in early November 2019. A key word search and affinity analysis has been conducted to identify themes in the perceived drivers and barriers to project implementation. Additional quantitative data will be collected after the formal conclusion of the programme in December, through participant surveys and business records of waste disposal, to validate the themes presented here.

The following findings are aggregated and anonymised to protect commercial confidentiality.

Findings

The set members, their businesses, and the projects selected are diverse and yet interesting similarities emerged, particularly in the perceived drivers and barriers to implementing resource efficiency strategies and participating in the circular economy.

The North-west Set comprised five participants from four businesses. One set member was an apprentice and younger than the other set members. The other participants were all in supervisory or management roles in their organisations. All the businesses undertook some form of manufacturing, although two were closely associated with agriculture.

The Northern Sets were formed through an analysis of the operational activities of the business, affiliated industries, nominated project focus and the existing skills and knowledge of the individual set member, with a view to balancing diversity of thinking with synergies of learning objectives. This objective analysis was countered by an intuitive guess, simply based on the perceptions of the facilitator, that certain people might work well together.

Northern Set 1 included an Ag-tech Startup founder; a project manager in a large engineering consulting firm; a systems manager employed by a family-owned manufacturing company; and a founder/operator of an established visual management company.

Northern Set 2 included a qualified cookery teacher working within a government funded training organisation; a craft beverage founder/producer, operating retail sales outlets (bar and ciderworks) and public events; and the general manager of an agritourism business.

Each project targeted waste at various stages in the product lifecycle. Most projects (8 of 11) targeted the manufacturing stage to reduce waste generated at the source. For 'problem wastes', such as highly contaminated plastic film, vinyl plastics and fibre composites, this was the only option as alternative end-of-life scenarios were not readily available. For those companies already recycling most of their production wastes (e.g. organic agricultural waste, metals), efficiencies in manufacturing held greater potential for measurable improvement. Six of the 11 projects focused on diverting waste currently going to landfill to alternative end-of-life scenarios, such as composting or existing recycling streams.

There were few projects implementing only known solutions for waste reduction, i.e. quality management, recycling programmes and inventory management. Most projects attempted something new – new to the business, the supply chain, industry or market. Three projects focused on new product development and two experimented with solutions for dealing with identified 'problem wastes'. Two new products were developed, one to prototype stage (drone swarm) and the other as a test batch trialled in the market (gin distilled from waste cider). A compelling business case was developed, including a closed loop value chain, for a third product (bio-fuel from plantation forestry residues) and trials are expected to occur in early 2020. Solutions could not be found for the two problem wastes in the time available, however the experiments conducted bring new information to bear on the problem. This information will be shared with industry and government stakeholders and the individual businesses will continue to pursue solutions.

Table 1 provides a summary of each project, targets and early outcomes over the period of the action learning programme. At time of writing, some projects are still underway and the final outcomes may not be known for another six months. However, it is clear that a number of projects will be more successful than others. An analysis of some of the reported barriers to achieving measurable targets may provide some insight, refer Figure 4. Conversely, the drivers for change are presented in Figure 5.

The most significant barrier to implementing resource efficiency strategies is time constraints and business priorities. This was repeatedly brought to set meetings for questioning by the set. In some cases, this was related to senior management engagement with the project. Even where leaders of the organisation were supportive of the project, they did not see it as a business priority but more as a 'nice to do'. Competing priorities meant that the set member was forced to complete actions 'off the side of their desk'. Internal resistance to change exacerbates the situation, isolating the set member and creating disillusionment, when they fail to inspire others to action. This finding is validated by the reported drivers for implementation; the greatest driver being the motivated individual, assisted by a supportive team and/or leader. Experimentation skills were a factor and set members that demonstrated a willingness to jump in and 'give it a go' achieved quick results and were able to let go and move on when their early ideas failed. High

Table 1. BREP Project descriptions and early outcomes.

Project A	
Description	**Outcomes**

• Find alternative disposal methods for fibre composite waste and cardboard and plastic film waste.	• Waste separation system implemented across site
	• Recycling services engaged for metals, cardboard and co-mingled recyclables
	• Education programme implemented for employees
	  ○ Waste separation at source
	  ○ Reduced waste during process, e.g. accurate measuring of resin according to BOM

Measure of success/target	• Alternative uses for fibre composite not found
• Reduce waste to landfill by 50% • Maintain or reduce current waste disposal costs	• Additional waste disposal costs recovered from scrap metal

Project B

Description	**Outcomes**

• Establish a value chain for pelletised bio-fuel and apply continuous improvement and quality assurance on briquette line to meet customer requirements.	• **Pellets**
	Agreements established with:
	  ○ Supplier of raw (waste) materials
	  ○ Retailer/distributor of final product
	  ○ Bulk commodity customers
	  ○ Transport company
	Equipment sourced and quoted:
	  ○ Bagging machine
	  ○ Dryer
	  ○ Pellet tooling
	Fully costed business case prepared

Measure of success/target	• **Briquettes**
• Sales target of 1000 tonnes p.a. of bio-fuel pellets • Sales target of 6,500 tonnes p.a of bio-fuel briquettes (up from 4,500 tonnes p.a.)	Quality issues resolved and new customers identified to take bio-fuel as coal substitute for industrial boilers ○ Sales targets not met due to major customer converting to another alternative fuel source • Sales target for pellets not met due to lack of capital funding for required equipment • Sales target for briquettes not met due to loss of major customer (installed new boiler)

Project C

Description	**Outcomes**
• Increase material yield and utilisation of sheet metal offcuts by using integrated software application to manage offcut inventory. • Seek efficiencies in the laser cutting process and reduce rework originating from design office.	• Obtained quote for integrated software application • Free Google Sheets solution implemented as an alternative to integrated software application has eliminated rework from the design office • Scheduling of work reviewed and 'nesting' processes refined to increase material optimisation at the source • Business plan prepared for complementary proprietary products, to utilise remaining offcuts, with variations on sales and distribution models
Measure of success/target	
• Reduce scrapped metal by 50% • Reduce off-cut inventory by 50%	• Performance against targets not yet known

Project D

Description	**Outcomes**
• Analyse cost benefits and test feasibility of various [waste disposal] scenarios with a view to implementing best case for diversion of wastes from landfill.	• Compostable plastic liners to replace single use plastic film trialled in production and composted on-site but found to be cost prohibitive • Various methods for separating and washing plastic film to remove purge contaminants investigated but not feasible
Measure of success/target	
• Zero waste to landfill from processing • Maintain or reduce waste disposal costs	

(Continued)

Table 1. Continued.

Project A
• Collection and transport system designed and implemented, resulting in 250 tonnes of organic waste diverted from landfill to industrial composting
• Waste management services streamlined to reduce handling fees and maintain costs
• Single use plastic aprons replaced with washable aprons

Project E

Description
- Establish best practice internal processes for waste management and small scale composting, with an associated training strategy for students undertaking a qualification in cookery.

Measure of success/target
- 1.4 t per annum waste diverted from landfill
- Landfill disposal costs reduced by 50% per annum
- Training and assessment strategy approved by TasTAFE

Outcomes
- Waste management procedures developed and implemented
- Students actively involved in managing waste following the established procedures
- Kitchen garden established to eliminate the need for store bought micro-herbs and leafy green vegetables
- New product development and customer discovery for compost underway
- Mapping and development of training and assessment strategy for vocational qualifications in Sustainable Operations started
  ○ Requires approval from regulating authority, project scoped for further work in 2020
- Performance against targets not yet known
  ○ Costs for disposal of waste to landfill and actual volume of waste generated were not consistent, suggesting that the organisation was charged, whether bins contained waste or not – further investigation underway

Project F

Description
- Evaluate the effectiveness of composting methods trialled to inform the adoption of larger-scale resource efficiency strategies across the site.
- Optimise supporting activities, i.e. separation and collection of waste and methods of disposal, etc., to ensure that waste management initiatives enhance manufacturing processes, food service and the customer experience.

Measure of success/target
- Reduce waste to landfill by 50%
- Reduce or maintain service cycle times
- Reduce or maintain product cycle times

Outcomes
- Full scale trial of composting completed and second trial designed and planned for summer 2019/2020
- Cardboard recycling programme implemented, including purchase of cardboard perforator
- Plastic bubble wrap eliminated from customer packaging and replaced with perforated cardboard
- Cafe operations streamlined, simplified menu reduces food waste at the source
- Waste separation procedures established and implemented
- Visual management of general waste bins to fill one bin at a time and reduce costs of pickup
- Performance against targets not yet known, data to be collected over 2019/2020 peak summer season

Project G

Description
- Undertake new product development for a spirit distilled from waste cider collected in drip trays during drink service.

Measure of success/target
- 100% of waste cider from drink service reclaimed
- Product launched to market

Outcomes
- Trialled methods of collection of waste cider at outdoor events
  ○ Performance against targets not yet known
- Developed brand 'story' and canvassed customer perceptions of gin made from waste cider
- Product trial conducted and tested by the set
- Product launched at Dark Mofo festival as pre-mix on tap

(Continued)

Table 1. Continued.

Project A

Project H

Description
- Explore the use of drones and related technology to reduce crop losses to birds.
- Assess the irrigation system on-site and evaluate the potential to achieve efficiencies with the infrastructure already in place, i.e. dam and pumps not currently in use.

Measure of success/target
- Maintain or reduce losses to birds
- Reduce water usage
- Reduce labour hours required to apply nets and water vines

Outcomes
- Technology partners identified and commercial agreement established
- Prototype drones built and swarm technology tested
- Promising results first trial, trials to continue into harvest 2020
  ○ If successful, nets may be eliminated in 2021
- CASA licencing obtained
- Investigated various sources of funding, including joint venture research partnerships and venture capital
- Infrastructure in place for irrigation found to be unsuitable, other improvements implemented to use potable water more efficiently

Project I

Description
- Divert waste from landfill by implementing best practice guidelines for waste management in shared tenancies. Including:
  ○ Recruitment of champions to collaborate and implement best practices.
  ○ Targeted communication and engagement of stakeholders.
  ○ Risk assessment and stakeholder consultation in establishing risk controls.

Measure of success/target
- Reduce waste to landfill by 50%
- Achieve and maintain accepted contamination levels

Outcomes
- Agreement in-principle obtained from majority of tenants for communal cardboard recycling bin
- Quotes obtained from waste management providers, significant reduction in costs achieved
- Investigated causes of contamination and current practices of tenants
- Reviewed known best practice for multi-tenanted buildings
- Signage and security cameras costed for bin locations
- Office paper and co-mingled recycling reintroduced under individual contract
- Envision Hands programme introduced in office kitchen to collect bottle caps

Project J

Description
- Improve materials handling on-site, specifically:
  ○ organise the central yard to optimise stock movement and goods receival, and
  ○ organise offcuts from the fabrication area for greater visibility.

Measure of success/target
- 35% improvement on time taken to locate and deliver materials

Outcomes
- Re-design of yard to create designated areas for material storage
- Quality checking on arrival and marking of materials for job allocation
- New software installed and deployed across two sites
- Inventory management for one business unit migrated to new software system
- Improvements in lead time indicate efficiencies created

Project K

Description
- Reduce wasted materials and labour by improving the accuracy of reporting of product non-conformances and reducing the occurrence of rework.
- Identify root causes, improve management systems in place, and raise employee awareness and engagement in seeking solutions to prevent recurrence.

Outcomes
- Device enabled App introduced for employees to enter rework reports on-the-job
- Daily quality report posted, based on rework reported by employees
- Weekly Toolbox meetings include Agenda item for discussion of quality report

(Continued)

Table 1. Continued.

	Project A
Measure of success/target	• Targets set for quality performance weekly, monthly, annually • Quality checking tools and processes introduced by employees in response to identified trends in own work • Accuracy of nonconformance confirmed through regular waste audits • Total costs of rework not yet confirmed • Volume of waste to landfill not yet known
	• Accuracy of non-conformance reported • Total costs of rework, in terms of material and labour • Volume of waste sent to landfill

levels of autonomy and authority made it easier to make decisions and allocate resources for implementation.

Capital funding featured as a driver and a barrier to implementation. Simply put, those projects where capital funding for specialised equipment and/or software was available, and the business case demonstrated feasibility, went ahead. There were a couple of exceptions, where the business case was compelling but the investment required did not fit the organisation's budget allocation models for capital expenditure. This relates back to business priorities and reflects organisational culture and internal barriers to innovation.

Systemic problems, such as lack of services or infrastructure available in regional areas, relate not only to the 'problem wastes' requiring significant new infrastructure and investment in research and development, but also to basic services, such as collection of recyclable materials, which are still not available in some rural areas in Tasmania

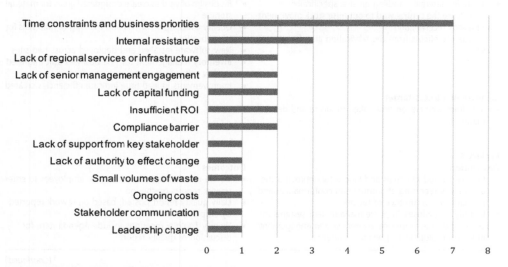

Barriers to implementation

Figure 4. Perceived barriers to achieving project outcomes.

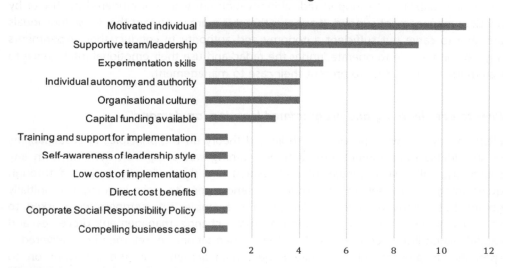

Figure 5. Perceived drivers for achieving project outcomes.

Discussion

Awareness, agency and association

There are many real and perceived barriers to sustainable development. We must learn how to do it by attempting to do it, in order to see, recognise and confront the forces that prevent us from achieving change. The effect of action and reflection moves awareness of individuals and organisations to the 'next level' and brings into sharp relief the issues preventing sustainable development. Set members become disillusioned by their lack of agency and the complexity of the problems they face. The problem, now seen, cannot be ignored. Support, if not received in their organisations, is sought from the set. As 'comrades in adversity', set members develop trust and gain confidence to mobilise and drive for change to overcome the barriers they encounter. This corresponds to the development of a contextual, theoretical and conceptual understanding of the circular economy (Ballard 2005).

Action learning for radical innovation

BREP delivered a number of innovative ideas and at least one truly radical innovation. This can be attributed to the individual set members' technical capabilities and skills in experimentation. One project has stalled at incubation stage, due to a lack of capital funding, and the other at acceleration, where the financial decision-making process of a large and established organisation prevents investment in market development over bottom line profit. This demonstrates the difficulty that established organisations encounter when adopting Startup thinking to achieve sustainability goals, and the tensions between economic, social and environmental values and the dominant corporate mindset of economic value creation. Individual set members, who were skilled at experimentation, were not necessarily working within organisations demonstrating 'dynamic capabilities' to support radical innovation but were not hindered by this, or by a lack of management support. It appears that it is more important that these individuals are able to carve out sufficient autonomy and authority to conduct their experiments anyway, or are able to operate 'under the radar' and use their emotional intelligence to determine the best time to present their case to management.

Peer to peer learning and programmed learning 'on-demand'

BREP participants were provided with limited theory on the principles of sustainability, or sustainable development. Programmed learning was sought on demand from any source (typically via a Google internet search) and then critically evaluated through questioning by the set. In the workshop series, peer to peer learning was initially guided but quickly became self-directed. For example, set members were asked to share examples of project management tools, change management processes and capital expenditure requests used in their organisations. A set member delivered a spontaneous presentation on Agile project management and the set went on to explore free online project management tools, used by some set members. Incidental peer to peer learning occurred throughout the set meetings. For example, a set member mentioned in passing that they would like to install solar power. Another set member (an engineer) questioned whether they had considered other aspects of their business that had a greater impact on the environment than electricity usage, such as replacing gas-powered boilers with electric, as Tasmania is powered by a hydro-electric system. This inspired a wide ranging discussion between all set members around environmental aspects and impacts and how to critically evaluate the perceived benefits of improvements.

This leads to a discussion about the role of the facilitator as an 'expert'. Experts do not sit comfortably in Pedler and Abbott's (2013) descriptions of the three roles of the action learning facilitator. However, the contract to deliver BREP would not have been awarded to BALT unless specialised knowledge and academic credentials in sustainable development could be demonstrated. An introductory seminar series was a deliverable of the programme, intended to provide the basic conceptual understanding of theory to be put into action, as typical of other action learning programme designs (Bourner 2011; Ellen Macarthur Foundation 2019). In the case of BREP, only four of the 11 participants in the programme attended any of the seminars and, of those, two attended one seminar, and two attended three of the four seminars. The waste audit report provided to each set member included a brief description of the theoretical models of product life-cycle assessment and the waste management hierarchy, but this was not required pre-reading. Throughout the workshops and set meetings, the facilitator observed set members naturally discovering the theoretical concepts underpinning the project work they were undertaking, as described above. Care was taken, by the facilitator as 'expert', to allow set members to make their own discoveries and avoid lecturing, where a simple answer or a redirecting question would suffice.

Revans held strong negative views on the ascendancy of the 'book' culture of higher education over the 'tool' culture of vocational education (Pedler, Burgoyne, and Brook 2005). The ascendancy of experts seems logical but there may be real harm being done through the continual retelling of existing knowledge. By doing so, are we eroding our ability to create new knowledge? Does force feeding information starve our natural curiosity and distract us from the problem at hand? Our growing inability to experiment and our deficiencies in dynamic capabilities may well be the symptoms of generations of students being delivered pre-packaged theory.

The outcomes achieved by BREP participants seem to suggest that an inaugurating theoretical framework is not required to get us moving in the right direction. This affirms Revans' view of the place of P (programmed learning) in his Learning Equation, as expressed by Boshyk & Dilworth:

> Rather than start with the P, as we have usually been programmed to do in both classrooms and our work life, action learning begins with the Q – the asking of questions – rather than immediately rushing to discuss possible solution sets. (Boshyk and Dilworth 2010, 8)

Mumford puts forward a revised version: $L = Q + P + Q$ and explains:

> The significance here is … that we must start with "Q". That is the process through which appropriate "P" is determined. (Mumford, 1994 via Boshyk and Dilworth 2010, 9)

The time sensitivity of climate change requires immediate action. The pragmatic argument is: we don't have time to wait for knowledge to be created as theory, tested in simulation, curated and transferred as abstract concepts to a business student, who must attain a sufficient level of autonomy and authority before re-constituting it into useful action. It's too late to learn first and act later, we must do both at the same time. Climate change is only one of a number of the disruptions occurring in society. If we can relinquish our dependency on known solutions, we may rediscover our ability to find unknown solutions for wicked problems.

At this stage, the circular economy is still a theoretical model that global economies are struggling to implement (Iles 2018). As such, it presents an ideal opportunity for action learning. Learning by doing overcomes the stasis of our education system, the deficiencies in our organisational capabilities, and our ongoing collective inertia in the face of an impending global crisis.

Conclusion

Limitations

The outcomes presented here are the very early impressions of set members and the facilitator. At an event planned for early December, set members will present these outcomes to a forum of government, waste industry representatives, peers and management. Questions will be put to the cohort and an entirely new perspective on the past 12 months will develop. The data collected throughout the programme and at the forum will be supplemented by a survey of set members to expand upon the themes emerging from this paper.

The sample set presented is very small and the exceptional quality of participants, and combinations of skills, personal attributes and professional contexts begs the question: 'could this be replicated?' As subsequent programmes are delivered, BALT intends to conduct a longitudinal study of the accumulative BREP alumni to determine longer-term effects of the programme across a larger sample set.

This programme has been delivered in on a small island state in Australia. The outcomes achieved may be predicated on the connectedness of individuals and direct access to key stakeholders in industry and government.

Contribution to knowledge

This paper adds to the body of evidence demonstrating the efficacy of action learning to achieve measurable progress toward sustainability goals. It supports Ballard's (2005) assertion that action and reflection develop the required conditions of awareness, agency and association toward developing the circular economy. The findings add new insights to Weissbrod and Bocken's (2017) observations on the dynamic capabilities required for radical innovation and the need for established businesses to apply Startup thinking to meet the challenges of disruptive times. The outcomes achieved in BREP, in spite of a lack of programmed learning provided to set members, prompts us to revisit the true meaning of Revans' Learning Equation. Above all, the findings presented here compel us to question the legitimacy of higher education as the solution to the really big problems of our age.

Disclosure statement

No potential conflict of interest was reported by the author.

Funding

This work was supported by Tasmanian Climate Change Office [grant number TCCO-2017-02]. The BALT Business Resource Efficiency Program was delivered in partnership with the Tasmanian government.

References

Ballard, D. 2005. "Using Learning Processes to Promote Change for Sustainable Development." *Action Research* 3 (2): 135–156. doi:10.1177/1476750305052138.
Boshyk, Y., and R. L. Dilworth. 2010. *Action Learning: History and Evolution.* doi:10.1057/9780230250734.
Bourner, T. 2011. "Developing Self-Managed Action Learning (SMAL)." *Action Learning: Research and Practice* 8 (2): 117–127. doi:10.1080/14767333.2011.581020.
Cother, G., and R. F. Cother. 2017. "Business Action Learning Tasmania (BALT) – An Account of Practice." *Action Learning: Research and Practice* 14 (2): 158–166. doi:10.1080/14767333.2017.1310688.
Doyle, A. 2019. *The Heat is On: Taking Stock of Global Climate Ambition.*
Edwards, S. 2009. "The Lowell Center Framework for Sustainable Products." Lowell Centre for Sustainable Production. http://www.sustainableproduction.org/downloads/LowellCenterFrame workforSustainableProducts11-09.09.pdf.

Ellen Macarthur Foundation. 2019. *The Action Learning Set Toolkit.* https://www. ellenmacarthurfoundation.org/our-work/activities/ce100/learning-resources.

Gatti, L., M. Ulrich, and P. Seele. 2019. "Education for Sustainable Development Through Business Simulation Games: An Exploratory Study of Sustainability Gamification and its Effects on Students' Learning Outcomes." *Journal of Cleaner Production* 207: 667–678. doi:10.1016/j.jclepro. 2018.09.130.

Iles, J. 2018. *Which Country is Leading the Circular Economy Shift?* Accessed November 22, 2019. https://medium.com/circulatenews/which-country-is-leading-the-circular-economy-shift-3670467db4bb.

Kirchherr, J., and L. Piscicelli. 2019. "Towards an Education for the Circular Economy (ECE): Five Teaching Principles and a Case Study." *Resources, Conservation and Recycling* 150: 104406.

Krishnamurthy, S., and V. Pradhan. 2018. "Anecdotes of Action Learning: Initiations of Sustainability Lessons by an Indian B-School." In *Cross-Disciplinary Approaches to Action Research and Action Learning*, 111–130. doi:10.4018/978-1-5225-2642-1.ch007.

Lambert-Pennington, K., L. Saija, and A. Franchina. 2018. "From Possibility to Action: An Interdisciplinary Action-Learning School Dealing with Waste." *Cambio* 8 (15): 73–87. doi:10. 13128/cambio-23216.

O'Connor, G. C., and R. DeMartino. 2006. "Organizing for Radical Innovation: An Exploratory Study of the Structural Aspects of RI Management Systems in Large Established Firms." *Journal of Product Innovation Management* 23 (6): 475–497. doi:10.1111/j.1540-5885.2006.00219.x.

Ormazabal, M., C. Jaca, V. Prieto-Sandoval, and Á. Lleó. 2017. *Developing Engineering Students' Engagement with Circular Economy practices* (Y. C. Ministerio De Economía, Ed.). doi:10.4995/ HEAD17.2017.5521.

Pedler, M., and C. Abbott. 2013. *Facilitating Action Learning: A Practitioner's Guide.* Berkshire: Open University Press McGraw Hill.

Pedler, M., J. Burgoyne, and C. Brook. 2005. "What has Action Learning Learned to Become?" *Action Learning: Research and Practice* 2 (1): 49–68. doi:10.1080/14767330500041251.

Resource Efficiency – Environment – European Commission. n.d. Accessed November 11, 2019. https://ec.europa.eu/environment/resource_efficiency/about/index_en.htm.

Rethinking Economics. n.d. *Rethinking Economics: UK Manifesto for Curriculum Reform.* http://www. rethinkeconomics.org/get-involved/why-reform-the-curriculum/.

Roobeek, A., and M. de Ritter. 2016. "Rethinking Business Education for Relevance in Business and Society in Times of Disruptive Change." The Academy of Management Annual Conference, Anaheim, CA.

TCCO. 2017. *Climate Action 21: Tasmania's Climate Change Action Plan 2017-2021* (DPaC, Ed.). http:// www.dpac.tas.gov.au/divisions/climatechange/tasmanias_climate_change_action_plan_ 20172021.

Weissbrod, I., and N. M. P. Bocken. 2017. "Developing Sustainable Business Experimentation Capability – A Case Study." *Journal of Cleaner Production* 142: 2663–2676. doi:10.1016/j.jclepro. 2016.11.009.

Williams, I. D., K. P. Roberts, P. J. Shaw, and B. Cleasby. 2018. "Applying Circular Economy Thinking to Industry by Integrating Education and Research Activities." *Detritus* 1: 10. doi:10.26403/detritus/ 2018.11.

Exploring the challenges of system leadership in the voluntary and community sector

Stephen Moss

ABSTRACT

LankellyChase Foundation works to bring about change that will transform the quality of life of people who face severe and multiple disadvantage. It set up the 'Promoting Change Network' (PCN) to foster learning, and to support 40 or so organisations which receive funding from the Foundation. This was in recognition of the challenges they face in their work to alleviate severe and multiple disadvantages – combinations of problems around homelessness, substance abuse, mental health, domestic violence and abuse, and chronic poverty. Action learning was a supportive intervention commissioned by LankellyChase for PCN grantees, covering London and the North of England/Glasgow. Two Action Learning Sets met five and six times respectively between November 2014 and July 2015. The Sets demonstrated the importance and value of standing back and questioning your approach – when you are part of the (complex) health and care system you are aiming to change.

Introduction and background

LankellyChase

LankellyChase Foundation works to bring about change that will transform the quality of life of people who face severe and multiple disadvantage.

> As an independent foundation we're working in partnership with people, across the UK, to change the systems that perpetuate severe and multiple disadvantage. Our mission is to get to a place where people want to, know how to and are free to create systems that are effective in responding to the interlocking nature of severe disadvantages such as homelessness, drug misuse, violence and abuse and mental ill health.

In 2015, LankellyChase released the most robust research to date on severe and multiple disadvantage in England. *Hard Edges: Mapping Severe and Multiple Disadvantage in England* drawing together previously separate datasets from homelessness, offending and substance misuse treatment systems (Figure 1).

It also took into account available data around mental health and poverty.

'Hard Edges' states in its conclusion:

- There is a huge overlap between the offender, substance misusing and homeless populations
- Local authorities which report the highest rates of people facing severe and multiple disadvantage are mainly in the North of England, seaside towns and certain central London boroughs
- People found in homelessness, drug treatment and criminal justice systems are predominantly white men aged 25-44
- As children, many experienced trauma and neglect, poverty, family breakdown and disrupted education. As adults, many suffer alarming levels of loneliness, isolation, unemployment, poverty and mental ill-health. All of these experiences are considerably worse for those in overlapping populations.
- The majority are in contact with or are living with children.

Figure 1. Key conclusions of *Hard Edges: Mapping Severe and Multiple Disadvantage in England* (Bramley et al. 2015).

> While this study was not designed to evaluate specific services, it is apparent from the outcomes data reviewed that current support systems struggle to deliver positive outcomes in more complex cases, no doubt in part because the 'degree of difficulty' in achieving progress is that much the greater in these instances.

This has implications for the people and organisations engaged to provide support to individuals with complex needs who experience 2 or 3 areas of disadvantage (of homelessness, substance abuse, mental health, domestic violence and chronic poverty). The report highlights that causal factors in the lives of the individuals have roots at a number of systemic levels both personal and structural: individual and family trauma; entrenched poverty; poor educational experiences; fragmented services focused on issues, not the person.

For leaders of voluntary sector organsiations and projects operating at the 'frontline' of service support for people with multiple disadvantage, we can see that there is a challenge, especially when resources are often limited, to create the conditions for staff and volunteers to feel personally resourced, safe and supported to cope with this 'degree of difficulty in achieving progress'. The leader has to look to create these conditions in a psychologically-informed way, and often in quite hands-on ways themselves (direct work with staff and service users).

However, these leaders also operate within a care and service system that is fragmented in how it responds to people with severe and multiple disadvantage.

Leading in complex environments: changing practice in a fragmented system

> A new person-centred approach to help specific groups and individuals with multiple and complex needs. Services should be designed around the needs of the person to deliver better outcomes. (Bolder, Braver and Better: why we need local deals to save public services, p5; Service Transformation Challenge Panel (2014), Department for Communities and Local Government and HM Treasury)

The challenges of bringing about changes in the lives of people experiencing severe and multiple disadvantage are complex, reflected in the complexity of the systems and services serving these groups of people. Individuals with complex needs face considerable barriers to getting help, in particular the fragmentation of funding and services, which tend to focus on issues (homelessness, substance abuse, offending, mental health) rather than integrating around the person.

The 'Promoting Change Network' (PCN) was set up to foster learning and support amongst 40 or so organisations funded by the Foundation in recognition of the challenges they face in their work to alleviate severe and multiple disadvantages. In particular, these projects were funded to:

> ... shine a light on hidden aspects of the experience of people facing severe and multiple disadvantage, shift commissioning practices, find new ways to give power to service users and provide excellent, person-centred, transformative services. (See http://www.lankellychase.org.uk/promoting_change_network)

In addition to the challenge of creating conditions for staff and volunteers to support their own practice and needs in working with individuals with complex needs, leaders of these largely Voluntary and Community Sector (VCS) (charities, community and voluntary) organisations faced systemic challenges on a number of levels to grapple with as they guided these projects. These challenges mattered to the leaders because they represent barriers to meeting the needs of individuals their projects are supporting in a number of deeply embedded structural ways.

The funding environment, local statutory budget constraints and the sustainability challenges facing the VCS presents difficulties for sustaining change. At the time of this intervention, austerity was biting hard into public services, and a consequence of this was to raise thresholds for receiving them. Whilst this increased the demand for help from the VCS, 'austerity' was also being reflected in less available funding for the VCS and reductions in 'safety net' services this sector traditionally provided.

Therefore for many VCS organisations, there was and still is a real financial, structural and psychological pressure for leaders: delivering projects with different funding streams, responding to distressed service users, creating safety, engaging service users more in co-producing services and responding to a call to work more in partnership with statutory, VCS and NHS organisations to transform local care and health systems.

Operating in local and national environments where not all parties agree or cooperate, nor always share the same values about how to respond to people with multiple disadvantage, is challenging; whilst 'integration' and collaboration are considered key to meeting needs, this presents a real personal challenge for VCS leaders as system leaders in a system where they do not control funding or commissioning strategies.

Social action: the PCN projects

The funded interventions presented by set members fell into two types: projects delivering direct services and those aimed at improving policy or research. They included:

Direct services

– Explore and evidence how integrated services are intrinsic to success when working with the most vulnerable client groups; to improve joint working, particularly to improve underpinning systems and remove institutional barriers.

– Work to create pathways into employment for people experiencing severe and multiple disadvantage.
– Flexible, person-centred and intensive work with young women and girls in or at risk of entering locked institutions in one region, sharing the lessons learned from practice with local commissioners and policy makers.
– Work to further develop and share an 'Appreciative Inquiry' asset-based approach to providing support to newly arrived Pakistani women.
– An intense mentoring model of engaging and working with young people with multiple problems.
– Work to support highly vulnerable women during the perinatal period, to develop evidence of effective practice and to influence statutory agencies.
– Work to bring measurable long term change to the lives of multiple disadvantaged young people and adults by offering intensive support.
– A project to use systems thinking to analyse demand for advice by people facing severe and multiple disadvantage including demand generated by the failure of public services.

Policy/research

– Develop a new narrative around women facing severe and multiple disadvantage, to engage with key national agendas and to make the case for women-centred solutions.
– Define ways to bring about radical change in society to understand (a) the key transitions or turning points and, where relevant, their triggers in the human life course of people experiencing severe and multiple disadvantage; (b) how a highly effective system could (or does) ensure the best possible outcomes following these transitions
– Collect and use compelling evidence to ensure the needs of homeless people and the impact of work by homeless charities is understood locally and internally.

The projects could deliver social impact in a number of ways:

• Short term through impacting directly on service users
• Locally and for local people with complex needs by joining up local services in more integrated ways
• More widely by sharing practices that are effective and reflect a systemic change in how services are delivered (more person-centred and integrated around the individual)
• Longer term through policy and research focusing on creating the conditions for system change and early help

When we put together the intrinsic challenge of creating conditions for staff and volunteers to be effective and feel supported, with having to deliver the project in the context of the systemic challenges described, we can see that the pressures, confusion and dynamics of the environment are massive for these leaders. For those working on policy and research, all these factors interplay across a wide spectrum of settings in which they intended to influence. Where could these PCN leaders go to step back, to make sense and meaning of this complexity and change?

Action learning as a space to step back and reflect on these challenges

The Promoting Change Network (PCN) has helped LankellyChase grantees to connect with each other through providing a forum for learn from each other's experiences. As part of the PCN offer, grantees were asked about what support and development they considered to be useful in helping them to deliver their projects. Action Learning was requested by a number of grantees and an Action Learning intervention was commissioned and offered to leaders from the projects.

Two sets were established from self-nominations by leaders of funded projects; one was based in the north of England and one around London. 11 participants joined the sets across the two regions. Action Learning provided a generative, challenging method and process where these leaders could explore their own complex leadership challenges in a systematic, supportive way. A 'classic' method was adopted based on a combination of active listening/inquiry, helping the individual to explore the challenge in depth and consider options/actions to move it forward. Each session included a check in, bid for time to present an issue, and usually 2–3 people had an opportunity to present an issue. We concluded with a group review of learning and process. The 'generative' quality of open questioning encourages movement towards insight and action and reflection on the process. In the context of social action objectives, we considered challenges from the perspectives of system change and leadership of that change.

Over the 5 or 6 sessions, each set member had 2 or 3 opportunities to bring issues relating to their PCN project. Other members provided the questioning process and observations to help the individual to explore her or his issue. In this context, there was often a resonance between the issue presented by one person and those issues of others; the process works to harness this whilst ensuring that the focus is always on the person bringing the issue.

We also reviewed what they were learning about system change from exploring these real scenarios. Given the challenges and complexity encountered by these leaders, the early action learning sessions very much aimed to create a safe space to share and reflect, even as participants grappled with the idea of asking open questions and not giving solutions.

Learning about system change

Recurrent themes emerged from reflecting upon the challenges being brought. These were developed with the Sets and shared with the LankellyChase Team to feed into the knowledge-base and funding-policy development.

Method

The primary focus of this intervention was to provide a learning and supportive space for the leaders of the projects. As a practice, rather than a research intervention, learning from our experiences in the Sets was reviewed at each meeting, and more formally half way through and at the end of the programmed number of Set meetings.

Learning reviews involved facilitator asking three questions:

- What are you learning about system change leadership?
- What are you learning about yourself as a leader?
- What have you learned from the action learning process?

As the Sets were conducted within limits of confidentiality, the method was to ask the questions and for myself as facilitator to write up on the flip charts the answers verbatim and check accuracy of the notes with the Set members. At the end of the feedback, it was agreed that answers would be typed up by myself, then circulated to the Set members for checking regarding accuracy and confidentiality. On that basis of that check, permission was sought to share the amalgamated outputs from the Sets with LankellyChase,

Figure 2 shows the learning outcomes from the halfway review, which brought together the outputs from the set review sessions.

A key theme emerging from the first 3 set meetings was that *developing and providing person-centred services is at the heart of achieving system change*. Being person-centred (as in Figure 2) shifts how you see, frame and support people with multiple needs – from the personal perspective, through the community and service perspectives to the whole system. This is then reflected in the adjacent themes: viewing the person in the system; how commissioners develop and commission services; the effectiveness and leadership of the Voluntary and Community Sector in shaping the system. As discussed earlier, the fragmentation of services experienced by someone with multiple needs is a barrier to change and/or recovery.

We observed a tension between taking a strategic focus for changing outcomes in a local system and taking a more emergent approach. Taking a more emergent approach, based on values – for example being person-centred at all times – involves working through what that means in practice, for funding, for how groups and organisations work together through a process of learning and adaptation. As Figure 2 suggests, being able to *see the bigger picture* is important for these leaders, who can get so focused on delivering their own service.

To develop a person-centred system also requires a *change in the way that commissioning as a function works*. Local authorities and NHS are commissioners in social care and health, with charitable foundations and Big Lottery also playing an important role. To create more joined up and integrated services means these leaders need to have the confidence and evidence to influence these commissioners. Another key theme from Figure 2 is that the VCS needs to develop its own effectiveness. *Leadership from the VCS* requires courage as well as vision and an ability to identify and share the stories that show that working in a person-centred and joined-up way can make a difference to lives.

In the final meeting of each Set we built on this earlier work to summarise the learning about system change. These learning themes included:

1. Enhanced leadership at a system level is required

- It is challenging leading a Voluntary and Community Services (VCS) service organisation providing services to individuals and communities with complex needs, whilst

System Change: learning from Action Learning Sets to date: March 2015

Commission the system, not just the service
- Inter-connections need to be mapped
- No organisation is operating independently – what are the relationships – dependent/independent/ interdependent?
- If one organisation is commissioned to change/work in a different way, need to look at the knock on effect on other organisations in the system and commission accordingly
- Build capacity in organisations for system change
- Commissioners and VCS have to work to develop an integrated response based on learning from experience of people using services

We have to see the bigger picture
- Not just 'the system' failing – families and community have a role in supporting people
- Work with the idea of re-storying – changing the prevailing narratives

Overcome limitations of the commissioning process
- Need to improve VCS evidence base
- Need to ensure that local expertise and specialist knowledge are not lost in the actual commissioning and procurement processes
- Ensure diverse responsive approaches do not lose out to large scale one size fits all approaches

Put person-centred services at the heart of change
- Built on respect for the individual
- Love is needed at the heart of it
- We have learn to be responsive – to be ready to be 'client led' – have confidence to help bigger partners to implement this
- Relationships key to delivery
- Important to employ 'experts qualified by experience' – however, critical standards still need to be met

Leadership from VCS
- We have to have courage and personal confidence
- Provide vision and strategy for own organisations and in the system
- Articulate the stories that create system change – keep the story and detail alive in developing pathways
- Give clear messages

Need to look at effectiveness of the Voluntary Sector, as well as statutory sector
- Build from where interventions are working
- Define what information needs to be shared and how
- Build organisation capacity to model the change
- Work towards cooperative bidding?
- Looking internally at relationships at all levels and with trustees – how do these reflect the system?

Requires both strategic and emergent approaches
- Participating organisations need to invest in continuing process of learning & reflection
- Experimentation and trust in an emergent approach to deliver better outcomes
- Can a strategy focusing on outcomes and an emergent approach be reconciled?

Figure 2. System change: learning from Action Learning Sets (March 2015).

influencing for whole system change (pulled in sometimes conflicting directions). Articulating this also reflected a sense of how the Action Learning Set had enabled the participants to acknowledge and share this.

- Experienced leaders in the VCS who have pioneered and consolidated new approaches into sustainable and established organisations may need to be freed up to impact on whole system change through developing a kind of 'eldership' role
  o Bringing-through successors to run operations
  o Focusing experience to influence the network of commissioners and local authority members and chief officers, health officers and providers
  o Bringing together Voluntary and Community Services to support needs – not competing but in collaboration
  o Helping establish sustainable responses to need locally – encouraging self-organising communities, whilst sharing 'what works'
  o Providing advice and guidance

2. System change needs to be acknowledged by commissioners when they commission new, system-changing services

- Consider how the wider network of services might need to change when commissioning/funding/supporting a project that is bringing about change through a service
- Consider how transition to person-centred services can be funded in order to realise benefits from a whole systems approach?

3. There is a real tension between implementing 'what works' at scale and facilitating ground-up innovation and participation in communities

- Relationships within growing VCS organisations can struggle when working with 'chaotic clients'; with a need to control (budgets, Health & Safety) whilst enabling delivery staff space for empowered creativity
- Shows up between VCS innovators who grow and are under scrutiny – Key Performance Indicators (KPIs), Financial accountability, safeguarding – and funding agencies
- What is the balance of applying the evidenced-based model with enabling local responses to local challenges and needs?
- There are no universal truths – some things just feel right to do
- Is 'system change' the right language? We need to focus on sharing values, intentions and culture

The participants were very experienced in their own fields of work, and the Action Learning process drew out the challenges of being 'system leader' and influencing how a local system supports people with complex needs. This requires them to look beyond their own place in the system to influence others: how to influence a local authority chief executive; getting alongside commissioners to shape services in a local place through genuine co-production; working with local community groups to implement an intervention that has worked somewhere else, whilst enabling that community to bring its own ideas and energy to what is needed there locally.

Action Learning enabled these tensions to be expressed, clarified and explored. Leading system change when reliant on funders' expectations whilst the rest of a system's powerful partners – Local Authorities, NHS commissioners and large NHS providers, Police – are in a different way of operating, is clearly challenging. How these leaders then influence that wider system to try new, more person-centred approaches is complex, involving culture change, relationship building and openness to try new ways of working and organising. Having to report against many Key Performance Indicator (KPI) measures (required by funders and regulators) inevitably starts to shape focus and behaviours in how a service is provided – and for some participants collecting KPI data was a major undertaking that influenced how they used their time and on what they focused.

Learning about self as leader

One participant, with many years in a leadership role of a large local-based service summarised the learning:

> I was surprised at how useful this has been. I learned most from the opportunity to listen to peers reflecting deeply and honestly on their work, because most of the issues discussed resonated with my own experiences and challenges. I learned a lot from the questions that were asked, which opened up new ways of thinking about my work ... It has given me, as the leader of the organisation, opportunity to reflect and think about leadership issues and to engage in the sorts of conversations that I do not normally get a chance to have. I have learned a lot, I am a more reflective leader and I have strengthened networks and relationships with other people in this field. (CEO, charity providing services and community activities in an inner-city centre)

The following verbatim feedback from participants summarises their own learning:
Working differently

- Helped with the project – I tried to do my element of the project feeling it is my responsibility, but now I am working with others and understand it is more powerful and interesting to be open help and working with others
- I'm thinking in a differently way about my work (questioning)
- The power of listening and inquiry
- Learned huge amount, not just presenting my issue, but also listening and gaining from the insights offered
- Hearing how other people have identified challenges to discuss and how they plan to overcome also gave a lot of useful learning
- Incredibly useful experience ... have done a lot of personal development work over the years, and I think this was great – the group was a valuable resource

A space to think and reflect

- Valued the space and the high trust and mutual respect that developed; space to focus – supportive with like-minded people (I can often feel isolated)

- Unexpected – not just getting ideas, but helping me to develop my own thinking
- Initially uncomfortable … see need for space for reflecting (now)

   Learning from and with each other

- Everybody's issues, also have been my issues
- Enjoyable, nurturing and left much to ponder upon. I listened a lot and gave me time out from having to come up with the answers. Found it reassuring because I have been around a long time and it allowed me to be involved in something that involved peeling back the layers and reminding ourselves that these are the issues that we all wrestle with on a daily basis

Clearly participants benefited from having the opportunity for reflection on the complex environments they are leading in. Trust and relationship-building in the Set came through as an important condition for being able to reflect in an open and adaptive way.

A further observation is that listening and the spirit of inquiry transferred from the Set process into their approach to leadership; in ways that they found to be positive in creating both a personal shift from feeling mainly responsible, to one in which more responsibility is shared with colleagues with a positive effect on outcomes.

One interesting discussion in a learning review was about how working across a system as a VCS leader might require a shift into a style of leadership more akin to 'eldership' as a way of influencing the power relations in health and social care systems. VCS organisations tend not to hold funding or the statutory powers that keep those systems in crisis through service eligibility threshold effects, or distanced from person-centred approaches to meeting needs. Building from the learning output, this 'eldership' could involve: stepping away from operations; influencing partners; creating collaborative relationships across the VCS to focus on needs; encouraging local communities to both self organise and learn from 'what has worked' somewhere else; providing a questioning and guiding presence to support leaders across the system; holding local memory about community development.

Learning from action learning

In many respects the Action Learning process provided unexpected learning for many participants, most of whom had not experienced it before. Key conclusions were:
   Benefits of reflection and inquiry

- Feedback identified clearly the benefits of reflection and peer-based inquiry on individual capacity to work with complex and challenging issues in their work as leaders

   Being part of a supportive space – needs time to build trust

- They saw this intervention/support as part of the LankellyChase PCN package 'PCN is big and can be difficult to find a space to "be in it"'

- Building trust and working together as a group to develop the methods takes a few sessions, but can lead to fresh insights to apply to their situations and new openness as a leader

Transferable skills and application of the Action Learning techniques:

- The (action inquiry) methods are transferable to apply to leadership in their own contexts
- Highlights the learning about the power of inquiry in exploring challenges and working where there is conflict – shows that this approach has practical application to real issues
- The importance and value of standing back and questioning your approach – when you are part of the system you want to change

This feedback highlights learning about the power of inquiry in exploring challenges and working where there is conflict and shows that this approach can be applied to other social action projects. Participants appreciated the importance and value of standing back and questioning your approach when you are part of the system you want to change. Specific comments illustrate these points:

Applying questioning and action inquiry as an approach

- Talking through dilemmas, not just (re)acting
- I'm going to think about its *(action learning)* application to implementation projects
- More exploring and questioning in approach – and need for reflection
- Bringing time to reflect into my own organisation with my team
- Waiting and listening more before I speak

Creating the space to think and connect for others

- The sector has a lot to offer – will be connecting more on advocacy and research
- Learning from peers, drawing on the experience of others
- Creating a positive thinking environment – can use this type of space to support others
- See the human side when people are struggling

Looking outwards as a leader

- Be more outward facing
- Looking at what are the right models to survive and thrive in the sector
- Changed approach – towards more preventative and early interventions, taking on board welfare cuts

These comments indicate participants' increased confidence as leaders to influence and create conditions for change and in particular, an understanding of how questions and action inquiry can support change.

Personal learning	Learning outcomes	Application	Potential social impacts - Outcomes for system
Working differently	Benefits of reflection and inquiry	Applying questioning and action inquiry as an approach	Staff development and support leading to improved support for service users
The power of listening and inquiry	Being part of a supportive	Creating the space to think and connect for others	Joining up local partners to improve services around the person (person centred)
A space to think and reflect	space – needs time to build trust	Looking outwards as a leader	Influencing through questioning how services are commissioned
Learning from and with each other	Transferable skills and application of the Action Learning techniques		Policy development is informed by action inquiry approach to research

Figure 3. Model of change: learning into social impact.

Conclusion

This Action Learning intervention demonstrated the effectiveness of the process for exploring complexity and issues about system change through the lenses of personal leadership stories.

> Bringing a tried and tested service to a new neighbourhood and seeing the grassroots community bringing their own ideas. Stepping back and appreciating the power of that local energy. As a leader, standing back and managing how best to build on the local ideas whilst sharing what has worked somewhere else.

> Building a strong organisation and service ethos, and yet having doubts about influencing the wider system's statutory leaders. Needing to step back and enable others in the organisation to lead, to create the space to engage with the system differently.

The spirit of inquiry within the set followed by taking that questioning practice back into the workplace relieved a sense of 'over-responsibility' felt by many participants and opened a wider collaboration in their local interventions. Reflective practice as leaders became a tool for leading in systems supporting people with complex needs.

The sets provided a space for these leaders to reflect and their feedback on learning indicates that they were able to take that learning into practice. Figure 3 shows a pathway from personal learning to the strengthening of local systems and how these learning outcomes can lead to the influencing of social impact outcomes.

Disclosure statement

No potential conflict of interest was reported by the author.

References

Bramley, Glen, Suzanne Fitzpatrick, Jenny Edwards, David Ford, Sarah Johnsen, Filip Sosenko, and David Watkins. 2015. *Hard Edges: Mapping Severe and Multiple Disadvantage in England*. London: LankellyChase Foundation.
Service Transformation Challenge Panel. 2014. *Bolder, Braver and Better: Why We Need Local Deals to Save Public Services*. London: Department for Communities and Local Government and HM Treasury.

Using action learning to tackle food insecurity in Scotland

Chelsea Marshall &Ruth Cook

ABSTRACT

In the context of a dramatic rise in food bank use in Scotland, the A Menu for Change project, delivered by Oxfam Scotland, Child Poverty Action Group in Scotland, Nourish Scotland and The Poverty Alliance, aimed to reduce the need for emergency food aid by improving local responses to food insecurity. Between 2017 and 2019, project officers worked with key stakeholders in Dundee City, East Ayrshire and Fife to identify and address challenges that people experiencing acute food insecurity face in accessing all the financial support and advice to which they are entitled. The project employed a cross-sectoral and multi-level approach in these three local authority areas. This account reviews the way action learning was used by the A Menu for Change project in Scotland, including an example of how one presentation led to practical changes in local referral patterns. The project demonstrated that action learning can be a useful approach for creating, supporting and developing relationships across complex systems and a mechanism for establishing the groundwork for social change. Facilitators learned that there is a need to work closely with stakeholders inside and outside the set to ensure the benefits of reflective learning influence policy and practice change.

Background

Food insecurity is the experience of not having enough money or other resources to feed yourself and your family well. It is a spectrum that includes being worried about not having enough food, not being able to eat the quantity, quality or variety of food you need, skipping meals, running out of food in the house and going hungry, sometimes for days at a time (Ballard et al. 2013). Food insecurity is a symptom of poverty, and the effects include 'considerable physical, psychological and social impacts on individuals and families' (MacLeod 2019, 9). It is also accompanied by significant levels of shame, embarrassment and stigma, which can prevent people from seeking the support they need (MacLeod 2019). Though the experience of food insecurity should not exist in Scotland today, it is unfortunately the reality for far too many people.

In the context of a dramatic rise in emergency food aid provision and concern from the United Nations (2016, para 53) about the 'lack of adequate measures to reduce the reliance on food banks', the Scottish Government established a short-life working group on food poverty to explore ways to improve their response.[1] The Independent Working Group on Food Poverty (2016) recommended a series of actions to reduce and remove the need for food banks in Scotland and to transition towards increasing incomes and developing community food initiatives based on the principles of dignity and inclusion. The working group emphasised the need for a rights-based approach that recognises everyone's entitlement to be able to feed themselves and their families without needing to rely on charity.

Four members of this working group decided to work together to explore how this transition away from emergency food aid might happen at local authority level. These organisations chose action learning as a method for supporting diverse stakeholders to explore local problems and solutions in three practice development areas.

A Menu for Change

A Menu for Change was a three-year partnership project funded by The National Lottery Community Fund and delivered by Oxfam Scotland, Child Poverty Action Group in Scotland, Nourish Scotland and The Poverty Alliance. It aimed to reduce the need for emergency food aid by working with key stakeholders in three local authority areas (Dundee City, East Ayrshire and Fife) to identify and address challenges people experiencing acute food insecurity face in accessing all the financial support and advice to which they are entitled. Given the scale of food insecurity in Scotland, and considerable rise in charity-based models of emergency food provision at community level, the project focused on engaging all relevant statutory and third sector local actors in greater collaboration and coordination to ensure that cash and rights-based options were prioritised.

A Menu for Change project officers recruited and facilitated action learning sets in each practice development area between 2017 and 2018. The project officers undertook a 3-day training programme with Action Learning Associates in July 2017, alongside the evaluator and some of the originators of the programme. They then kept reflective learning logs and were accredited in Action Learning Facilitation with the Institute of Leadership and Management.

This account of practice reviews the method and approach used by the A Menu for Change project, focusing in particular on the lessons that emerged for how action learning has been used in this context to improve local responses to acute food insecurity.

This project demonstrates that action learning can be a valuable methodology for supporting social change, though there are challenges associated with complex systems that will require facilitators to work closely with stakeholders inside and outside the set to ensure the benefits of reflective learning influence policy and practice change.

How action learning was used

Project officers recruited sets of 10 members in three local authority areas – Dundee City, East Ayrshire and Fife – and acted as co-facilitators of monthly meetings held between October 2017 and October 2018. Process reviews were conducted after four and 12 months to ensure the members felt the method was helping them to meet their goals.

In each local authority area, project officers also worked with an advisory group of people with lived experience of food insecurity. These advisory groups provided important insight about the local issues and challenges people in the community faced in relation to accessing financial advice and support, which the project officers were able to draw on to inform discussions and suggested actions within the set.

Building on existing work

The three local authorities involved already had existing commitments to improving their responses to food insecurity and saw this project as useful in furthering their aims. The action learning elements of the project helped groups of key stakeholders in the three areas to review and improve current policies and practices supporting people in acute food insecurity. Additionally, the project funded seven pilot projects aimed at improving various specific responses to food insecurity.

A key component of initial engagement was to determine how the project would build on and support ongoing work at a local level. Project officers joined regularly held strategic meetings focused on financial inclusion/welfare reform and anti-poverty/food insecurity agendas. Staff shared informal updates from the action learning sets at these meetings, and these groups agreed to consider how to take forward and implement any issues that required strategic action. These arrangements were also agreed with the set members, and facilitators were clear with participants about the information they intended to share outside of the group.

Recommendations based on the learning from the action learning process and initial pilot project results were published in spring 2019. Many of these recommendations were accepted by and implemented at strategic level.

Set composition

The project faced an early challenge of establishing a small enough set to support trusting relationships, while ensuring the group was diverse and representative enough to have credibility to progress the complex issues identified by key stakeholders in the local area.

Each set included 10–12 set members from agencies and organisations that provide financial advice in a crisis and/or referred people to emergency food aid on a regular basis. Seeking members from different parts of the system aimed to build stronger connections between relevant agencies and organisations, support advice providers to be reflective about the accessibility of their service and encourage better and more coordinated working that would make it easier for people facing financial crisis to access the money to which they were entitled.

Sets were cross-sectoral and multi-level. Members were recruited to bring knowledge and experience from their perspectives across the referral pathway (council and independent advice providers; Scottish Welfare Fund; local authority teams such as social work, housing and health; and community food initiatives, including emergency food providers) and of a mix of frontline workers and more senior managers with the capacity to influence changes.

Each set also included one community member with lived experience of food insecurity, recruited through their involvement with local organisations. In the set where this member attended and participated regularly, their contribution was valued highly by all the other members. This led in at least one case to a specific and significant change to local practice: the text message notification a person receives when their application for a Scottish Welfare Fund crisis grant[2] has failed was amended to include information about onward financial support and advice.

Not all organisations and agencies were willing to participate in the action learning process, and their absence affected the scope of issues considered and resulting actions. For example, issues related to the implementation of Universal Credit, an important policy and practice change that took place during the project, were outside the set's direct influence.

Each action learning set had a complex system of cross-pollination (Figure 1), which involved (a) input on up-to-date issues related to food insecurity responses in the local area and (b) sharing their learning and proposed actions with relevant stakeholders. This included direct and indirect lines of communication and accountability, such as: direct representation on local strategy groups (either set members specifically or others within their agency/organisation), formal updates at strategic group meetings (via A Menu for Change representation), indirect input from an advisory group of people with lived experience of food insecurity (through A Menu for Change facilitators) and project staff's informal but regular discussions with other stakeholders such as local food bank managers and JobCentre Plus staff.

Non-neutral facilitators

A Menu for Change did not take a neutral role as facilitators of the action learning sets – it was a stated objective that the groups were working to identify actions for reducing the need for emergency food aid. Project staff balanced this objective against action learning's focus on supporting individual reflection and empowering members to take ownership over specific actions to resolve these issues.

Wider stakeholders in each area raised important questions about how a small group, working on its own, would be sure to identify and prioritise 'the most important issues' for improving responses to food insecurity. While it would have been inappropriate for the

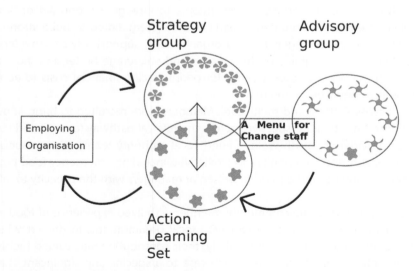

Figure 1. 'Action Learning System' in each of three areas.

regional strategy group to agree the set's agenda, the project did place constraints on the issues and themes discussed. Set members were asked to present on issues related to, for example, 'barriers people experiencing food insecurity face in accessing the support they need in a crisis' or 'reducing the need for emergency food aid in the local area'.

This was not always easy, however. At times, set members struggled to think of a presentation that fit both within the sphere of their/their organisation's influence and the broader issues of food insecurity. Some members – and facilitators – felt concerned that the specific nature of individual presentations meant it was unlikely the group would have the opportunity to discuss the full breadth of issues related to the complexities of the referral system.

Project staff trialled various techniques for addressing these concerns, such as using a 'themed approach' to meetings so that each month covered a key topic raised by stakeholders within and outside the group and using traditional group work to build set members' collective knowledge and capacity on issues related to food insecurity.

Case example – from presentation to implementation

In each area, at least one issue raised by set members was developed into a pilot project, with funding from A Menu for Change. The following is an example of how this happened in Dundee.

The largest food bank referral agency in Dundee when A Menu for Change began working in the area was an independent community centre. With close proximity to the city's largest Trussell Trust food bank, and opening hours that coincided with the food bank's opening times, this community centre was the easiest place to go for people to access a required voucher for a 3-day food parcel and collect the parcel in the same journey. In 2017, the centre provided more than three times as many food bank vouchers as the next highest referral agency. In November of that year, this was about 50–60 vouchers per month.

The centre's project manager was a member of the action learning set, and she presented on the challenges the centre staff and volunteers faced in offering consistent, robust support to people who approached them seeking a food parcel referral. The Trussell Trust voucher system relies on the principle that referral partners have the time, knowledge and capacity to offer those in crisis additional support, signposting and/or referrals to other agencies that may be able to provide longer-term support beyond the three-day emergency food aid. In theory, this would ensure that only those who had no other options would need a voucher for a food bank parcel.

What was clear from this set member's presentation was that operationally, voucher recipients were not always receiving the type of support that may have helped maximise their income to prevent recurrence of food crisis. When the project manager had time and was available to issue the voucher, she would do her best to offer suggestions for additional services – such as financial advice agencies or local community food initiatives – but given her role in the centre, it was not always possible for her to stop her work and sit with someone to offer this level of support. Their priority was to ensure that people received timely support, so if someone presented with a request for a voucher while she was busy, other staff members or specified volunteers would issue the voucher. She recognised that not all her staff and volunteers had the knowledge, capacity or confidence to offer alternatives for people.

Through her presentation, and in response to the questions from the set, she reflected on the role of her organisation and the pressure that was being placed on her service by the current system. This session encouraged her to think of actions she could take to lessen the pressure on her centre while improving the service they were able to offer those who approached them in financial crisis. The set member has described this as a 'eureka moment' and credits the opportunity to slow down and think reflectively about this challenge as the reason for looking at this problem differently.

Her aim was to (re)focus on supporting people in her community by offering a positive and inclusive space and a range of engaging projects and activities. She recognised that their role in providing substantial numbers of food parcel referral vouchers had drawn focus away from this aim and that the quantity of referrals they were offering meant that they were not able to provide the quality of support to each person that she felt they deserved.

The actions she and the group identified from this session were directed towards: (a) making more referrals to financial advice and support agencies before or alongside the food parcel referral, (b) reducing the pressure on the centre as the main referral agency in the city, e.g. by asking the food bank volunteers to refer people presenting directly to them to an advice agency instead of routinely sending them to the community centre, (c) promoting the centre's other activities, such as a project for people to grow, cook and share food together.

At this stage, only minor and exploratory actions were identified about how to address the core concern: people receiving inconsistent support from the centre if their request was handled by staff or volunteer members with limited knowledge, capacity or confidence to engage in conversations about addressing the person's underlying financial situation.

Follow up on these actions over the coming months demonstrated that some progress had been made on improving referrals to financial advice and support agencies but that potential for further improvement was limited by factors beyond the set member's influence or control. People seeking a food parcel referral were not always willing to think about or discuss longer-term issues when experiencing an acute food crisis, meaning that there would always be some people who received a food parcel voucher without further support.

Importantly, limited progress had been made on actions that required change in others' practice. Although all the set members had good relationships with the local food bank, for example, their actions to encourage and influence changes in food bank procedures and operations were much harder to achieve. This revealed some limitations of the action learning method for progressing change in a complex system of referrals towards and away from state- vs. charity-based responses.

The other issue was that it was too time- and resource-intensive for the project manager to build the knowledge, capacity and confidence of every member of her team to offer the same level of support to everyone seeking a voucher from their service. It was simply not practical to implement a strategy for this without additional resources.

Based on the learning from the action learning process – including the barriers this set member faced in implementing the actions she had identified – A Menu for Change project officers approached the centre to host one of the pilot projects.

Funding was awarded to employ a part-time support worker, available for drop-in ses-sions or by appointment on consistent days/times each week. This was a non-specialist post with an aim to ensure that anyone presenting at the centre requesting a food parcel referral would be offered clear and consistent information and support. She devel-oped a strong working knowledge of the range of support available to someone facing acute food insecurity (including cash-based statutory and discretionary entitlements, money/debt/benefit advice and community food initiatives). Other action learning set members in the advice and community food sectors provided part of her induction and continued to act as important sources of information and points of contact.

Over the next year, having a dedicated worker in place at the centre had a significant effect on the level of support people were offered. In the two months prior to the worker being in post, 91% of vouchers were 'food parcel-only', meaning a food bank voucher was issued without any additional support or referral. During the same two months the follow-ing year, with the worker in place and handling almost all of the requests, 'food parcel-only' referrals had fallen to 23% of visits. More than three out of four people presenting at the centre were now receiving information about their wider options, including active referrals to advice agencies co-located within the centre, encouragement to take part in other activities and forms of support the centre offers or signposting and referrals to other services and agencies in the city.

This is a practical example of how the action learning method led to changes in the system. The main referrer to the largest food bank in Dundee had the opportunity to reflect on their role in the flow of people towards charitable food aid, identified and sought to implement actions that would improve their own service and coordination with other services, exposed further barriers to progress based on these actions and developed a new initiative to address one of the key issues in the system – knowledge, capacity and confidence of referral agencies to support people to access alternatives to emergency food aid.

Set members' reflections

Set members were invited to consider the usefulness of action learning to meeting the group's aims through internal process reviews after four months and in the final meeting. They also shared feedback on the positive and negative aspects of each meeting monthly, which the facilitators worked to address throughout the process.

The main benefits of action learning that members identified were: having a safe space to discuss challenges; the protected time to reflect on the 'big issues' and get out of the 'day to day' and 'firefighting' approach; that the meetings were focused on actions rather than 'just another talking shop'; learning more about what each other's organisations did.

Overall, despite the challenges some members faced in committing the time to attend the meetings each month, participants were broadly positive about the use of action learn-ing as a way of thinking more deeply about the issues related to food insecurity and for the time to focus on issues beyond crisis intervention. The key value of their involvement seemed to be a feeling of empowerment from the opportunity to discuss important issues in a solution-focused way rather than the many networking-type meetings people normally attend.

On the other hand, there was a frustration about how much influence the set members had to address the important issues they were identifying and discussing. Although facilitators regularly shared the group's learning and recommendations with strategic level bodies in each of the areas, and held meetings with organisations who had not felt able to join the sets, some group members still found it difficult at times to see how the commitment they were putting into the monthly half-day meetings would make a difference.

This related both to the level of influence members had within their own role (often in the local authority context) and to what could be achieved without key stakeholders in the room (such as the local food bank or particular government officials). In some instances, frontline workers who were best placed to identify solutions to the *specific* problems someone in crisis might experience in accessing their service were not best placed to affect the change needed to overcome these. This question about whether it would be more advantageous to have frontline workers with detailed knowledge of the daily practice, managers with strategic influence or a mixture of both may need further consideration.

Conclusion

The A Menu for Change project used action learning to support better connections between relevant agencies, create the opportunity for stakeholders to identify new and practical solutions to the barriers people were facing in accessing cash-based entitlements and encourage these stakeholders to begin to take practical steps towards implementing change. This happened in each of the three local authority areas, and there were clear benefits for the set members involved.

The opportunity to focus specifically on a complex and evolving issue such as how to tackle food insecurity benefited from the structure and framing of action learning. Many of the set members were already attending networking meetings in their local area, on related issues such as welfare reform and anti-poverty, health and wellbeing or community cafés and meals. Action learning brought a renewed focus and purpose to food insecurity as an urgent issue across multiple sectors by supporting a small group of participants to think more deeply and reflectively about practical actions and possible next steps. Along the way, set members gained a better understanding about each other's services, built relationships with individuals within these organisations and had the opportunity to consider their work within the wider contexts of poverty, human rights and social justice.

It was less clear how the action learning process affected improvements in the local referral pathways more generally. In some ways, this to be expected, since change takes time and good ideas often have to percolate through the system before showing tangible results. It may also be a sign that greater clarity was needed about who was responsible for ensuring that the set's work would pay off. Many practical and significant actions were identified and progressed by set members. However, the set's freedom to present on issues over which they had most influence and authority (and may have been most pressing for them) was constrained by the project's overall objective to reduce the need for emergency food aid. This meant that in some instances, the sessions exposed important changes that required action at a higher and more strategic level. Given the stated purpose of the project, it was even more important that accountability for progressing change outside the sphere of set members' influence was made clear.

As an example of action learning for social change, there are important lessons about the potential for systemic change.

Accountability for progressing change should be discussed and agreed both within and outside the action learning set. This should include set members, their host organisations and relevant local and strategic stakeholders. Apart from the practical challenge of dedicating the time to the meetings, this appeared to be the most significant frustration for participants who occasionally felt more disempowered than empowered by the process.

Some actions will require resources beyond what the set members bring to the room and can commit to achieving themselves. This relates to the point above about accountability but is more specifically about recognising that some elements of social change may indeed require investment or realignment of resources. The A Menu for Change project included some dedicated resources for actions that required funding, and this account of practice includes an example of where that developed into an effective initiative for improving the response for people experiencing food insecurity. Others exploring the use of action learning for social change will need to consider the relationship between the set's work and wider structures and influences across the system.

Finally, there are benefits to developing an 'action learning system' when tackling complex social problems. The A Menu for Change project used a series of action learning sets as the centre of its stakeholder engagement (from community-level advisory groups of people with lived experience of food insecurity through to strategic-level groups of senior managers in the council and third sector). The method brought credibility to a small group's work on this issue, and the communication with outside groups strengthened the set's resulting actions and recommendations.

This project has demonstrated that action learning can be a useful approach for creating, supporting and developing relationships across complex systems and a mechanism for establishing the groundwork for social change.

Notes

1. This cross-sectoral working group was tasked to make recommendations about how to better address the complex drivers of food poverty, create a more dignified and sustained food strategy that supports vulnerable people and develop and align collective resources to eradicate food poverty in Scotland.
2. In Scotland, people on low incomes may be able to get a grant from the Scottish Welfare Fund in the event of a financial crisis. This is a one-off payment that helps someone cope during an emergency or disaster, or due to unexpected expenses. Crisis grants may be given as cash or as vouchers, e.g. to buy food or fuel. The applicant may be required to request a hardship payment or benefit advance before being awarded this grant, but crisis grants do not have to be paid back (i.e. not a loan).

Disclosure statement

No potential conflict of interest was reported by the authors.

References

Ballard, T. J., A. W. Kepple, and C. Cafiero. 2013. *The Food Insecurity Experience Scale: Development of a Global Standard for Monitoring Hunger Worldwide*. Rome: Food and Agriculture Organization of the United Nations.

Independent Working Group on Food Poverty. 2016. *Dignity: Ending Hunger Together in Scotland*. Scottish Government. https://www.gov.scot/publications/dignity-ending-hunger-together-scotland-report-independendent-working-group-food/.

MacLeod, M. 2019. "Found Wanting - Understanding Journeys into and Out of Food Insecurity: A Longitudinal Study. A Menu for Change." https://menuforchange.org.uk/wp-content/uploads/2019/10/Found-Wanting-A-Menu-for-Change-FINAL.pdf.

United Nations Committee on Economic, Social and Cultural Rights. 2016. "Concluding Observations on the Sixth Periodic Report of the United Kingdom of Great Britain and Northern Ireland." E/C.12/GBR/CO/6.

Developing empowered and connected leaders in the social sector: the Rank Foundation's engagement with Action Learning

Sam Anderson, Caroline Broadhurst, Siobhan Edwardes & Michelle Smith

ABSTRACT

This paper gives an account of how Action Learning Sets (ALS) are used in two of The Rank Foundation investment streams to support the social action impact of charities and social enterprises. With the aid of two Case Studies, the paper illustrates how the ALS can help to connect, sustain and support the social action responses of the local organisations involved. The first case study considers the impact of diversity and the importance of composing sets reflecting the diversity of sector, community, age, gender, and sexual orientation. The second case explores how the ALS process helps participants reflect on the actions that are most congruent with their values and then supports them in their social actions. The paper concludes that the ALS structure offers a safe and critical thinking space for participants who are working with high degrees of complexity in the absence of simple answers. The opportunity for a deep connection between people and their issues, can helpfully connect individual challenges and local social actions with wider societal struggles.

Introduction

In the paper, we explore how Action Learning Sets (ALS) are used in two of The Rank Foundation investment streams to support the social action impact of charity or social enterprises. The premise of our paper being to use ALS help connect, sustain and support the social action responses of these local organisations. We offer a brief background to The Rank Foundation and how it became involved in offering ALS, describe the Action Learning Set process of two of the investment streams before going on to offer our arising questions, reflections and conclusions.

The rank foundation and action learning

The Rank Foundation is the major charitable legacy of James Arthur Rank, Baron Rank (1888–1972), flour-miller, filmmaker and philanthropist. Today, the Rank Foundation is a pro-active, research-driven foundation, which takes an engaged approach to philanthropy.

As well as traditional 'giving', it is an operating foundation, in that it develops and delivers programmes to address key issues affecting the social sector.

Time to Shine is one such programme, and was created in order to enable people with skills, talents and ambition to gain work experience full time for 12 months in a charity or social enterprise in the UK. The programme aims to provide a unique opportunity for a person who is interested in a career in the social sector, to demonstrate and develop their skills and talents within a Rank-funded organisation, and build and challenge their leadership skills, by completing a time-limited and skill-based activity. At the same time, the programme supports the improvement of an aspect of the funded organisation's development so that it becomes more sustainable in meeting the needs of people accessing its services and the wider community.

Time to Shine has been running for nearly a decade, and now includes strands of work funded by the National Lottery Community Fund in Northern Ireland and across the UK.

Siobhan Edwards, a freelance coach and facilitator was brought in by Rank to introduce ALS to the *Time to Shine* programme from 2015. Siobhan trained in Action Learning facilitation with Action Learning Associates in 2007 and, as Fellowship Director for the Clore Social Leadership Programme, from its inception in 2008, brought Action Learning to the Fellowship programme.

When Action Learning was first offered as part of the *Time to Shine* programme, it was available to peer groups of interns and managers. From early on, it was clear from feedback that both managers and interns were benefiting from the peer support and challenge provided by ALS, and the rigour of the open questioning approach. In the programme evaluation report in 2016, it was noted how the interns embraced the methodology, asked open questions, and avoided giving advice. The interns have become supportive of each other, and reflected positively on the experience:

> At first I wasn't sure what to expect from the Action Learning Sets and was quite nervous going to the first one. I quickly settled in and got the grips of the process a lot easier than I expected … Personally, the process brought about some really big changes for me by allowing me to look at my issues in a new light and think differently, I don't believe I would have managed to solve some of it without the process and the support from my peers. (Intern, 2016)

> To me the Action Learning Set was a valuable experience. It helped me develop my problem solving and listening skills, which I can now use in my everyday life. It was a great opportunity to share this with other alike young people in the charity sector who appear to also face similar problems to me. (Intern, 2016)

The evaluation noted that the managers also worked well together, and came together as a group, but seemed to struggle more with open questions. The evaluator wondered if this suggested that the more experience you have of being a manager, the less familiar you are with 'not knowing' and the more you have a desire to tell other people what to do.

Feedback from managers was also very positive, and showed how the skills developed in Action Learning supported development in their organisations, as well as for them personally:

> I must admit, I was a bit sceptical at first as it is something that I have never done before, and I've always been used to solving the problem not guiding others to do so. However, this process has been a real eye opener to me and taught me to take a step back and look at things a little differently … I think it was a great skill that I will continue to use in the future. (Manager, 2016)

The Set learning process, strange at first, became clearer as the group began to discuss issues with people and day to day problems … I now believe the process has added a new dimension to my ability to analyse, manage and deal with issues in a much better and more concise way. (Manager, 2016)

… being able to have time and space to chat through issues with other managers was invaluable. Very often situations which arose were relatable to the group and the method was fantastic for problem solving and offering a proper chance for reflection. (Manager, 2016)

In 2019, the decision was taken to make Action Learning a requirement for all interns, now known as 'Time to Shine leaders'. This year, the ALS bring together the leaders, in groups of 7 or 8, to explore their emerging practice in the social sector; to support and challenge their ideas, influences and (often) insecurities, and to invest in the professional well-being of the new generation of charity leaders in the UK.

Since 2016, Rank has been building a network of Action Learning Set facilitators from within its network, by funding some Action Learning Set participants who, once accredited, deliver Sets on behalf of Rank. This 'network leadership' approach to ALS translates into an emerging programme of Set facilitators who have the experience, understanding and skills to stretch, challenge and support their Set members and to inform the wider Time to Shine programme and other programmes, on a confidential basis, on the key themes emerging from this new generation of leaders.

Case studies

One of the network leaders trained with funding from Rank is Michelle Smith, who shares her reflections on facilitating ALS for Time to Shine in the case study below.

Case study 1: ALS and the impact of diversity

My journey with the Rank Foundation began in 2009 when I joined Blackpool Carers as its Chief Executive Officer. As part of the funding that Blackpool Carers Centre received from the Rank Foundation's Time to Shine programme, I was invited to take part in a facilitated ALS with other managers from funded projects. As someone with a finance background, ALS was definitely outside my comfort zone. The ALS facilitator for my group was experienced, and the improvement in my self-awareness and leadership practice quickly became evident. Following involvement as a participant, Rank offered training in the facilitation of ALS for interested managers. In return, we agreed to facilitate four sessions for Time to Shine interns in the following intake.

During 2017 and 2018, I facilitated groups from Belfast. This year, I have been working with two groups: one in London, and one taking place in Edinburgh with Set members from both Scotland and Plymouth attending.

My first experience of ALS facilitation was with an intern group based in Belfast. The Set members lived and worked mostly in and around Belfast, and seemed to have a strong shared heritage, community and culture. From a facilitation viewpoint, the group connected quickly, and they developed a good level of trust from the first meeting. The Sets offered a safe space for sharing, and the Set supported each other to shift their thinking. However, despite the enthusiasm of Set members, I felt as a facilitator that the homogeneity of the group limited the experience on which they could draw, and the level of challenge they were able to provide for each other.

The ALS I am facilitating this year include Set members with very diverse backgrounds, life experiences and heritage. They include participants from the USA, New Zealand, Nepal,

Nigeria and the Philippines. I have noticed how much energy, challenge and fresh thinking they have injected into the ALS. The diversity of the group gifts each member an extremely broad range of experiences to draw upon, and allows them to challenge and be challenged by perspectives they may otherwise have had no means of encountering.

For example, one non-European Set member found it difficult to comprehend why others felt unable to ask their line managers for support. It was this participant's bafflement that led to an opening up of the questioning, and moved the Set further on. Their myriad of cultural viewpoints, combined with their broad personal and professional experiences, appears to provide an opportunity to offer new and alternative perspectives, and a degree of supportive challenge that is inspiring to facilitate.

In addition, some of these participants had left family and communities behind to move their careers forward and, as such, demonstrate courage and commitment, which seems to add depth to the learning process for all participants.

My experience facilitating this group has led me to reflect on the importance of considering the diversity of experiences within each Set, including diversity of sector, community, age, gender, and sexual orientation.

As part of my ongoing, personal development, I am planning to train in Virtual Action Learning facilitation in order to be able to bring Sets together from across communities, without the potential constraints imposed by travel.

In conclusion, I have been left with a question: if a group of people have very similar life experiences, how effectively are they able to challenge each other's assumptions?

Case study 2: ALS and the Catalyst pilot, profit for good programme

Another Rank programme, piloted in 2018, is Catalyst, created by Rank Foundation to 'advance enterprise within the social sector' by encouraging organisations within the Rank Network to consider enterprise and to explore opportunities for generating both a social impact and a financial return.

In the case study below, Sam Anderson, another of the network of ALS facilitators, tells her story of facilitating on the pilot Catalyst programme:

How I became an action learning set facilitator

As the founding Director of the Junction, a young person's health and well-being organisation, my first experience of ALS was through my participation in the Clore Social Leadership Fellowship where it was included as a core element of the programme.

I experienced the process as immensely powerful, offering a deep level of connection with peers while recognising and offering a different way of supporting me in exploring the complexity I was living in.

Following on from this I was awarded a bursary by the Rank Foundation to train as an Action Learning Set Facilitator. Being Edinburgh-based, I did my ILM Facilitator's training with Acorn Principle, who had trained with Action Learning Associates.

The Catalyst programme

The stated intention of the ALS offer in the Catalyst programme was to encourage reflective learning and create a network of peer support. A four-set offer, with Sets every two months over an eight-month period was the initial plan. However, at the Set three review, the participants requested the length of the Set be extended. We negotiated this with Rank, and the Set ran with an additional three sessions over an extra four-month period. The focus of the additional Sets was on the group further developing their capacity to facilitate their own Sets.

Open to all, seven Catalyst Pilot grant holders the offer of ALS was accessed by six. The participants were the people from their organisations responsible for the delivery of the Catalyst

Grant. The participant ages ranged from twenties to sixties. Three identified as female, and three as male. Only one had previous experience of ALS, although it emerged to have been a much looser format than the process we followed. The youngest man withdrew after Set two, citing work pressures. The areas of social action the participants were involved in include:

- Part of a place based development project with a strong sustainable approach to developing a city farm to support local people on low incomes to grow their own fruit and vegetables improving both physical and mental health through good food, activity and connection. The ALS supported the pioneer in their thinking during the launch phase.
- Supporting women moving out of the criminal justice system through 13 different pathways including an accredited training centre offering an environment sympathetic to their needs. The ALS set supported the lead in setting up a charity shop to provide supported training opportunities and income.
- A community based Bee Project created by young people at a local urban youth organisation where young people maintain hives, design and produce honey based products alongside creating educational resources about the importance of bees. The ALS process supported the lead in creatively exploring how best to support young people in developing their bee businesses.
- Responding to a locally recognised need a local community project started collecting donated sports clothing and equipment via 'donation stations' in leisure centres and schools then selling it on at affordable prices in the local community with profits invested back into sports programmes. Since participating in the ALS they have a number of large sports organisations donating kit, have negotiated a store within a larger social enterprise open seven days a week and offered several accessible sports programmes.

  In recognition of the pilot nature of the programme a gathering themes round was added to the end of the standard Action Learning Set Process steps we experienced together. This additional round supported us in capturing the learning to help shape future iterations. The gathering themes round proved to be a helpful way of visually demonstrating what was regularly articulated by participants throughout the ALS process. For small community-based organisations involved in social action, the connecting of individual challenges with wider societal struggles was important in helping people recognise their important contribution, reduce a sense of isolation, and overwhelm. For set participants it offered a shift in mindset of individual focussed solutions around 'if only I do more, work harder, am more skilled' to also recognising the contextual tensions and contradictions within which people are working.

The themes that emerged from the Catalyst Sets included the following: managing managers; sustainability; change leadership; values; connection versus isolation; managing volunteers; governance; looking after people; feeling valued; self-care; entrepreneurialism. To offer an example in relation to entrepreneurialism. The Action Learning Set process supported participants in first recognising and then exploring the tension in balancing the quality of the experience of those involved in the creating process, usually people accessing a service to access support while developing skills and experience with having an end product/experience, which customers would want to purchase at a profit. The ALS process helped participants reflect on what action would be most congruent with their social action values and then act on this.

Valuing the process

I knew from my own introduction to ALS how important the introductory session had been in creating enough safety for deep exploration to happen. Participants in this Set offered similar perspectives:

From the very beginning she set the tone for the group by her willingness to be vulnerable and to share. By doing this, she gave us permission to do the same. It also gave me confidence that she could hold the group and could be comfortable with any uncomfortable feelings that may come up.

I feel that because we all shared so much in the first session our group had a richness that would not have been there had she not taken the risk in the first session.

A number of participants struggled with open questions having built successful careers on advising people what to do. For me, I felt I was holding a 'wobbly line' of honouring the process while avoiding 'shutting down' participants from not yet being able to ask an open question or getting stuck while they searched for the 'perfect catalytic' question. I came up with two ways to address these challenges: by sharing a range of examples of open questions between session one and session two, and in session three, using a set of coaching cards which were placed in the middle and drew cards from to use as their questions. These cards gave participants the powerful experience of asking participants open questions and witnessing the presenter going to places the questioner had never foreseen they would go.

Interestingly my perception of the tension was not reflected in participant's feedback, either during the process review section or at the end evaluation.

... allowing participants space and time to learn, gently correcting us when we'd strayed into asking questions that didn't help the process and helping us reframe our questions into ones that would help the presenter.

... a conscientious facilitator, allowing participants space and time to learn, gently correcting us when we'd strayed into asking questions that didn't help the process and helping us reframe our questions into ones that would help the presenter.

This feedback was useful to hear and underlined for me the importance of reviewing the process as part of a Set process and gathering end evaluation.

The participant's evaluation of the Catalyst ALS offers useful insights and confirmation of the value of this kind of very structured ALS process, the connectivity to others and the 'permission' it gave them to behave differently:

I valued the space and time to reflect on my work and what was working and what was not working. It was helpful to know that you could bring a situation that was not working and that it would be explored in depth and the underlying cause of the problem would be revealed and often it would be very different from the presenting problem.

It was also very enlightening to listen to the problems that other people brought. I learned a lot from everyone and could always recognise something in my own situation which mirrored what was going on for them and by exploring their situation it gave me greater insight into mine.

The realisation that the answer to a particular problem is already within us. This happened with the chance to talk through a particular situation without interruption. It was refreshing not to have other people justify their selves with offering what they think are helpful suggestions.

I find the experience of Action Learning empowering – I felt valued. When sharing circumstances where I couldn't see the next step, the Action Learning process enabled me to clarify my internal 'storms' and realise that it was not beyond my ability to know what to do next. It has also helped me to improve the way I communicate with others; I think Action Learning teaches an essential life skill- the ability to listen well, and hold back on offering judgement or advice.

What the Catalyst Pilot Programme ALS confirmed for me was the power of the process.

Questions, reflections and conclusions

In drawing this paper to a close, some of our questions, reflections and conclusions are:

If a group of people have very similar life experiences, how effectively are they able to challenge each other's assumptions?

Is there anything, which could be done differently to support participants who choose to discontinue?

My experience facilitating this group has led me to reflect on the importance of considering the diversity of experiences within each Set, including diversity of sector, community, age, gender, and sexual orientation.

Like so much social action all the participants were working within a high degree of complexity with no simple answers. The ALS structure, through offering regularity, accountability, equal voice and critical thinking space creates a safe container for us to 'bring our questions not our cleverness' (*Reg Revans*).

In our shiny, individualised, performing world where there is a lack of opportunity for a deep connection between either people or issues, the ALS process can helpfully connect individual challenges and local social action activity with wider societal struggles. ALS can offer a shift in mindset of individual focussed solutions around 'if only I do more, work harder, am more skilled' to also recognising the contextual tensions and contradictions within which people are working. ALS can create what the leadership writer Margaret Wheatley calls 'islands of sanity' for participants to come and experience another way of being.

The Rank Foundation is an 'engaged funder', which seeks to support people and projects to learn and develop. For Rank, Action Learning is a powerful tool for supporting the development of empowered and connected leaders in the social sector, and to support the sector as a whole to find new, diverse and sustainable social action solutions to society's ongoing, ever-changing challenges.

Disclosure statement

No potential conflict of interest was reported by the authors.

DIAL: the rise of cafe-based, drop-in action learning

Paul Levy & David Knowles

ABSTRACT

Different styles of Action Learning that have evolved from the original form by Reg Revans, the originator of Action Learning. In this paper, we offer a further development of Action Learning which we name DIAL (Drop-In Action Learning). DIAL is a facilitated or self-managed form of action learning that has the specific quality of being a 'drop-in' process. Participants do not need to sign up to attend, nor do they need to attend regularly. This drop-in quality has lent itself to the choice of venue being in informal meeting spaces such as cafes. This paper outlines the history of DIAL, the project to experiment with and research it (The DIAL project is based in Brighton and Newhaven in the UK), and the specific challenges and advantages of the drop-in element. That is one part of the paper and the project. The second part refers to the location of the action learning meetings. We are researching how we believe flow and creativity in the DIAL meetings is enhanced (as is the drop-in element) by them being located in non-formal meeting spaces, such as cafes and pubs. By being community-based they are also a form of social action.

Introduction: the DIAL approach to action learning

DIAL has been in operation for over five years and over 300 people – startups, freelancers and pre-startups have attended. In this paper, we examine the effectiveness and potential of DIAL as a new form of action learning and also the specific benefits of non-formal meeting spaces to support the effectiveness of DIAL. We are at the beginning of a more formal data collection stage and much of what is presented in this paper is based on facilitator diaries, direct observation and informal post-meeting interviews.

We draw parallels with self-managed action learning (Bourner 2011) which enables groups to practice action learning without a facilitator, and also with auto-action learning (Pedler, Burgoyne, and Brook 2005), where one-off or occasional attendees set their own reflection and review points and milestones for action outside of the action learning process (Revans 2016). In other words, a participant may decide to only attend once but set a date for personal review of actions. In some cases drop-in action learning motivates attendees to attend on a regular basis; in others they may transition into auto-action learning. So DIAL can be a catalyst for other types of action learning. It is also a programme exploring self-discipline as a cause of commitment to action learning rather than explicit rules (Pedler and Abbott 2013).

DIAL enables and even invites participants to be tentative and spontaneous in their commitment to attending an action learning meeting. Regular attendance is possible but not a formal (Or even informal) requirement of the process. A DIAL participant may attend only once in their life. Others may attend sporadically, and yet others may become regular, ongoing attendees. The core element is that there is no formal require-ment to attend. This runs against the grain of many action learning programmes which require or encourage regular attendance, seeking continuity which is viewed as important to the success of the action learning process. Lack of regular attendance is viewed as undermining the process, even a weakness (Stark 2006), or even viewed as a problem to solve. Formal attendance requirement can also create a sense of the group being a kind of task force, where attendance is a control mechanism to ensure tasks are achieved (Dixon 1998). These formal rules have often been seen as the 'minimums', part of the 'Gold Standard' laid out as founding principles by Reg Revans himself (Willis 2004). Yet more informal approaches to meeting such as Open Space Technology point to different prin-ciples that do not necessarily undermine action and reflection (Owen 2008).

Drop-in action learning meetings are often set on a particular date and at a specific time at the same point each month but participants can drop in to meetings without prior com-mitment. (There is scope in the future for DIAL meetings to be 'pop-up', organised via social media where participants become the instigators of, and inviters to self-managed action learning meetings.)

There is a current expectation that participants will be there at the advertised start time and commit to attendance at the particular meeting they have chosen to attend, though this is not always the case. Indeed as DIAL has developed the facilitators (also the authors of this paper) have discussed how important commitment on the day really is. A societal norm of equating professional behaviour with reliability and punctuality is still in play at DIAL meetings, but this is less the case in comparison with action learning that takes place in formal meeting venues.

At the start of the DIAL project we had brought in some taken for granted assumptions from our own training in, and experiences of action learning. Regular attendance was one of these assumptions (Wade and Marilyn Hammick 2011). As DIAL progressed we noticed the informality which included a more relaxed approach to attendance led to more relaxed participants as well as better and more immediate conversational flow.

In locating meetings in cafes, we have noticed that DIAL suits these venues. Commit-ment is more informal and there is permission to be more spontaneous and emergent with attendance. There have even been cases where a person not attending DIAL, who happens to be sitting at a nearby table drinking coffee, interrupts a DIAL conversation and joins in! There are obvious implications for issues of privacy and confidentiality here. In post-meeting interviews this has been more welcomed than worried about – a cafe venue is clearly a place of assumed openness. (In further research we would like to examine this issue and its impacts in more depth, but it is beyond the scope of this paper).

Cafes (coffee & tea shops) have played an important role in literature, philosophy, poli-tics. For example, legendary cafes such as Les Deux Magots played host to the likes of 'intellectuals such as Simone de Beauvoir and Jean-Paul Sartre, and young writers, such as Ernest Hemingway. Other patrons included Albert Camus, Pablo Picasso, James Joyce, Bertolt Brecht' (Wikipedia 2019a: October). Intellectuals and political thinkers such as Freud, Trotsky, Stalin and others frequented the Cafe Central in Vienna. History also tells us that Lloyd's Coffee House, frequented by merchants and sailors, was a place where deals in the shipping industry were conducted. As a result, it became the major insurer Lloyd's of London. In the seventeenth century, stockbrokers also gathered and traded in coffee houses (Wikipedia 2019b: September). They were places of debate, discussion, transacting and occasional fist fights!

There is a long history to this kind of cafe culture, documented (and still celebrated) via further examples such as the cafe culture of Paris from the seventeenth century to this day (Scott Haine 1992). Ideas were exchanged, decisions taken.

Stylist Team (2016) speculate on the distinctive qualities of cafes and how their energy stimulates not only informal but also a kind of conversation that helps introvert behaviour and also encourages less self-critical flow. Formal meetings rooms, by their very nature are potentially places where the 'buzz of conversation' is lacking.

> Perhaps it's the smell of the coffee; the air lightly laced with caffeine and conversation. There's a wonderful sort of anonymous social contact gained from a day in a cafe; the short exchanges with serving staff, the moments tuned in to other people's gossip. As an introvert, this suits me – it distracts both me and my inner critic just enough to get stuff done, without causing me to lose focus.

More recent authors confirm this view in relation to freelancers and micro-businesses.

> Some independents try working in cafes because of the liveliness and the atmosphere, but the trouble is that cafes can be noisy and impractical (think for example of going to the loo, wondering whether you take your laptop with you or not). (Meet and Brinkø 2014)

Our current research agenda is broad as we move beyond the fairly anecdotal findings as we reflect on the development of DIAL. We have identified the following questions going forward:

> How does DIAL work and what are the challenges and benefits we have experienced?

> How does the action learning process work without regular attendance or fixed cohorts?

> How do cafes and non-formal meeting places appear to enable flow and creativity more effectively than formal meeting rooms?

> What specific types of actions do participants in DIAL discover and commit to?

> What are the weaknesses of DIAL?

> What further research questions arise from our initial research into dial?

DIAL as social action

At the heart of our most work is the notion of DIAL as a form of social action. Based in Brighton in the UK, DIAL has focused on helping startups to launch successfully, and pre-startups to progress towards startup phase in the development of the enterprise.

Brighton has a high proportion of micro and small businesses. The location of meetings has encouraged start-up activity and brought participation in ways that locate the process right at the heart of the community. Over twenty startups have been recorded since the beginning of DIAL.

Brighton also has a high number of creative businesses and these find a friendlier home in the cafe community for the practice of DIAL than in formal meeting rooms in places such as enterprise hubs and university business schools. We can compare participation levels in each of these. Brighton is often called the cafe city by visitors and those who live there (Shrimpton 2017). Whether the city as a cafe cultural hub is more of a social focus for cafe meeting than any other city is yet to be proven,

In Brighton, we have worked with local cafes and community organisations such as the North Laine Traders' Association whose aim is to encourage local small business startup and survival.

More recently in Newhaven we have partnered with the Newhaven Regeneration Group who seeks to support the regeneration of the town and the local area. DIAL can enable local startups, micro-businesses and projects to meet in the heart of the community, using AL to further develop that regeneration agenda and reduce business failure. The informality of the process as well as the use of local business locations (such as the Hope Inn in Newhaven) bring DIAL into the heart of that community and the informality and 'drop-in' nature pays respect to busy, unpredictable working and lifestyles.

DIAL has been described by users as being 'very directly accessible', 'welcoming,' 'adaptive to unpredictable work schedules' and its informality in the cafe locations has helped participants to 'feel and work more creatively'. Of all of our participant entrepreneurs pre-startups and startups, a high majority have pointed to the cafe location as an appropriate place for exploring the development of their ideas, enterprises and projects. Their reflections were recorded in our diaries and confirmed our own reflections on the practice of action learning in these community-based, informal meeting spaces.

Several participants claimed the 'smell of the coffee' was a contributing factor and compared to this to the often mediocre catering offerings in formal meeting spaces. As one participant said: 'A decent cappuccino is not the same as a poor filter coffee from a huge press down dispenser!' Quality coffee, the energy of a cafe at the heart of the entrepreneur community, also seems to confirm the benefit of the cafe as a place of informal, energised, creative interchange, where openness encourages reflection, and the energy is motivational supporting experimentation and commitment to action (Scott Haine 1998).

What makes DIAL unique is its novel approach to action learning. What makes it relevant to the special issue is its location with communities looking to generate and support small creative and many social businesses as well as aid community and town regeneration. Researchers have highlighted the importance of cafes as meeting places for conversation and getting things down in recent centuries.

But, as far as the authors are aware, there has been little or no study of the role of the cafe and its informal, drop-in nature in enhancing action learning for small enterprises. We have anecdotal evidence that actions were recorded from participants at an earlier action learning programme for startups we ran in a more formal meeting setting tended to result in more rational, 'safer' decisions; there was a tendency towards more logical decision-making and a cautiousness in the chosen actions. For example, in the earlier project, a participant might commit to 'revisiting the business's website'. A typical DIAL meeting action would be a 'radical redesign' or even a 'totally new' business website.

Whether these actions are also more reckless in a DIAL setting is yet to be researched. Our diary reflections and informal follow up suggests that DIAL meetings tend to lead to more radical innovation and risk taking. This more radical thinking tends to remain grounded and evidence-based due to the peer group scrutiny from fellow action learning participants around the table. One participant referred to the cafe environment as both 'a place for honest peer criticism, reality checking and also more creative and radical thinking'.

As innovation researchers and advisers in small business in the UK, we began to realise that the most effective forms of help and advice for small businesses were those businesses themselves in an informal, community located, peer setting. This was essentially a soft hypothesis, largely intuitive.

Entrepreneurs are often passionate about their businesses and many have long experience of both the highs and lows of managing one. Tapping into that experience, and only topping it up with specialist advice when really relevant is the best way to help businesses survive and thrive. General business advice doesn't usually help small business leaders solve their nitty gritty problems.

Learning from experience and sharing that with a group of people going through similar and different challenges – reflecting together, experimenting, taking action and then learning from that action – that's what action learning is all about – a cycle of learning in a small but powerful group.

The core idea of 'drop-in action learning' idea is to bring groups of small business leaders and owners together, on a monthly basis to act as free consultants, advisers and guides to each other. The process to enable this is called Action Learning, which was invited in the 1970s by Reg Revans.

Work was carried out with over 250 local businesses and freelancers between 2009 and 2015 across 5 local venues. Partners included The North Laine Traders' Association, Emporium Brighton and Newhaven Regeneration Group.

We collected data informally and due to funding limitations did not survey in depth. Diary methods were pragmatically chosen. As the programme progressed over time we collected more post-meeting actions and also informally interviewed participants about their experiences. Our findings and conclusions below are more indicative than definitive. More systematic data collection and data analysis will help to address our research questions more specifically.

We began our analysis of cafe meeting spaces by reflecting on our experiences of more formal meeting spaces we had used in previous work on drop-in action learning. (This was a project in 2009 called ALPINE (Action Learning Pilot in New Enterprises) which had been funded by the then Department of Trade and Industry in the UK).

From our diary notes:

Formal meeting rooms exude the atmosphere of formal decision making and formal hierarchy. Many have square tables, neon lights, office-style chairs, formal info recording and data collection tools such as flip charts (rectangle on metal stands), wipe boards etc. Any art tends to be corporate or formally placed on walls, suggested controlled decision-making even in the choice and placement of art. Sound systems, projectors and other audio-visual tools and technologies reinforce the formal nature of the meeting place.

Attempts are sometimes made to soften these effects with round tables, cushioned seats, help-yourself tea, coffee and juice, executive toys, creativity resources, sofas and even table tennis tables. Bean bags are not far away in some organisation cultures and windows look out over gardens with plants in the rooms. These are attempts to incorporate notions of play, flow, relaxation, self-organisation and freedom into the meeting place. Some of these rooms are also located

in more open plan offices with cafe area near to the meeting spaces. Some companies and organ-
isations are large enough to include a high street coffee chain within the building.

The DIAL project began back in 2009 in such buildings, a building on the University of Sussex Campus called The Freeman Centre, where meeting rooms, though formal, were not far from a kitchen, sofas and a cafe area where people could make their own coffee. We also used DIAL at a business hub called Basepoint in Newhaven where meeting rooms, though formal, were near a kitchen area, coffee point and self-service snacks machine. Relaxation areas with sofas were nearby as well.

The two facilitators (myself and David Knowles, senior researcher at the University of Brighton) began to record actions and noticed the conservative nature of many of them from meeting members. Using our own auto-ethnography, we noticed our own facilitation styles were conforming to the formality of the meeting spaces. Ironically, we often met before the DIAL meetings in a concession cafe in a building nearby at the Sussex Innovation Centre. It was there that we noticed we were having some of our most creative conversations, and generating our most interesting and radical ideas – at the cafe table, where the smell of coffee and the sound of the coffee machine sending steam upwards was only feet away. We noticed the buzz of conversation in the cafe that was distinctly lessened and sometimes absent in the more corporate spaces our action learning was taking place in.

This was, of course, subjective in terms of our observation of ourselves, others and the impact of the meeting space. It was only over time, as more set meetings took place, and when we experimented with different meeting places, that we began to notice and record more systematically the impact of the type and quality of meeting place on the flow, quality of decisions and atmosphere of the action learning meetings. A simple typology emerged as follows:

Traditional, formal, corporate-styled meeting rooms

Formal meeting rooms enhanced with attempts at creativity encouragement and informality

Informal meeting places in a formal context, including onsite cafes

Informal, cafe-based and off-site meeting places

It was at the same time that one of the researchers began to research the history of cafes and found a repository of historical images showing how important cafes and taverns were for the conducting of formal business in the 18th and 19th centuries. Out of those cities such as Prague and Vienna became well known as places where cafes entertained financiers, philosophers and artists. Some still have the private booths to attest to the fact!

Since the rise of digital technology, cafes have created dedicated places, plugs and other features to encourage work-based cafe meeting. Co-working has also arisen and a cafe usually forms the heart and even the core design of those places. They are designed to prioritise noise over silence, dialogue and creative flow between colleagues and even businesses. The buzz is seen as a driver of innovation over the formal meeting space. It was into those places and realisations that we took the DIAL project.

The process of noticing

We have found the concept of 'Noticing' useful in our attempts to understand why cafes become places of better flow, creative thinking and the creation of more telling actions for DIAL participants than formal meeting spaces (Burden and Warwick 2015). There was much to notice and the researchers kept diaries (Alaszewski 2006), and verbally debriefed before and after sessions. Indeed, we used a version of pair action learning where we reflected on our respective and joint experiences of action learning meetings, and set actions for ourselves before the next meeting.

We were also working as a team so this also included some joint commitments to action. For example, one personal reflection was that were becoming too involved as experts in the process, especially where certain challenges on small business failure to attract clients were concerned. This was an area both of us had past research and practical experience in.

We became drawn in more quickly in the cafe context where conversation was more informal, flowed more quickly and easily and the cafe itself was a place with more of an atmosphere of 'permission to speak and engage' than in a traditional, more formal meeting room that was experienced as a place that defaulted to silence, politeness, formal process, and expectation of a 'chair of the process'. To ensure self-awareness we engaged in our own reflection on practice, both self-managed and peer guided, partly to be as aware as possible of our own enjoyment of cafes and tendency to become subjectively too immersed (Johns 2000, 2002).

This reflection led to experiments in less interventions, even leaving the group to themselves under the excuse of getting another coffee! We also discussed the issue with the groups on some occasions when we checked out at the end of a particular session. Some participants and groups welcomed the higher level of facilitator involvement with selective expertise, others noticed it inhibited their own offering of advice. Our role evolved over time; sometimes it was higher in terms of expert knowledge input, in others we left a group entirely to themselves and sat together at a different table. There is a lot more to reflect on and research on this issue and it is beyond the scope of a paper of this length.

In all of these cases, we noted down first what we 'Noticed'. In hindsight, our note taking should have been better. A more thorough and comprehensive study could have gone beyond verbal reflection and diary notes and collected more systematic data. What we did do was simply shared what we noticed first, without judgment. Only later did we begin to more systematically analyse these reflections (along with participant reflections and feedback) and draw tentative conclusions.

We noticed ...

An almost immediate settling in and opening of participants to the rest of the group in the cafe setting compared to more reserved behaviour in the formal meeting setting. Participants tended to share their needs and feelings much more quickly.

I'm feeling very stuck in where my business is going

I don't have enough clients and I am feeling frustrate

I know I should get a better web site and I am not sure why I have done nothing about it.

This instant familiarity with strangers, and also with people who may have only been to the meetings once or twice before seemed to be a function of the social qualities of the cafe – a place where friends and families often meet, compared to colleagues in the formal setting.

It was only later that we linked this to a mindset that can automatically kick in from life outside of the working environment. Does a cafe setting trigger more immediate open, social norms when participants practice action learning? Do we become more immediately open and risk vulnerability?

We noticed ...

The 'ease' within the group dialogues, perhaps for reasons just mentioned, also seemed to engender more challenge. Language was more emotional and participants hold each other to account more, in some instances, and less so in others. One participant hadn't completed their agreed actions over several meetings and a new drop-in participant picked up on this immediately and gave themselves permission to the other of 'stalling' or 'making commitments they had no intention of keeping'.

Finding the flow state (which cafes seem to encourage also seems to encourage what is known as the breaking of the collusion of mediocrity or niceness, where people avoid the zone of discomfort created by direct honesty resulting in mediocrity in the zone of perceived and experienced safety), can lead to almost instant group cohesiveness. Ice doesn't need to be broken in the cafe-based DIAL group because it was never assumed in the first place. The assumed awkwardness and politeness of the norms at the start of a meeting in a formal meeting room falls away instantly at the DIAL session or was simply never there in the first place.

We noticed this didn't happen in all cafes to the same level. On one level there was a cacophony because the cafe became very full. We noticed insecurity arise in the group as they tried to cope with increased volume in the whole space; also some participants became more reserved and guarded in terms of awareness of people not in the group conversation sitting at other tables. Would we be overheard? Were we disturbing others? Becoming a member of a DIAL action learning meeting was, as with other forms of action learning, different for different participants (Beaty, Bourner, and Frost 1993).

Part of our response to that and a realisation of those issues playing into the openness and quality of the group flow state was to choose times where the cafe was not empty, but was also not too full for vicinity of non-participants and noise to be negatively influencing factors. Paradoxically, at some group meeting someone on another table suddenly joined in a group conversation and offered invaluable ideas and suggestions for action! In another instance, one group member said the louder the noise, the more they felt comfortable and inspired! This lack of usual formality seemed to create a more immediate form of peer trust (Levy 2016).

We have noticed that different cafes – their design, noise quality, mood, style of service can have different effects (Sayers 2009) on different participants and facilitators. A formal meeting room can be more consistently controlled. This standardisation and consistency can ensure a more predictable and controlled experience for the action learning process and the attending participants. However, that formality can also feel 'clinical' and less conducive more creative and radical thinking and decision-making. On the other hand, the cafe environment can be less predictable and lead to more or less satisfying experiences for different types of people attending. The 'ideal cafe' has not been defined by our research so far.

Further research and tentative conclusions

Our research so far is interesting, potentially offering a new form of action learning that locates within communities. It builds on past research where we began to notice that more informal meeting spaces, even in formal organisations had an effect on the quality of conversation and idea creation (Levy and Knowles 2004; Levy, Knowles, and Junkar 2005a, 2005b, 2006) It is also methodologically limited. Further research will need to be more systematic, comparative and also grounded in both facilitator and participant experiences.

Initial observations we have noticed suggest that cafe informality and the permission to 'drop-in' maps well onto the more emergent and unplanned nature of startups, pre-start-ups, freelancers and creative entrepreneurs. The rise of cafes as meeting spaces and the notion of 'getting around the table' combined with the positive 'smell of the coffee' are intriguing concepts for possible innovations in action learning.

Our research has only really just begun. Further research could involve more systematic use of diaries and statements of relevance kept by participants. The risk here is the very informal and less administratively cluttered approach to action learning that cafes and 'drop-in' norms offer could be undermined by the bureaucratic nature of formal data collection.

Collecting data in terms of recording actions and participant experiences could be both formal in terms of action lists, comparing actions gently recorded at meetings with (facilitators as non-intrusive note takers) then followed up by interviews at a later stage to record actions actually taken. A defined period of measurement time could also compare intended and achieved actions at cafe meetings with a parallel programme taking place in a more formal meeting session using more traditional forms of action learning.

Keyword analysis could attempt to compare how radical, adventurous and creative actions are in formal and informal settings. Assessing the impact of meetings that are drop-in by also looking at the type of actions identified and implemented.

There is also scope to research the difference between in-community meeting location to action learning meetings in more formal venues such as conference meeting rooms.

The first stages of DIAL have yielded fascinating insights. The potential for DIAL to become an important approach to supporting pre-startups, startups, freelancers and creative entrepreneurs is, we believe, significant. Further research is needed. Watch this space.

Disclosure statement

No potential conflict of interest was reported by the authors.

References

Alaszewski, A. 2006. *Using Diaries for Social Research, Introducing Qualitative Methods Series*. Thousand Oaks, CA: Sage.

Beaty, L., T. Bourner, and P. Frost. 1993. "Action Learning: Reflection on Becoming a Set Member." *Management Education and Development* 14: 350–367.

Bourner, T. 2011. "Developing Self-Managed Action Learning (SMAL)." *Action Learning: Research and Practice* 8 (2): 117–127.

Burden, P., and R. Warwick. 2015. *Leading Mindfully*. Scotts Valley, CA: CreateSpace.

Dixon, R. L. 1998. "Action Learning: More Than Just a Task Force." *Performance Improvement Quarterly* 11: 44–58.

Johns, C. 2000. *Becoming a Reflective Practitioner*. London: Blackwell Science.

Johns, C. 2002. *Guided Reflection: Advancing Practice*. Oxford: Blackwell Publishing.

Levy, P. 2016. "The Rise of Horizontal Trust and its Implications for Organisation Development, Practitioners." *AMED Journal* 4–5.

Levy, P., and D. Knowles. 2004. "Product and Process Innovation in Small and Medium Sized Firms Using Action Learning." In *Proceedings of the Management of Innovative Technologies MIT 2003/ 4, Piran, Slovenia*, 41–46. Ljubljana: Slovene Society for Abrasive Water Jet Technology; Laboratory for Alternative Technologies. ISBN 9616238817.

Levy, P., D. Knowles, and M. Junkar. 2005a. "The Role of Action Learning in Supporting Continuous Innovation in Small to Medium Sized Firms (SMEs)." CI Net, Brighton, UK, September 5–6.

Levy, P., D. Knowles, and M. Junkar. 2005b. "The Application of Process Thinking to Enable Artful Innovation in Manufacturing Firms." MIT 2005: 8th International Conference on Management of Innovative Technologies, Fiesa, Slovenia, September 22–24.

Levy, P., D. Knowles, M. Junkar, and C. Stagg. 2006. "The Twelve Death Signs of a Growing Manufacturing Company." *Journal of Mechanical Engineering* 52 (7–8): 515–525. ISSN 0039-2480.

Meet, J. V., and R. Brinkø. 2014. *Working Apart Together*. FMWorld. https://backend.orbit.dtu.dk/ws/portalfiles/portal/88598737/Working_apart_together.pdf.

Owen, H. 2008. *Open Space Technology: A User's Guide*. 3rd ed. Oakland, CA: Berrett-Koehler Publishers.

Pedler, M., and C. Abbott. 2013. *Facilitating Action Learning: A Practitioner's Guide*. Maidenhead: Open University Press.

Pedler, M., B. Burgoyne, and C. Brook. 2005. "What has Action Learning Learned to Become?" *Action Learning: Research and Practice* 2 (1): 49–68.

Revans, R. 2016. *ABC of Action Learning*. New York: Routledge. ISBN 978-1-4094-2703-2.

Sayers, J. 2009. "Flat Whites: How and Why People Work in Cafes." *New Zealand Journal of Employment Relations* 34 (2): 77–86. Accessed 10 September 19. https://search.informit.com.au/documentSummary;dn=960610867583736;res=IELBUS. ISSN: 1176-4716.

Scott Haine, W. 1992. "'Café Friend': Friendship and Fraternity in Parisian Working-Class Cafés, 1850-1914." *Journal of Contemporary History*. doi:10.1177/002200949202700403.

Scott Haine, W. 1998. *The World of the Paris Café: Sociability Among the French Working Class*. Baltimore, MD: Johns Hopkins University Press.

Shrimpton, J. 2017. "Café Culture." *The Post Magazine*. http://www.thepostmagazine.co.uk/brightonhistory/cafe-culture.

Stark, S. 2006. "Using Action Learning for Professional Development." *Educational Action Research* 14 (1): 23–43.

Stylist Team. 2016. "Forget Working from Home: Why Coffee Shops are the Key to Freelance Success." *Stylist Magazine*, April 4.

Wade, S., and M. Marilyn Hammick. 2011. "Action Learning Circles: Action Learning in Theory and Practice." *Teaching in Higher Education, Critical Perspectives* 4 (2): 163–178.

Wikipedia. 2019a, October. https://en.wikipedia.org/wiki/Les_Deux_Magots.

Wikipedia. 2019b, September. https://en.wikipedia.org/wiki/English_coffeehouses_in_the_17th_and_18th_centuries.

Willis, V. L. 2004. "Inspecting Cases Against Revans' 'Gold Standard' of Action Learning." *Action Learning: Research and Practice* 1 (1): 11–27.

Index